Off the Beach
in the
Caribbean

Raymond A. Saraceni is a professor, dramatist, and performer who lives in Philadelphia, Pennsylvania. He has traveled extensively in the Caribbean over a period of many years. He holds a Ph.D. in drama from Tufts University, and his work has been published in several scholarly journals. Raymond is currently engaged in research focused upon playwrights of the Leeward Islands. He is a company member of Iron Age Theatre in Philadelphia and teaches in the Center for Liberal Education at Villanova University.

Travels in the
LITTLE LEEWARD ISLANDS

Off the Beach
in the
Caribbean

RAYMOND A. SARACENI

Matador
9 Priory Business Park,
Wistow Road, Kibworth Beauchamp,
Leicestershire. LE8 0RX
Tel: 0116 279 2299
Email: books@troubador.co.uk
Web: www.troubador.co.uk/matador
Twitter: @matadorbooks

ISBN 978 1800461 413

British Library Cataloguing in Publication Data.
A catalogue record for this book is available from the British Library.

Printed and bound by CPI Group (UK) Ltd, Croydon, CR0 4YY
Typeset in 11pt Adobe Garamond Pro by Troubador Publishing Ltd, Leicester, UK

Matador is an imprint of Troubador Publishing Ltd

CONTENTS

Kate McLenigan Altman © 2016

PREFACE

This is a small book, with small ambitions. It is a recounting and a recollection of my own travels through a very small part of the world at a very particular moment: the Leeward Islands of the northeastern Caribbean, during the second decade of the twenty-first century. The Caribbean is a region at once familiar to and remote from the experience of most North Americans, even (perhaps especially) for many of those who have themselves traveled there. While hundreds of thousands of vacationers head to the Caribbean every year, for most this means either a week at the all-inclusive resorts of Mexico and the Dominican Republic—Cancun, Riviera Maya, Punta Cana—or a ten-day cruise (often out of Miami or San Juan) through the Virgin Islands and down the eastern chain of the Antilles, terminating at various southerly latitudes. Nevertheless, the islands often elude such travelers.

This is a book that eschews both cruise ships and all-inclusive resorts, in an attempt to discover and articulate a different kind of travel to the region. One gets to know as little of these islands from the decks of the former, as from the eateries and golf courses of the latter. But this is not a work of history or anthropology, and I do not claim any expert knowledge of these places, beyond what the curious and attentive traveler might discover for him- or herself. Still less is this a work that looks down its literary nose at the meretricious, middle-class traveler who should just stay home if he or she lacks the resources to rub shoulders with the elite on islands like Nevis or Anguilla. I could not (and cannot) afford to keep pace with the bountiful "haves" who annually make the region their playground. But travel is not just about money; it is about a particular disposition born of the encounter with an unfamiliar place; ironically, money is often used to purchase the sort of comfort and familiar experiences abroad that make the trip itself superfluous. And the Caribbean islands are not playgrounds, or even "destinations", they are real places, full of actual people and particular histories. One of the challenges of traveling in a region that strives so determinedly to present itself as little more than a series of luxurious resorts—places where there is "something for the entire family", but which also cater to a carefree hedonism, places where you can swim with dolphins and blast across the beaches aboard all-terrain cruisers, where you can "get close to nature" without setting down either your frozen cocktail or your smartphone—is that one is not often encouraged to get off the beaches and away from the resorts, so as to catch a glimpse of what the island itself is like. This is a book about traveling in a region where most of us are encouraged to simply vacation.

There are some 7,000 islands and thirty nations in the Caribbean. This book is about five of them. The Leeward Islands (particularly the smallest members of the archipelago) constitute my focus. There is something of a problem, however, even in the designation itself. First of all, these islands at the northeastern edge of the Lesser Antilles do not really lie to the lee at all. The Trade Winds and the equatorial currents that help to determine the balmy, breeze-befallen Caribbean climate embrace equally the Windward and the Leeward Islands; it is thus not the case, as the designation would seem to imply, that the Leewards are positioned somehow *behind* the Windward Islands, and thus "out of the wind". The Spanish correctly referred to all the islands of the eastern Caribbean as Windward Islands, calling them *Las Islas de Barlovento*, while the small islands close to the South American mainland— Bonaire, Aruba, Curaçao, Aves—they named the Leewards (*Las Islas de Sotavento*). Likewise, the French continue to refer to all the islands of the Eastern Caribbean as *Les Îles du Vent* (Islands of the Wind).

It was the British who confused matters when they designated their own early holdings in the Lesser Antilles— Antigua, St. Kitts, Nevis and Montserrat—as the "Leeward Caribbee Islands" once their collective government had been separated from that of Barbados in 1671. These were the days when sugar was rapidly transforming the islands and the planters in the Leeward group were convinced that Barbados refused to come to their aid during the Second Dutch War (1665–7) because its planters were only too happy to see the cane fields of their fellow countrymen devastated by the French and the Dutch, in hopes that this would drive up the value of their own Barbadian sugar. Sir Charles Wheler was the first governor-in-chief of the English Leeward Islands, but he seems to have bungled negotiations with the French for the return of lands lost by the English to their Gallic foes on the island of St. Kitts. Having lost the confidence of the planter class, he was unceremoniously cashiered and replaced by Sir William Stapleton—an Irishman who successfully governed the new colony from 1672 to 1685 (and who won the favor of the Lords of Trade in London in no small measure because he was able to placate his fellow countrymen in the Leeward Islands and to convince King Charles that his Irish subjects in the West Indies were not exclusively treasonable rogues). Of course, the ascendency of sugar led also to the ascendency of slavery in the Leeward Islands and throughout the Caribbean; the horrors of the institution cannot easily be overstated. Numbers alone begin to make this clear. Whereas some 275,000 slaves were brought from Africa to what would become the United States between 1607 and the end of the eighteenth century, some 1.2 million slaves were brought to the British West Indies between 1708 and 1790 alone—more than eight times as many slaves in less than half the number of years. This discrepancy is due in part to the fact that there was an annual population loss of slaves in the Caribbean (more died than were born on the plantations) that endured for more than two centuries. By the end of the 1700s there were some 750,000 black men and women living in the United States, but well under 400,000 in the British West Indies. The Caribbean sugar estates were killing fields.

Traveling in this part of the world, then, carries with it the weight born of such a reality—or at least it should, as St. Lucia Nobel Laureate Derek Walcott reminds us with terrible irony when he writes of the souls of dead Africans tossed overboard during the Middle Passage asking to be remembered to the black waiter who brings privileged white vacationers their poolside beverages. Indeed, it is not easy to escape the cordon of facilitators that the tourist industry employs to segregate travelers and residents from one another; even the desire to reach beyond the bars and the pools and the hotel grounds for something "authentic" may also have about it something grasping and appropriative. The following pages may occasionally exhibit just such difficulties. But such are the contradictions and tensions born of travel in the twenty-first century. There are only two alternatives: refusal to acknowledge these contradictions and tensions, or staying at home.

But back to names. Today it has become conventional to count even those nearby islands that were not subject to British control—French St. Martin, Guadeloupe and St. Barthélemy, along with Dutch Saba, St. Eustatius and St. Maarten—as Leeward Islands. In the Anglophone world, then, the Windward Islands begin in the north with Dominica and include all the southerly archipelago: Martinique, St. Lucia, St. Vincent and the Grenadines, Grenada, and (for some) the sister islands of Trinidad and Tobago. Dominica's status had been contested for some years: until 1940 it belonged to Britain's Leeward Federation, leaping that year into the less centralized administrative family of the Windward Federation. I have found that the Leeward Islands are very rarely considered in either the scholarly literature that is focused on the West Indies or in the more leisured and casual writings about the Caribbean. Most North American tourists travel elsewhere while most Anglophone historians have long been more interested in the larger and traditionally more important regional players like Jamaica, Trinidad, and Barbados: the economic and political heavy-hitters of the Caribbean. Windward Martinique is the cultural and historic heart of the French West Indies, while the Dutch were always more concerned with the East Indies than with the West—not to mention more concerned with Aruba and the refineries of Curaçao than with their poorer, smaller Leeward holdings. Thus, these little Caribbean outliers are usually off the radar screen, often overlooked and discounted by historians and travelers alike. Too close to North America to feel "exotic" or "foreign" enough in the minds of travelers from the States, their individual populations supposedly too small to sustain true and various cultures, their several landscapes generally lacking the impressive natural features of St. Lucia's grand Pitons, say, or Dominica's sulfur-clad peaks and stunning biodiversity, the Leeward Islands have long been the forgotten players in the rich and tumultuous history of the region— their people (despite a cache of impressive artists, authors, and musicians) all too often voiceless on the larger West Indian stage, at least when considered from abroad.

This book is about my own discovery of five of these remarkable and overlooked islands—but it is hardly an exhaustive account, even of the relatively small region of the northeastern Caribbean. The French islands, for example, are woefully underrepresented in the following pages. Here you will find two Dutch islands, two British islands, one independent and ambivalently-confederated island. This distribution seems fairly reflective of one of the only regions left in the world where territories maintaining a direct political affiliation with European "mother countries" remain the rule rather than the exception. But there are caveats—for even the so-called "British Islands" are themselves more or less autonomous while the "French Islands" (overseas departments, administratively speaking) have evolved creolized cultures that make them very much their own places, their peoples (as are all of those represented in these pages) unique and decisive contributors to their own histories and values.

I wish to thank David and Christine Peterson for the use of their villa as a jumping-off point for each of these several adventures and to Nadia and Pamela Hodge for their many kindnesses. Thanks as well to all those whose hospitality, careful attention, and delightful conversation served to enliven and ornament my time in the little Leeward Islands—particularly Liz, Alan, Matthew and Marissa Mycek, John Rae and the Reverend Stacey-Kyle Rae, Randall and Cheryl Wise, Anthony and Jennifer Giampetro, and Carolyn Bell. So as not to perpetuate the vulgar and sometimes racist errors of those who have traveled to the West Indies from abroad—laying authoritative claim to histories, facts, and traditions which belong to others and not to themselves—I frankly acknowledge both my status as respectful, enthusiastic non-belonger as well as my indebtedness to West Indian residents, commentators, artists, scholars, and keepers-of-memory: Colville Petty, Courtney Devonish, and Colonel Harrigan of Anguilla, along with Howard Fergus of Montserrat and the Leas of Gingerbread Hill, to name only a few. I am indebted to many for their knowledge of the region, while I lay exclusive claim to any mistakes that appear in the following pages.

As I write the final words of this preface, the novel Coronavirus has already come ashore upon several of these islands. No doubt, its effects will soon be felt throughout the Caribbean archipelago. While final outcomes are unknowable during these unsettled early days, two facts are uncontestably true. There will be significant suffering and change upon these various islands, change that even now must begin to recast parts of this manuscript as artifact. But it is also true that these islands and the good men and women who people them will endure. Here I pause for a moment to wish all of them well.

Finally, I wish also to thank my mother and father who first taught me to travel lightly, with generosity and attentiveness. Special thanks to Erin, the best and kindest of companions—traveling or otherwise.

Paoli, Pennsylvania
April, 2020

SABA

My first glimpse of Saba was on a radar screen. I had heard about a sheer mountain of rock and ravine looming dramatically out of the ocean, and had anticipated a gradual approach from the sea, one that would allow for a thoughtful, measured progress into Fort Bay, giving me time to experience the inevitable combination of delight and anxious anticipation that a traveler feels when gazing upon an island that he has never visited, except in the pages of old books. However, when I discovered that a boat ride from St. Maarten would have meant ninety minutes at sea, and when I further considered the likelihood of a good hour's worth of rolling nausea aboard the little boat called *Dawn II*, I willingly sacrificed the romance of an approach by sea to the glum, practical convenience of a twelve-minute flight upon a twin-engine propeller-driven airplane. I was to discover that Saba is one of the few islands on earth where an arrival by air—for sheer adventure—might surpass the agreeable authenticity of a landing by boat.

Earlier in the afternoon I had flown into St. Maarten and spent a few hours at the Princess Juliana airport, watching the sky above the tarmac turn from turquoise to gray and finally to an ominous black, while I awaited my 4:50 Winair flight to Saba. I would be flying aboard a de Havilland, the sturdy airborne pack-mule of the Leeward Islands, a tiny aircraft with a mere twenty seats. By the time we began boarding, a steady rain had begun to fall, and I clambered urgently into a seat directly behind the cockpit. A curtain that would normally have separated the pilot and copilot from the passengers had been tied back, which afforded me a view—one that I was not certain I wanted—of the windshield and the cockpit instrumentation. I had read that the runway on Saba was the shortest commercial landing strip on Earth, and I was hoping to conjure up some distraction for myself once the airplane began its descent. Gazing into the cockpit, this now seemed unlikely. As I took my seat, the copilot, a large black man in a crisp, white shirt and blue tie, was attempting to placate two young men from Holland whose luggage had been mislaid somewhere between Amsterdam and St. Maarten, and who were faced with the prospect of traveling on to Saba without their island attire. They had flown from the Netherlands to Newark, and had been told that their bags would be checked directly through to St. Maarten, but their luggage had gone missing. The copilot, determined to depart exactly on time, assured them that there was nothing to worry about; their clothes would no doubt arrive only a day or two after them. The pilot himself blithely checked his instruments. It was a peculiar conversation, moving from Dutch to English and back again, the copilot implacable in his dark sunglasses, his polite detachment grounded in a firm awareness of his own absolute authority. I shared the copilot's desire to get the plane off the ground, as the rain was becoming heavier the longer we idled on the tarmac. At last the twin propellers coughed to life and the airplane bounced roughly down the runway. We buckled our seatbelts. The airplane made a 180-degree turn and paused for a moment. The pilot placed his hand upon the overhead throttle and the copilot placed his own hand behind the pilot's. As they both pushed forward, the airplane shook and lurched like a wild, metal seabird struggling to gain confidence and altitude. Suddenly we were airborne, Philipsburg dropping away beneath us as the horizon pitched and angled outside the cockpit window. We turned through the wisps of low clouds toward the southwest.

Once we had reached our cruising altitude the little airplane settled itself into a layer of smooth air, while the low, constant pulse and whir of the propellers gradually enveloped the handful of travelers aboard and nudged us toward a meditative silence. The precarious physics of flight do not hide themselves on small vehicles such as these, and I imagined that I could feel the plane surge forward, straining to keep itself afloat amidst a sea of grim, charcoal clouds. The young men from the Netherlands were silent; an old black man wearing a pair of rough, green overalls rested his eyes, while a woman—perhaps his companion—sang a melancholy song quietly to herself. Rain swept the windshield of the plane; no radio chatter at all came through the console. The cabin was dark. Knowing that our approach would place the island to our right, I was seated on that side of the aircraft, straining my eyes for the first glimpse of Saba. Initial impressions are important, and I wanted my own to be rich and full of wonder.

The airplane was suddenly filled with a soft silver light as the heavy rain clouds began to uncouple themselves one from another. Quickly glancing ahead into the cockpit, I saw an ungainly shape appear on a console screen: a blue-green electronic facsimile of the island that lay somewhere beneath and before us, still invisible, but now tantalizingly close. There was a nearly imperceptible sharpening of focus aboard the airplane, a quick, reflexive attentiveness from the passengers and crew. The woman stopped singing and her companion opened his eyes; the pilot and copilot ceased their desultory dialogue and leaned forward in concentration. Those pilots who fly into Saba's Juancho E. Yrausquin Airport are required to demonstrate exceptional proficiency before they are licensed to bring their aircraft in and out. Failure to touch down upon the tarmac as quickly as possible means that the pilot would have a reasonable chance of losing runway before bringing the aircraft to a complete stop. This would mean a precipitous plunge from the edge of the rock face at the end of the landing strip into the churning waters of the Caribbean below. I later heard—from one of those pilots who ferries passengers between Antigua and Montserrat—that the Saba fliers were actually able to approach the airport from the northeast, setting their planes down perpendicular to the runway and with only about one-third of the available landing strip at their disposal. Such a feat would be impressive indeed, but I cannot vouch for the authenticity of the tale.

The Juancho E. Yrausquin Airport is perched upon a narrow promontory of rock jutting out from an otherwise sheer cliff face, just above the Flat Point Tidal Pool and the adjoining sea.

I would soon discover that this is one of the only level spots upon the entire island. During the late 1950s this area was cleared by a work crew that struggled for months to remove large rocks and fill in the holes with tightly packed earth. It was

4

here that the first airplane landed on the island in 1959, piloted by one Rémy de Haenen—his most trusted flying companion, José Dormoy (also known as "Captain Pipe," for the one that perpetually dangled from his lips), later took up the route to Saba and would represent the island's primary aeronautical link with the outside world for several years (small displays at the island's airport commemorate both of these pioneers). De Haenen himself is one of those daredevils and swashbucklers whose exploits seem to unfold at the place where legend meets history. Born in London in 1916 to a French mother and a Dutch father, he joined the French merchant marine and sailed into the Caribbean in the 1930s; from that moment, the Antilles became his home. De Haenen made a name for himself as a smuggler during World War II, moving alcohol and cigarettes through the islands and avoiding customs officials of various nationalities, all the while (so the story goes) keeping an eye on activities in Martinique—home of a Vichy-appointed government that was sympathetic to the Nazis (and also the home of Gisele, the woman who would become de Haenen's wife). Stories abound of his daring escapes and adventures. One such tells of de Haenen, having been arrested for smuggling, convincing the gendarmes to let him out of jail in order to attend to a problem with his aircraft.

Agreeing to the policemen's demand that they accompany him to the airfield, he managed a sudden takeoff with the two constables on board—depositing them on a nearby deserted island with only their wounded pride for company. Eventually he settled on St. Barthélemy, where he opened the first salting facility on the island, thus allowing local fishermen to preserve and sell more of their catch. He would later open one of the first hotels on that island, the Eden Rock. This inn quickly became the luxury destination for an exotic international clientele: guests included Greta Garbo, David Rockefeller, the King of Sweden, and Jacques Cousteau—one of de Haenen's greatest, lifelong friends. De Haenen also created one of the first Caribbean airlines, the Compagnie Aérienne Antillaise, with a fleet of surplus United States transport planes that had been mothballed after the Second World War; the small fleet was based on Tintamarre—a long, flat island belonging to nearby French St. Martin. Most of the aircraft were destroyed by a hurricane in 1950, but de Haenen was adept at picking up whatever pieces he could find and fashioning something new. Later in life he would become involved in the political scene on his adopted island. From 1962 until 1977 he served as councilor-general of St. Barthélemy, bringing electricity and telephone service to the island as well as negotiating a more advantageous relationship with Guadeloupe, which serves as the administrative capital of the French Antilles. The terms of this agreement were cemented when President Charles de Gaulle dropped in for a visit in 1964. De Haenen was never far from the cockpit, however, and by the time he retired from flying at the age of seventy-five he had logged some 18,000 hours aloft. He died in July 2008, at the age of ninety-two. Less than a year later, we began our final approach toward the little airstrip he had inaugurated in the days before the cruise ships and the all-inclusive resorts, before offshore banking and the tourist-industrial complex remade the Caribbean. I wondered if, on Saba, I might find the image of an earlier, more spacious moment.

*

Despite my attentiveness, the island had appeared from nowhere; the suddenness and nearness of Saba took me by surprise as the airplane began its precipitous but smooth decent. Our approach took us past the Pirate Cliffs on the island's north side, and through my window I saw the towering rock face soaring into thick gray mists swirling above us. The sun had sunk low toward the ocean so that the escarpment had receded into pools of jagged, variegated shadow, giving the impression of patches of dark mountain heather as we hurtled past, while other outcroppings of rock were touched with faint traces of crimson and orange. The scene was desolate, brooding and melancholy, despite the thrill and velocity of our decent. Directly before me, the pilot and copilot completed their preparations for landing, while through the windshield I glimpsed for the first time the little airstrip itself. It seemed impossibly small, a gray tarmac wedged tightly between the cliffs and the ocean—glumly expectant and absent of any other aircraft or sign of life. An electronic voice from the cockpit recited a list of measurements that diminished rapidly as we neared the runway. 'Five hundred meters... four hundred meters... three hundred meters.' A gust of wind swinging down from the Pirate Cliffs blew up under the airplane's right wing and the horizon went momentarily askew before the vehicle righted itself, the pilot driving her forward with a determined and vigorous concentration. 'Two hundred meters... one hundred meters.' We were nearly atop the runway now, yet it looked only slightly larger than it had when I first spotted it from a much higher altitude. I noticed that I had a firm grip on the arms of my seat. The two Dutch travelers looked around anxiously, while the young woman who had been singing glanced out of the window; the black man wearing the overalls appeared, improbably, to be sleeping. Suddenly, instead of the gray swells of the Caribbean, there was tarmac just several feet below the airplane, and no sooner had the runway appeared than the craft dropped forcefully onto the ground. There was not much room to spare. The sound of the engines roared immediately into a higher register, while we all lurched forward in our seats. The flight crew was bringing the old de Havilland to an expeditious halt, and the airplane thudded and shuddered to a near-stop. The copilot looked back toward us and grinned as the airplane turned gracefully toward the small terminal building, from which one or two airport personnel emerged, followed by three travelers who would be taking the return flight to Philipsburg. The only thing that I enjoy about most flights is having put them behind me and gotten to where I wanted to go. Despite my reservations, however, the trip had been a smooth one and the landing exhilarating. I felt for a moment that all of us had come through some aeronautical rite of passage together, and half-wished that a traveler who landed on Saba would get some kind of special certificate, as sailors used to when they crossed the equator. At this moment I had no doubt that those tales I had heard about the Saba fliers were true: these men could have landed the aircraft harmlessly upon a dolphin's back at midnight.

It was about twenty minutes until sunset, and a heavy rain had only just passed across the island. As I stepped from the plane the air was cool, sharp, and fresh. A *zouk* beat hammered out from the direction of the little airport bar where a handful of taxi drivers had collected. Just beside the terminal a sign proclaimed: "Welcome to the Unspoiled Queen". I glanced across a tiny assemblage of galvanized red roofs into Cove Bay and up onto Kelbey's Ridge, beside which a narrow switchback road snaked upwards through a sizable mountain covered with dense scrub forest and sinuous tendrils of mist. Scattered here and there high along the road were a number of houses, some huddled together in groups of twos and threes, others standing apart, faintly unsociable outliers amidst the fringes of thick tropical growth. Lights had begun to appear in a few of the windows as the side of the peak slowly receded into an early twilight. In the faint gloom, the houses themselves seemed almost to be moving—creeping slowly up and down the road, stopping for a moment to glance out to sea while perched at precarious and even impossible angles along the steep rise of the forested cliff. This assortment of homes was the village of Hell's Gate, one of only four very small communities scattered about the tiny island. Despite the name, there seemed to be nothing particularly infernal about the rambling little town—also known as Zion's Hill. This flip of the theological coin is said to have been effected by several island pastors who considered the original name to be inauspicious and thus pressured the government to change it. Most people I spoke to seemed to prefer the diabolical to the celestial designation. The serpent rustling of the shak shak and the low growl of a bass guitar grew louder as I headed toward the airport bar, where old comrades gathered nightly to tell familiar stories, tales wrapping themselves in light clouds of cigarette smoke and pausing for a moment in the soft evening air before passing down over the water and out into the twilight. I would be traveling alone to Saba, as Erin had found it impossible to get away on short notice; perhaps my solitary situation contributed just a touch of melancholy to my first, crepuscular impressions of the place. I wondered how the island would have appeared from the sea at this hour—slumbering and a little ominous, I imagined, its gray mass punctured by small points of bluish light, the mournful sound of amiable laughter lost amidst the low murmur of the synthesizer and the surf—all slowly receding into a rolling, imminent Caribbean dark.

The night was rich with noises. As I clambered up a tall, narrow flight of stone steps (there were over seventy of them!) that led from an empty street to the El Momo Cottages, I became aware of the strange amphibian chorus that would come to define the sound of the island during my stay. While they remained largely invisible to me, legions of little frogs introduced their sets of melodies: eerie suites of clicks, sighs, chirps and weird pulsations that would permeate the hours from dusk to dawn and quickly became an essential counterpoint to sleep. Only the young males of the species engage in these vocal arabesques, however—demure and respectable by nature, the females do not sing. On the flatter and drier Leeward Islands, these tiny frogs are largely absent, or present only in very small populations. Given her much higher elevation and thus her regular wardrobe of heavy mists and clouds, Saba is overrun with the sort of dense tropical plant life and insects that prove most appealing to such creatures. Foremost among the Saba specimens is the arboreal *Eleutherodactylus johnstonei*, the so-called "whistling frog" (or land frog) whose ancestors seem to have arrived from South America some thirty million years ago. The *eleutherodactylids* represent an especially successful family, and various members of the clan may be found throughout the Antilles. Presumably their forbears were early stowaways aboard that primeval method of West Indian inter-island commerce: storm-tossed bushels of mangrove, tenuous nets of scattered fronds, or buoyant trunks of mahogany, rolling hazardously across the narrow sills that separate one island from another. The frogs probably continued to diversify as sea levels rose and further isolated various islands from one another; thus the whistling frogs assume a variety of different appearances throughout the Caribbean: here a dull spinach color with black markings, there a deep obsidian, flashed with touches of kelly green. All of these creatures are able to accomplish an unusual reproductive trick, for the young frogs hatch fully formed from the female's eggs—which she lays beneath a wet awning of leaves—without having to pass through a tadpole stage. The whistling frog was given the name *johnstonei* in 1914 to commemorate a chief justice on the island of Grenada, who set aside funds for the collection and taxonomic classification of Caribbean flora and fauna. Whatever the whistling frogs' unusual reproductive skills and however they got to Saba, I was told that the island's red-bellied racer snakes were happy to welcome them.

The El Momo Cottages consist of six tiny wooden cabins arranged along a steep ridge that climbs to a height of some 1,600 feet. The cabins themselves, white clapboard with galvanized red roofs and ornamented with a touch of gingerbread trim, were smartly painted and sparsely appointed: two mattresses, a few shelves, and a low table with a sprig of bougainvillea set in a little glass of water. A maze of narrow stone paths, perpetually damp and often broken by tree roots or deep-green splashes of fern, linked the individual cottages with a breakfast room and a common shower and lavatory (a private sink and shower adjacent to one's cottage cost just a little extra). A small swimming pool, bounded by a slightly ramshackle terrace of wooden planks, was grappled to the side of the steep hill. The individual bungalows were hardly elegant, but the place possessed real charm, a charm characterized by unpretentious simplicity. The common breakfast room was an A-frame structure with a few tables, a bit of inexpensive latticework, and a floor with smooth wooden planks. The small vegetable garden that sent its finest produce onto the dinner table in various guises was a reminder of the hotel's determination to position itself as an unembellished destination for ecotourism, which, by and large, is the island's project too. Upon arriving I was introduced to a young Dutch couple who were the temporary managers of the place. Richard and Chloe were friendly without being effusive or fussily overaccommodating. He was fit but stoutly built, with a round face, light-reddish hair, and a neatly trimmed beard. Quiet and deliberate, Richard never wasted a remark or a glance. Chloe, his companion, was a small young woman with full features and an open face beneath a head of fine chestnut hair. Her bright eyes, round cheeks and easy, radiant smile belied her ferocity, however, when the rooster from a nearby farm would begin his cannonades of shrieks around one or two o'clock in the morning. For several successive nights Chloe hurled her own deluge of noise right back at him, the guttural growl of her Dutch and the detonation of its sharp consonant clusters rising out of the dark in a barrage of ear-splitting vengeance. I was fortunate to arrive when I did, as Chloe and Richard were soon to assume managerial responsibilities at another resort on a nearby island, a place with carefully manicured grounds, a

12

golf course, and an Olympic-sized pool with a double-helix set of slides full of gleeful, screeching children. The brochure they showed me certainly made the place look attractive, but I detected some ambivalence from the couple as they spoke of their new assignment. 'Probably fussier people there,' said Richard, taking back the brochure. 'After our next job, it's home to university. We both hope to take degrees in business management,' said Chloe, a barely audible accent manifesting itself in her longish vowels. I wondered if the couple might not regret moving on from the hard, worn charm of this place, from its stone paths and passion fruit trees and its bevy of curious, anxious lizards.

There was a small dinner party in the breakfast room on my first evening at the Cottages. Chloe and Richard had invited a handful of friends, and I was asked to drop by as well. The menu was casual and eclectic: everything from an excellent fondue with warm, crusty bread, to curried shrimp, Cuban smoked sausage, rice and peas, Trinidadian pelau (a stew made from chicken or beef seared in caramelized sugar) and homemade brownies. It was a kind of bilingual castaway's party: relaxed, economical and unself-conscious. Chloe, Richard, and their friends politely sought to converse with one another in English—largely for my benefit—but the ratio of Dutch to English increased as the night wore on, while the empty bottles of Carib lager began to mass along the cluttered tables, leaving small wet rings like ghosts to mark their agreeable passage from point to point, conversation to conversation. Outside the darkness was thick and vast, while a heavy mist began to roll down from The Level, creeping slowly through the breakfast room, daubing the lanterns and small wicker-framed lamps into faint aureoles of pink-orange light, light that was more like the memory of light, or the strange iridescence of haunted wrecks at the bottom of the ocean. Night-time on Saba seemed to invite all sorts of dark musings, and I half-wished for a good ghost story to take back to my room with me. Surprisingly, no one seemed to know any; instead there was some discussion of politics.

The Netherlands Antilles—consisting of St. Maarten, Saba and St. Eustatius in the Leeward Islands, along with Bonaire and Curaçao off the coast of Venezuela—was in the process of being dissolved and was to be wholly abolished by October 2010. Instead of the former administrative system, established in 1954, each individual island would be free to become either a special municipality within the Kingdom of the Netherlands or a largely autonomous self-governing territory. The Dutch island of Aruba had already chosen the latter option; Curaçao and St. Maarten would soon follow. In 2004, 555 people (86% of those Sabans who participated), had voted for direct ties with the Netherlands, meaning that the island would soon become an extra-territorial municipality, essentially enjoying the same status as a small town within the Dutch kingdom. The people of Saba would thus be able to vote in Dutch parliamentary elections, as well as for representation in the European Union. There remained some question as to whether they would also be forced to accept legalized prostitution and same-sex marriage; neither is especially palatable to the socially conservative West Indian subjects of King Willem-Alexander (they were still the subjects of Queen Beatrix at the time of my visit), although Dutch law serves to protect both institutions. Significantly for all the islands concerned, the

Dutch government had agreed to assume responsibility for the debt accumulated by the Netherlands Antilles during the fifty-five years of its existence, as well as to address directly some of the islands' more pressing concerns: drug smuggling, youth unemployment, and substandard education.

In the European dependencies of the Leeward Islands, political history often unfolds in subtle ways. The significance of all the fuss and bother, the abstruse legalese that makes a municipality or overseas territory of a former dependency (as well as the heated wrangling that shapes such undertakings) is often lost on visitors from the United States, for whom a binary logic tends to prevail. A state is either independent or not, a benighted colonial backwater, or modern, dynamic and progressive republic. In the Leeward Islands, however, a kind of attenuated gradualism tends to color colonial and post-colonial questions into a number of different hues. While the British Windward Islands eventually embraced independence during the 1970s, their smaller cousins to the north (whether British or Dutch) have generally remained a bit more circumspect about outright separation from their respective parent states. Only St. Kitts and Antigua have made the leap, and these quite recently. Independence for Saba was, of course, an option, but for an island of eight square miles with a population of just over 1,400, the advantages of union seemed undeniably more sound than the burdensome vagaries of complete sovereignty. Curaçao has long engaged in the lucrative business of refining petroleum, while St. Maarten benefits from a thriving tourist economy. Saba, however, is poor in industrial materials, and with only a single beach—accessible for a few short weeks in late spring, after which it disappears—the island attracts a comparatively small number of visitors from the outside world. Union with the Netherlands thus seemed the most sensible option and only five Sabans had voted for independence in the 2004 referendum. However, there was some concern among several of the guests that evening at the Cottages that the government in Curaçao (capital of the Netherlands Antilles) was dragging its feet when it came to respecting the various wishes of her various peoples. Apparently reluctant to surrender its position of prestige, the government was insisting that the parliamentary elections scheduled for 2010 still be held, even though the body to which winning office-seekers would be sent was to be dissolved just a few weeks afterwards. I did not realize at the time that this issue would come to quite a head by September 2009, just a few months after my departure. Chris Johnson, the Saba Commissioner of Constitutional Affairs, would even go so far as to inform Dutch prime minister Peter Balkenende that the local government was prepared to break off relations with Curaçao (in effect, to secede) if the government of the Netherlands Antilles continued to behave in ways that seemed to be obstructionist. There were accusations and counter-accusations; angry but unfailingly polite letters traveled back and forth across the Atlantic before frayed tempers were stitched up and wounded feelings appropriately salved. However, as there was political consensus among the guests at El Momo that evening, everyone appeared to be much more interested in whether or not I had enjoyed my flight than in discussing particular points concerning the upcoming dissolution of the old administrative infrastructure. Mildly unnerving the new arrival seemed to be something of a party game; it was Richard who informed me that, when

16

the airplanes were full, they tended to drop off the end of the runway and struggle for a moment or two before finally gaining altitude. I told him I was grateful for having arrived off-season, when the planes were largely empty—and thus lighter—than they might otherwise be.

Around eight-thirty, a tall, square-jawed and muscular man arrived with a bound manuscript in his hand. He had a military-style brush cut and wore a broad, disarming grin. I hadn't realized that Richard and Chloe had organized the party to celebrate the première of a one-man show written by Tom Judson, one of the other guests at the Cottages, who would be presenting an informal staging of the play this evening. Tom was from New York, and the play introduced us to his colorful career as a Broadway hoofer, bartender, gay activist, and adult film performer. In the adult film industry he was better known by his screen name, Gus Mattox. While I can't say that this was how I had imagined spending my first night on Saba, Judson was a charming performer, and the play itself more mischievous—and genuinely touching—than I had anticipated. When he described standing on an elegant Italian hotel balcony and releasing the ashes of his deceased partner into the night air, watching as they danced and tumbled in sharp pillars of light shining up from the garden below, it was impossible not to be moved, especially while the Saba mists contributed their own chiaroscuro effects. His audience was appreciative: the yearning amongst the residents for a voice from the outside—from beyond the confines of the little island world and its too-familiar stories—no doubt contributed something to its enthusiasm that night. The performance was a success, the author and I discussing his plans for the piece, and the future of the American theatre, with the support of a growing ensemble of beverages (and an attendant, fuzzy-headed eloquence), while the number of partygoers quietly diminished by twos and threes. Apparently, Judson had acquired and restored a 1950s-style camper, which he compared enthusiastically to Ken Kesey's Further Bus and Joel McCrea's Land Yacht from the film *Sullivan's Travels*; with this as his studio-cum-living quarters, he planned to tour the play throughout the United States. He would call the piece *Canned Ham*. I have since learned that Judson has revised the play and performed it to some acclaim in New York City, New Hope, Pennsylvania, and in various locales on the West Coast. A solicitous and kind man, as well as a puckish and brave performer, I was glad to have met him and I wished him well. As I fell asleep later that night, the whistling frogs offered their own musical entertainment.

*

Christopher Columbus was apparently the first European to set eyes on Saba, when he returned to the Caribbean on his second voyage in 1493. Unlike the expedition of the previous year, which involved only three ships and a crew of about eighty-five men, this undertaking enjoyed the generous financial support of Fernando and Isabella of Castile (in addition to a number of Spain's wealthiest aristocrats). Thus the Genoese admiral and viceroy of their Most Catholic Majesties had at his disposal a much larger fleet of seventeen ships and 1,500 men in the fall of 1493, when he first discovered and began to explore the Leeward Islands. Saba's rocky shores must not have presented a particularly hospitable picture, for Columbus did not set foot upon the island. In this context it is also interesting to note that Saba is one of the few islands in the Eastern Caribbean to have escaped (or at least to have sloughed off) its European designation. Columbus conferred upon those islands he discovered the names that they would be fated to carry with them into their various futures, names that situated them firmly within a network of alien political, cultural, and theological traditions. Guadeloupe was named for a famous Jeronymite monastery in Extremadura, for example, while Antigua was named in honor of Santa María de Antigua, the famous Virgin associated with the cathedral of Seville, the city that would soon become the headquarters of the *Casa de Contratación*, the House of Trade, and thus the unofficial mercantile capital of the Spanish Empire in the West Indies. Whatever name Columbus may have given to Saba, however, seems to have been put off by the rugged coastline just as decisively as the admiral was himself, for this appellation has been eroded by time and lost to memory. Instead, the island's name appears to have been derived from an old Arawak word, *siba*, meaning "rock." This is one version of the story, but there is also a persistent legend on Saba that Columbus must have been reading from the Old Testament when he first spotted the island, choosing to name it "Sheba" after the queen of that fabled realm with whom Solomon was so enamored. Most historians discount this tradition. An Amerindian people known as the Ciboney seem to have lived upon the island by 1500 BC (perhaps even earlier), though they left hardly any artifacts behind to mark their sojourn. Sometime around 800 AD, subsequent arrivals—the Arawak-speaking Taíno—settled in the area around Spring Bay (not far from today's airport), where some carved stone tools, decorative shells and pottery sherds have recently been discovered. These were the people who apparently named the island "Saba." Several centuries earlier, forbears of the Taíno began moving into the Caribbean from what is today Venezuela, climbing the ladder of the Lesser Antilles from Trinidad to the Virgins, and then moving on to settle the larger islands of Puerto Rico, Hispaniola, Jamaica, and Cuba. One wonders what might have drawn the Taíno from the flatter, more easily settled islands of Antigua or St. Eustatius to such a forbidding and glowering home. It is hard to resist the glum conclusion that these inhabitants were motivated primarily by self-defense, for by at least 1200 AD, the Taíno of the region were already coming into conflict with the Kalinago (also called the Carib), more recent arrivals from South America. Surprisingly, there were no Amerindians whatsoever on the island when the first Dutch settlers arrived in 1640. It may be that the Taíno (or the Kalinago) left on their own. Perhaps, however, they were forcibly removed from the island by Spanish raiders sometime in the preceding century, set to work as slaves on Hispaniola, where the native inhabitants had died of overwork or exposure to disease soon after contact with Europeans. From the beginning, then, the settlement of Saba was marked by waves of emigration: forced, voluntary, gradual, sudden; Taíno and Kalinago, Spanish and Dutch. And as with other of the Leeward Islands, emigration would long exist as a way of life there, even into the twentieth century, when many Sabans sought work in the oil refineries of Aruba and Curaçao, or in the United States. During the early 1900s still others went to Bermuda, where they were employed by the British as guards at a Boer prisoner of war camp. A few Sabans returned from these migrations, but many remained in their adopted homes.

*

A cool coral light crept across my room, brushing aside the curtains that framed the small windows beside my bed and casting delicate gray shadows upon the far wall. The chorus of frogs now emitted only a faint gurgle of sound; just one or two persistent vocalists remaining at work. The morning air was crisp and chilly, something of a surprise in the tropics, but there was also that sharp, luminous clarity—the sky a fathomless, lacquered blue—that served to demarcate the lower latitudes. Looming directly before me as I sat upon the little porch adjacent to my cottage was the most impressive physical feature of the Saba landscape: brooding Mount Scenery. At nearly 3,000 feet, this is the highest point on the island, the "highest point in the Kingdom of the Netherlands," in fact, as I would be told several times. The tip of the mountain was capped with mist, a Caribbean parody of an Alpine peak topped with snow. The summit of Mount Scenery is rarely visible, and hikers are urged to use caution should they travel there, as the effect of the mists is often disorienting. A hike to the top is an arduous endeavor, and many who have taken the trouble have complained that there is often little reward by way of a view: a wall of heavy clouds instead of the anticipated expansive ocean vista. What one finds atop Mount Scenery, however, is more haunting, more unsettlingly beautiful, than one might expect. The peak is covered by a dense cloud forest, thick with moisture and heavy with a strange light, gray-green and silver. Clusters of *prestoea* palms hover round like covens of witches, solemn and indifferent, with their spider roots and their trunks ringed white and green beneath a canopy of feather-shaped leaves. Most impressive, perhaps, are the large mountain mahogany trees, their gnarled limbs festooned with hanging mosses like shreds of tattered garments. Ferns grow in profusion here, and there are philodendrons the size of small dinosaurs; orchids—purple, white and claret—often glance through the gloom. Then there are the *heliconia*: a blaze of red leaves with yellow tips, twisted round a green stem like a ladder of tongues of fire, each strangely aglow in the primordial twilight of this mist-bedecked summit. The stillness and the silence become disconcerting; you think perhaps you are being followed, but by whom and to what purpose are unclear. You may notice the low canopy, the relatively small trees; this is the result of hurricanes that periodically tear across the crest of Mount Scenery, driving winds and rain that toss the trees aside and furrow sudden rivers through the tumult of the forest. On such evenings it must seem that the gods of the first peoples have returned, wrathful and not well-rested. The topography and history of the island still hold the memory of these terrible storms: a particularly severe hurricane in 1772 decimated the coffee and cotton crop, neither of which ever recovered. In 1998, when Hurricane Georges roared onto Saba as a category three storm, the cloud forest atop Mount Scenery was in a climax stage; most of the tall trees were lost, unable to withstand the winds that bludgeoned the peak. Rainfall atop Mount Scenery is always heavy, averaging close to eighty-five inches annually, thus the deep ravines, called "guts" by the local population,

22

that run in a radial pattern from the top of the mountain down to the ocean, fracturing the island into an agglomeration of scored rocks and cracked scrub forest at the lower elevations. These guts tend to intensify the spinning of storm winds; it is thus likely that, within and along these trenches, the actual wind velocity generated by Hurricane Georges was significantly greater than the official measurements of 150 miles per-hour. Standing atop Mount Scenery just as the daylight begins to thicken—and the late-afternoon winds to insinuate darker things—one inevitably begins to imagine the deep, trembling terror of one of those frightening storms moving across the mountain during a windswept, howling August evening.

*

During my second night on Saba I met Tom van't Hof. I had taken Richard's advice and decided to have dinner at the Ecolodge Rendez-Vous, a small, ecologically friendly resort situated in the middle of the rainforest along the Crispeen Trail. There are very few cars on the island, and this fact—coupled with the intimacy of the place and the unusually steep landscape—means that drivers will almost inevitably stop to offer a ride to whomever might be working their way by foot up the nearest incline. On Saba, such courtesies are commonplace, even obligatory, and I have been present when rides were offered and received in complete silence; help is politely proffered and gratitude assumed. On this occasion, however, I asked Richard if he might call a taxi for me. Moments after he hung up the phone, I saw a white minivan back down the driveway of a small house situated directly across the street from the steps leading up to the El Momo Cottages. The driver's name was William, a light-skinned black man with a creased face, a salt-and-pepper mustache, and a quietly amused expression. He wore a loose cotton shirt with a pack of cigarettes in the breast pocket. A postcard from Venice was tucked into a strap that secured the visor above the passenger-side windshield. I wondered who had sent it. The radio played what sounded like music from a church service as William moved the minivan with conviction through the narrow streets of Windwardside, past the cemetery (where the tombs are situated above the earth), and down a set of sharp curves toward the Crispeen trailhead. 'You remember to bring your flashlight,' he said. It was a command, not a question. There is no road running to the Ecolodge, and after dinner the trail would be very dark. I mentioned that Richard had given me his own flashlight, and that I thus felt reasonably well-provisioned. William's initial reticence soon gave way to a series of interesting observations concerning Saba life in general and his own career in particular. He pointed out one of the little rest stations situated beside the road, a quaint chapel-like structure, with a set of benches framed by cut wooden shingles and a peaked roof with fluttering eaves, nicely complemented by delicately fashioned carpenter's lace. 'You can rest there if you get tired walking the hills and things, or when the rain catch you,' he said. When William was a young boy, his father had been a bit chagrined by the fact that his son became so easily seasick; as many Sabans still pride themselves on their seamanship, such an embarrassment was not to be borne. 'So they took me out on a boat and we floated around for three days. Three days!' A veritable tempest of seasickness apparently did the trick, for William claimed never to have suffered again

24

from this unseemly malady. He was happy, however, to be driving a cab on solid ground and he preferred to travel by air whenever he had to leave the island. 'I meet some interesting people doing this work, though. Last year a big ship pull up, a yacht, you know? The Prince and Princess of Denmark come by to see the place. They outdoor folk; I drive them all over. Nobody even recognize them.' I told him I hadn't heard about the visit. 'They fly under the radar, you know. No one even recognize them. Maybe that's why you didn't hear.' William sang along to the music for a few minutes, then turned to me and grinned. 'This here is a *royal* taxi you driving in tonight!'

The Crispeen Trail begins just beyond the last house in The Bottom, the capital of the island, and home to its governor. Climbing several hundred feet, the track passes through thick jungle and over a forested ridge into open pasture, meandering past Peter Simmons Hill to the right. Accessing the trail from the road, however, I saw only a small portion of the Crispeen track, where it runs alongside a crumbling stone wall and past the ruins of what appeared to be a small mountain farm. An enormous bull was tethered to an iron stake beside the trail, and he watched me pass by with a soggy, sullen indifference. The Ecolodge is the work of Tom van't Hof—an eminent marine biologist who began his career over twenty years ago on the island of Bonaire—and his wife, Heleen Cornet, a respected artist, responsible for (among other work) the lively murals that grace the sanctuary of the island's Roman Catholic Sacred Heart Church. Here vivid, kaleidoscopic rainforest scenes dissolve into a condensed wave of radiant faces—portraits of local men, women and children—splashed and unfurled across a half-dome above the altar in a rainbow of variegated hues.

Tom van't Hof has helped to create marine parks not only on Saba and St. Eustatius, but as far afield as Kenya and Indonesia. He created Saba's Conservation Foundation in 1986 and helped to organize the island's first national park. It took the couple some three years to construct the twelve individual units that make up the Ecolodge Rendez-Vous, along with the Rainforest Restaurant. The cottages are white clapboard with bright yellow trim, each with a small porch and tastefully spare interiors: a canopied bed, a few pieces of wicker furniture, and white walls trimmed with stenciled hibiscus and bougainvillea. Each unit is made from recycled materials, while solar panels harness the sun's rays as the primary power source for the resort. The restaurant itself is delightful. It consists of a small room with about twelve tables; the walls are painted green and white beneath five simple chandeliers, each holding a ring of hurricane lamps, their muted, honeyed light shaping the corners of the room into shadowed undersea caverns amidst the accumulating dusk. Traditional West Indian windows are propped ajar with small sticks fitted into grooves, while bits of jade-colored sea glass and honeycombed coral are arranged along the windowsills. A set of large glass windows are situated along the side of the restaurant; their purpose only became clear toward the end of the evening. Tree frogs are not uncommon here; one perspicacious visitor sat upon my table for half an hour, possibly contemplating whether to use my mozzarella salad as a hiding place. The menu is small and there is only one sitting each evening, but the meals are remarkable: the seafood freshly caught, and the vegetables grown in an onsite organic garden. My red-curried coconut shrimp was prepared alongside a bed of rice, bananas and Jalapenos, testament to the chef's expertise in joining traditional Caribbean with South Asian ingredients. Wednesday nights at the restaurant are particularly happy occasions, for on these evenings—after the diners have ordered their meals—Tom van't Hof himself arrives to discuss the ecological history of the island.

He will tell you that Saba was formed about half a million years ago; it is perched at the top of a volcanic mountain (now dormant) that first became active during the late Pleistocene era, when wooly mammoths still trumpeted across the northern wastes, and glaciers stretched southward toward the approaches of Manhattan Island. While the volcano has not erupted in the last 5,000 years, one does not have to look far to discover the effects of geothermal activity as these continue to shape the island. Hot springs still percolate on Saba's north coast, near where a sulfur mine was operated by the McNish Company for a few seasons in the late 1880s. He will tell you that there are eight different microclimates on Saba, and that the whole mood and texture of life in The Bottom, for example—resting upon the floor of a vivid and viridian crater—remains quite different from what one finds in a town like Windwardside, perched along the narrow rim of what had been the erupting mountain. If the latter feels more like a highland hamlet, with its cool temperatures, regular mists and chilly winds, The Bottom, with its humidity, heavy heat and damp good humor, belongs decisively to the tropics. Of course, the natural history of the island is compounded by the man-made variety. While the kind of de facto racial segregation that once characterized the four primary communities on Saba has happily begun to dissolve in more recent years, it is nevertheless true that the descendants of Dutch, Irish and English settlers tend to cluster along the Saba rim, while the descendants of the island's slave population (which, in the absence of extensive sugar estates, was never very large) are to be found generally in The Bottom. Tom will conclude by reminding you that the volcanic and tectonic forces that have shaped the island do not cease their work at the water's edge. Millennia of geothermal shifts and plumes have shaped vast canyons of pinnacles, vertical walls dropping to depths of over one hundred feet and adorned with pink and yellow gorgonians. Sea fans curl with musical grace to a silent, aqueous sonata and are towered over by soaring barrel chimney sponges, from whose brims one might glimpse whole universities of angelfish and blue tang—further out, perhaps, a prowling hammerhead, or even a pod of gray whales, aloof and ancient and slumbering northward. Some say that in March, on particularly still nights, you may even catch the songs of these barnacled, baleen-bearing giants from your bed, as they shuffle heavily toward cooler climes. At the conclusion of his lecture, Tom darkened the room and instructed those of us with flashlights to shine them toward the large glass windows: a constellation of small frogs croaked back at us, bellies pressed to the glass, eyes bulging and limbs akimbo, a panoply of whimsical amphibian curiosity.

*

Without the white sandy beaches that traditionally entice North Americans and Europeans to the region, Saba is a late arrival to the tourism game and has taken its place on the field thanks to imaginative and careful marketing of its own particular assets. The island has positioned itself as a high-end

28

destination for eco-tourists, primarily hikers and divers. My assumption that I was a somewhat experienced hiker—even if I knew that strolling (which remains my wont) is decidedly not the same as a vigorous hike—nearly wrecked my own trip, and within a few hours of my visit to the Ecolodge. As I left the cab that evening, I asked William if he would transport me to Hell's Gate early the next morning, where I planned to hike the Sandy Cruz Trail to the point where it intersects the All Too Far Trail (the name should have served as a warning); here I would follow the latter down along the Rainforest Ravine to the old sulfur oven before circling back up to Hell's Gate and hailing another cab to return me to Windwardside. All of this seemed a lot more plausible on a map than it would be in the flesh. Unused to the demands of extended physical exertion in the West Indies, I had equipped myself quite poorly: in my backpack I had only a small bottle of water and another of orange juice, while my cell-phone was without a signal and would prove useless in the event of any unpleasant eventualities. I mentioned my plans—although not the specifics of my itinerary—to Chloe and Richard, who were drinking with some friends in the breakfast room and who had invited me to join them. As I planned to rise around 6.30 the next morning, I politely declined. Richard thought it a good idea to begin my trek early, before the sun got too high, and Chloe promised to rise early and to fix me a big breakfast before William arrived, which, fortunately, she did.

The Sandy Cruz Trailhead was marked by a handful of large gray stones, and tall grasses turned strangely in the breeze as I began my trek under a low, leaden sky. As is typical on Saba, a heavy mist lay thickly upon the high hills, and helped to reinforce a mood of gloomy, prehistoric desolation. The vegetation was dense and dark, illuminated here and there by a sudden spray of wildflowers or fluorescent devil's weed. Vines dangled from the canopy like tattered curtains in a ghostly spider's theatre. Muddy and rather steep in places, the trail sometimes required that I move forward hand-overhand, or clamber from tree trunk to tree trunk, much as a ground-dwelling, slightly inebriated monkey might travel. Once or twice I caught a glimpse of the sea through a tunnel of foliage: gray-green, topped with whitecaps, and impossibly far away. At these moments, I felt a kind of giddy isolation, a vertiginous upwelling of uneasy pleasure coupled with deep loneliness, as though I had come away from time and from the earth itself, glancing down at a little ocean from the utter silence and trackless void of space. When I came to the head of the North Coast Trail, I was momentarily tempted to change my plans and follow this new path out toward the ruins at Mary's Point. A sign reminded me, however, that it was illegal to hike this trail without an experienced guide; broken by guts and sharp crevasses, the path is a dangerous one. As I turned south to follow the ravine, I broke out of the rainforest proper and found myself in a steep landscape dominated by scrub and a dry clay soil. By this time it was about mid-morning and the mists had begun to burn away, revealing a white-hot sun climbing quickly in the sky. I had dawdled a bit on the trail, while the humidity had compelled me to drink heavily: just a swallow of orange juice remained. It was at this point, unsure of precisely how far ahead the end of the trail lay, clambering up and down a number of dry ravines and disturbing large clusters of aggrieved lizards, that I began to become concerned.

I was nearly exhausted, uncertain of exactly where I was and unable to contact anyone who might be of assistance (I had not encountered another soul along the trail and no one else on the island knew where they might find me). William had given me a business card with his cell-phone number, but this was of little use at the moment. I finally spotted the entrance to the sulfur mine about a half-mile below, but realized that, had I made the trek down, I probably wouldn't be able to get back up the trail. Amidst the intense heat and with no shade available, I recall watching a sailing boat out at sea. I was amazed at how small and faraway it seemed, nearly identical with the tumble of whitecaps that silently surrounded the tiny vessel. I turned in the direction of what seemed to be the head of the trail and promised myself that I would wait until I had reached the end before I took my last swallow of juice. Fortunately, I had judged correctly, and within about fifteen minutes I reached the end of the trail. Here, however, I was faced with another problem: I was far from the main road through Hell's Gate and was unable to climb any further in an attempt to reach it. There was, to my good fortune, a solitary house situated near the trailhead, and I walked over to the small front gate, calling out to whomever might be at home. No one was there. Nevertheless, as the situation seemed an urgent one, and as the house (like most on Saba) had its windows propped open and its doors unlocked, I took the unusual step of letting myself in and using the telephone to call William and ask him for a ride back to Windwardside. The rights of life and liberty trump those of property, I thought, although I refrained from helping myself to the bottled water that had been left on the counter, a malicious if unintentional temptation. I was, of course, more circumspect in preparing for subsequent excursions, and later managed an ascent of Mount Scenery with much less to report in the way of near-disaster.

*

While Spain and then France laid early claim to the island, the first Europeans to arrive on Saba were Dutch settlers who sailed up from nearby St. Eustatius in 1640, although the island passed through many hands before the Kingdom of the Netherlands established decisive and permanent control in 1816, at the conclusion of the Napoleonic wars. During the Second Dutch War (1666–7), an expedition led by Colonel Edward Morgan—uncle of Henry, the infamous buccaneer— managed to seize the island for King Charles II, but English suzerainty proved to be short-lived. Père Labat, a French priest who traveled through the Caribbean from 1693 until 1705, stopped in for a visit and left a brief account in his delightful *Nouveau Voyage aux Isles de l'Amérique*. According to Labat, the Sabans heaped large boulders along the edge of the cliffs and beside the pathway that served as the only point of approach toward the island's settled regions; these rocks were apparently kept in place using a system of planks and posts that could be tripped by pulling a rope. The stones would then tumble down upon any enemy force that had been foolish enough to have attempted an ascent. No old wives' tale—as I had initially believed—this particular defensive scheme was bequeathed to the island following a period of English occupation which lasted from 1672 until 1679. It seems to have been decisive in driving off a French attack in 1690, but was apparently unable to deter the successful assault led by James Cockburn, who seized the island once more for Britain in 1781 (this time defeating the French, who had recently seized the island). Dispatched from St. Eustatius by Admiral Rodney following his occupation of that island, Cockburn waxed lyrical in his description of the successful attack on Saba. In a letter home he wrote:

> 'We climbed and climbed and waded
> Through a mass of shale and gravel,
> Sometimes backsliding, 'til we reached
> The borders of a level:
> With circumjacent hills
> That hemmed in every side –
> Then only did we realize,
> And not a moment later
> That this *top* was the *bottom* of
> An old volcano crater.'

Cockburn was incorrect in his last observation: The Bottom *is* at the base of a large crater, though this is *not* the caldera of the former volcano. Saba has spawned many travelers' tales, some of the tall variety, but not all of them. Labat himself—a *raconteur* and *gourmand* who writes with special zest about his Antillean repasts—manages the trick of maintaining an anthropologist's curious detachment while at the same time refusing to permit a dreary fastidiousness to get in the way of a good story (or a dietary fussiness to get in the way of a good meal). According to the priest, the island was peopled by forty or fifty families, including some French refugees who showed him particular kindness. Given his enthusiasm for all subjects that touch upon the palate, Labat also reports that there were no regular butchers on Saba, but that the settlers in each quarter of the island took turns slaughtering animals and preparing meat for themselves and their neighbors. This was still the custom in the early twentieth century, as a perusal of Raphael Sorton's *An Inside Look* will confirm, the memoir chronicling a career that carried Sorton from goat-herding on Saba and schooling on St. Maarten to serving as Minister Plenipotentiary at the Hague. Shoemaking was the principal trade when Labat visited; an earnest Catholic pastor of souls, the good Father lamented that Saba had been settled by Protestants; had it been claimed by his co-religionists, it would inevitably have borne the much more picturesque name of St. Crispin, patron saint of shoemakers. The Crispeen Trail, however, preserves in its name a vestigial link with a small collection of Irish shoemakers who named their island guild for the patron saint of the trade.

After the Second World War, Alec Waugh, Evelyn's elder brother and himself a respected writer, visited Saba and lamented that the traditional lifestyle that had survived on the island from the days of Labat's visit was in the process of being forever (and unhappily) transformed. The culprit: roads and automobiles. The first motor vehicle had arrived in 1947, a jeep for the lieutenant-governor. According to legend, some of the islanders thought the vehicle was a living thing, and offered to cut grass for its provender. At the time, the only paved road on Saba ran from Fort Bay to The Bottom; a team of engineers from the Netherlands had concluded that any further road construction across such a mountainous island, cut by jagged cliffs, deep guts and thick forest, was impossible. Josephus Lambert Hassell disagreed. If there is a Saba folk hero, it is

34

the man affectionately known as "Lambee." A local carpenter who built cabinets, ships and various musical instruments, he was determined to prove that the team of professional Dutch engineers was incorrect. Lambee took a correspondence course in road construction from the University of Chicago and then set to work. Employing a team of island laborers, he undertook the construction of what would become nine miles of road, linking together for the first time the communities of The Bottom, Windwardside, St. John's and Hell's Gate. Using shovels and wheelbarrows, Hassell and his crew of volunteers opened up a road that begins at sea level and rises through a series of hairpin curves and switchbacks to a height of 1,968 feet. In the one and a half-mile span running from the airport to the village of Hell's Gate, the road climbs some 1,300 feet through a series of twenty curves. Saba's many volcanic stones became raw material for the reinforcement walls that were necessary to keep the road from collapsing under the weight of pressing mountains or from washing away in a hurricane. Work began in 1943; twenty years later Lambee's road was officially finished. On Saba it is still called "The Road That Could Not Be Built," an acknowledgement that even the fact of its existence cannot quite convince you that it was possible to construct such a thoroughfare. It remains an astonishment. Still a point of pride for the residents of the island, the road also enjoys a prominent place in Saba folklore: a stretch that runs from St. John's to Over-the-Peak became known as "the dancing place," due to the occasional apparition there of six men dancing around an open coffin at midnight. If any spirits are dancing along that road, however, I prefer to imagine a ghostly cotillion of Lambee's own work crew led by Hassell himself, armed with the great man's collection of musical instruments and dancing down the sky.

This road runs directly through the pleasant village of Windwardside, perched snugly along a narrow precipice that here crosses the base of Mount Scenery. The town itself is faintly suggestive of a small village situated at an implausible juncture of the highland moors with the Caribbean. Tidy, quiet and cool, Windwardside is characterized by a delightful profusion of traditional Saba architecture. The typical cottage is a one-story affair of timber-framed construction upon a stone foundation. The exterior walls are covered with white wooden shingles, while sash windows and storm shutters are painted green; the roofs are red. At one time the roofs were topped with wooden shingles as well, but most of them are now covered with galvanized sheets. The color of the original roofs has happily been preserved, however, while the uniformity of this architecture and color scheme is striking. One might be forgiven for thinking that one had stumbled upon a kind of fairy hamlet, unfolding from its typical wardrobe of morning mists to shade its eyes beneath the bright blue of a noontime Caribbean sky. England and Holland are equal players in terms of mood and atmosphere, with the nod going to the former more often than not. Everyone on Saba speaks English, after all, while (with the exception of a few official persons) almost no one speaks Dutch. Such a thing may be explained by the fact that the Dutch in the Caribbean (as opposed to those administrators sent out to the East Indies) never really thought about their work as involving any sort of "civilizing" mission, thus there was no real determination—as there was on the part of the French and British—to leave behind the accoutrements and flavor of their own culture. When, in 1997, the Netherlands Antilles sought to adopt a national anthem, it is significant that the authorities determined that, while English lyrics were acceptable, Dutch lyrics should be avoided.

I was especially pleased, during an afternoon walk, to have stumbled upon the Harry L. Johnson Museum, a wonderful example of the island's typical architectural style. Harry Johnson was a police officer and amateur artist who spent his spare time gathering various artifacts associated with Saba's past. By the mid-1970s, Johnson was in search of a building that might serve as a home for his impressive collection. He found an old cottage built some time around 1840 by a successful sea captain named Josiah Peterson. Because of the traditional connection between Saba and the sea—until very recently, most of the island's male population was obliged to make a living as sailors or fishermen—Johnson felt that this structure would be an ideal choice for a heritage museum. The original nineteenth-century kitchen is still intact, and was built with a large stone hearth for baking. On the other side of the cottage, the master bedroom is both grand and understated. A four-poster mahogany bed with pineapple carvings atop its posts stands in the center of the room, while in the corner there is a wonderful woven desk with slanted writing surface. The sitting room at the center of the house contains what is undoubtedly one of the finest antique pieces I have ever seen: an early twentieth-century piano organ donated by the Wesleyan Holiness Church, the milk-white ivory of the keys nicely offset by the rich cherry hues of the wood, with bursts of flower-shaped molding suspended above two centrally placed floor pedals. This organ arrived on Saba long before Lambee's road was begun; thus it would have been necessary to carry it by hand up the steep incline and rough steps from Ladder Bay all the way to the town of Windwardside. Museum curator Sherry Peterson (her husband is a direct descendant of the sea captain who built the cottage) was particularly proud of this piece. 'We are used to thinking of art and music as those things that come last,' she suggested, 'only after a place has acquired the more needful things that make life easy. Then we have to find ways to pass the time—because we *have* the time.' The silent presence of the organ, she asserted, argued against this way of thinking. Indeed, it was difficult to understand why such an isolated and hard people, situated at the very edge of the world, would have undertaken the unnecessary and toilsome labor of hauling an organ up nearly two thousand feet of cliff and jungle. 'But it's only difficult to understand,' said Sherry, 'if we imagine that what the instrument provided was simply a diversion. But if we can see that it's really about beauty... I mean, we need music like we need water, don't we? It sounds silly when you say it, but it's really true. When I think about that, then it makes sense, the awful job they must have had getting it up here. The music must have been very, very beautiful.' She lightly touched her hand to the keys. 'I wish I might have heard them singing.'

In back of the sitting room a set of double doors open onto a meadow that meanders gradually down toward the left, while on the other side of the house is a large cistern; there are no freshwater streams on Saba, so rainwater must be collected and carefully stored. Nearby one may also see a small family cemetery where Allen Peterson, the last Saba resident who owned the cottage, is buried. Beside him lies his daughter, who died in infancy. The museum is situated near a little public park, where a statue of Simón Bolívar stands proudly beside a couple of flagpoles, one flying the gold-starred Saba flag, the other the blue and white banner of the Kingdom of the Netherlands. I was surprised to find a statue of the Liberator situated here on a tiny Dutch island, many miles from South America, but it is a gift from the Venezuelan government, commemorating Bolívar's several visits to Saba. On this island, he gathered a small body of idealists, mercenaries and adventurers who fought with him in the series of long and bloody wars against Spain that served to bring to birth the independent states of South America during the early years of the nineteenth century. I soon learned that there is another significant connection between Saba and Venezuela. A young lady named Mary Gertrude Hassell Johnson had spent some years at a convent in Caracas during the later nineteenth century; here she learned the art of what became known on Saba as "Spanish Work," the fashioning of exquisite and meticulously wrought lace. A number of island women became adept at executing such work and eventually a few of them began a mail order business, selling pieces of what quickly came to be called "Saba Lace" to buyers in the United States and the Netherlands. Once a thriving cottage industry on the island, today there are probably less than ten women (mostly elderly) who continue to produce Saba Lace, although these ladies sometimes offer informal classes instructing adolescents in the delicate business of appliqué and open work. I purchased a fine, highly ornamental piece of blue and white trim (threads crossing and interweaving like the reflections of cloud on deep blue water). The work had been executed by a sad-faced and sweet-tempered old woman named Maggie; she had stood beside her cottage door as I passed and welcomed me into her small parlor, where carefully arranged lace work vied for space with a forest of photographs of siblings, children, and grandchildren, several, I was told, 'no longer among the living.' She was in poor health, but the lace was ethereal and fine, hovering in the faint morning light like a kaleidoscope of pale butterflies, momentarily alight but poised for an imminent departure. 'I remember before we had electricity,' she said, nodding toward the television humming and flickering in the corner as she handed me a small brown bag. 'I have it on all the time now, but I can't see the picture anymore, you know.' I asked how she managed her lace work if she suffered from such poor vision. Maggie shrugged. 'I don't have to look,' she said, wriggling her knotty fingers, 'they know what to do. And they still work sometimes.' She sighed and suddenly seemed far away. 'Before electricity the light was different.' How so, I wondered. 'Gaslight in the square then. It was just different. Like everything.' She smiled. 'You'll see.'

*

Lambee's road climbs upward through the community of Hell's Gate, after which a dramatic right turn spins the motorist along the narrow streets of Windwardside. Just beyond the head of the Mount Scenery Trail, you leave the town behind and pass out into a desolate and forbidding landscape: rugged and grim, with Mount Scenery itself glowering over your right shoulder and a stunning view of St. Eustatius to your left. Ahead is the tiny hamlet of St. John's, home to the island's primary and secondary schools, perched atop a jutting tongue of land and suspended many feet above the surf. I was told that these school buildings are some of the few structures on Saba equipped with air-conditioning, for the winds rage so intemperately here that the windows must be kept closed at all times. Outside of the campus, St. John's is more a smattering of cottages than a town, isolated and aloof even by the standards of such a singular and solitary island. This ramshackle little corner, however, possesses its own charms, including the delightful residence known as Trevelyn's Cottage. Built in 1910 by Tommie and Nellie Barnes, this was the home of one of Saba's most celebrated masons (residents can often tell you who lived in a particular house several generations and many decades earlier). Unusually for Saba, the exterior here is colored a kind of cream yellow instead of the more typical white, thus making the structure relatively easy to identify. Just past St. John's, the road executes a dramatic hairpin turn, bringing into view the village called The Bottom, named (as has been noted) for its location. It has been said more than once that Sabans are practical people, essentially immune to overstatement and grandiloquence. Place names here are thus more functional than poetical. Windwardside won its moniker because it is located on the windward side of the island. Likewise, a narrow plateau just outside of the town, where a dramatic rise flattens out for a moment, is known as The Level. Poinciana trees are called July trees here, because they flower in the month of July. In a flight of whimsy, however, an enormous rock formation that towers above The Bottom has been given the name of Willy the Whale. Indeed, once you are told where to look, Willy's flukes and bony, protuberant head may easily be seen rising beyond the rocky surf of the mountain rim in flamboyant guardianship of the town below.

The Bottom itself is a staid and sober place; the casual yet sophisticated restaurants, the hip shops and bars of Windwardside, are wholly absent. The mood is administrative and a little dour, but there are quiet treasures here that should not be overlooked. Perhaps the first thing one notices as one explores the town is that the sea has completely disappeared, not an unremarkable thing on such a small island, where the Caribbean is visible nearly everywhere else. In The Bottom, though, the silent streets (some paved, others cobblestoned) most often terminate in sheer, stunning walls of green. With the singular exception of the place where a switchback road climbs up from Fort Bay, the town is wholly enclosed by a dramatic ring of rock and forest. One of the most splendid structures in The Bottom is Crantson's Inn, originally known as Gezaghebber's House (the island's chief executive having long been known as "Gezaghebber" or "lieutenant-governor"). The two-story building features an elegant yet simple balcony beneath a roof trimmed in gingerbread and ornamented with handsome acroteria. The open rooms on the second floor are among the few places in the town where one might catch a desultory breeze, for the soaring crater rim blocks the Trade Winds from blowing through with their usual vigor. Originally, government offices and a library were located on the first floor, while the chief executive and his family slept upstairs; only later did the building become an inn. A story is told that many years ago three Dutch officials visited the island and slept in the grand stateroom, with its enormous four-poster bed: while the judge and the prosecutor slept lengthwise, the gentleman who held the less prestigious office of recorder was obliged to sleep across the foot. During her visit to Saba in 1955, Queen Juliana slept in the four-poster in Room One; whether it was the same bed that had earlier accommodated the judge and his staff is not known. The current lieutenant-governor resides across town in a grand two-story structure with spacious wrap-around balconies both upstairs and below, fronted by an elegant garden graced with a small antique cannon situated amongst bouquets of yellow allamanda. Traditionally, the Dutch appointed their West Indian governors from amongst the resident populations of the islands themselves, rather than following the British model of sending a royal representative out from the imperial metropole. The people of Saba in particular continue to take great pride in the fact that their lieutenant-governors are "sons of the soil," as I was told more than a few times. The wedding of Governor Jonathan Johnson caused quite a sensation on the island in the summer of 2012, as did his decision to spruce up the governor's house in preparation for the festivities: nearly everyone spoke approvingly of his decision to remove the whitewash on his garden walls in order to reveal the blue-green Saba stone hidden beneath. Down the street from the governor's house is a small district known as the Promised Land. While biblical resonances are inevitable, this is yet another instance of the islanders' predilection for pragmatism in nomenclature. Fearing that the entire village of Mary's Point might soon collapse into the crumbling ravines along the island's northern coast, the government many years ago encouraged the inhabitants to abandon their settlement and relocate to The Bottom. The land set aside for their relocation became known as the Promised Land. What little is left of Mary's Point might still be seen, but the hike is treacherous and should not be attempted alone. Such warnings are to be taken seriously on Saba. Several years ago a young man from New Jersey disappeared while hiking and remained missing for many months. This event led to a great deal of uneasy speculation on the island. Perhaps he had fallen into the sea somewhere along the North Coast Trail. Perhaps he had cunningly engineered his own disappearance for some personal reason that could only be guessed at. Nearly a year later, these and similar speculations were resolved in a dismal and grisly fashion. On Halloween, of all days of the year, a group of hikers exploring the sulfur mine stumbled upon the remains of the young man. He was sitting propped against his backpack, having apparently become disoriented, and was overcome by the suffocating vapors; it was reported that the body was in remarkably good condition, having essentially been mummified by ten months' exposure to the sulfur fumes. The promontory where the mine is located remains one of the glories of the island, though an awareness of the sad events of several years ago means that one treads lightly and reverentially there. As you pass out of the woods and onto the grassy plain of the clearing, you experience a strange kind of disorientation; the plain slopes vertiginously toward the ocean, while the view of the eastern cliff face—blue and purple and saffron in the sun—is at once majestic and a little frightening. Here and there grayish blooms of fearless mountain goats festoon the grassy slopes and towering rock wall, while just beyond the escarpment, the small airport may be seen. If you are lucky, one of the Winair flights from St. Maarten might hurtle past as you stand at the edge of the cliff and gaze out to sea. If you leapt at precisely the right moment, you would swear you might grab hold of a wing and ride the de Havilland onto the tarmac like a modern-day Pecos Bill. Nearby, the ruins of a stone furnace may still be seen. Here the sulfur was baked before being transported by a pulley system to Green Island, just off the coast, where it was hauled onto waiting boats, although the pounding surf that surrounds the scanty isle makes one wonder how on earth this was ever accomplished. The wind wails wildly here, while the frigate birds whirl and chortle in exuberant display.

Saba is a small island, and I very quickly came to realize that anonymity—despite a venerable tradition of minding one's own business—was not a possibility here. I frequently ran into guests from the party at El Momo; most of them waved at me or grinned sheepishly, as if faintly embarrassed by something they had said that evening, but unable to remember if they had any real reason for concern. I discovered Richard, Chloe and Tom at an elegant little restaurant named Brigadoon, where I enjoyed a glass of merlot and a filet of almond-encrusted grouper. I soon learned that the owner of the restaurant, a sharp-witted, smoky-voiced blonde American woman named Trish, had also been in attendance at the party (I received a complimentary dish of homemade passion fruit ice cream, one acquaintance to another). As I watched a second evening of heavy fog roll across the island, reducing the green and white clapboard houses of Windwardside into swirls of charcoal and ocean-gray, the town and its warren of spectral little streets began to resemble the lost, melodious hamlet for which the restaurant was named. I agreed to meet Richard, Chloe and Tom at the Swinging Doors after they had finished eating and off I went to explore the darkling town.

It was only a little after eight o'clock, but the streets of Windwardside were empty, and the cheerful, sunlit town I had seen earlier had given way to something more solemn and melancholy. Mist obscured the ends of the little stone lanes: narrow-walled avenues that terminated in groves of poinciana trees, rounded into deep caverns by the moonless night. The daycare center was shuttered and dark, the little playground empty and forlorn, while faint smudges of streetlamps pooled their light in unexpected (sometimes unsettling) ways: a few of the gray sarcophagi situated just across from St. Paul's Roman Catholic Church seemed to swim within a gray-green ocean, their rounded hulls and angular markers bobbing wanly in the night. Throughout the town, small back-garden family plots could be seen lying amidst tufts of grass and trees, headstones lightly illuminated in yellow streams falling from nearby windows, where the grandchildren or great-grandchildren of the deceased pass their evenings in intimate proximity to the departed. The little houses perched atop their stone foundations seemed remote and oddly separate from the empty, shadowed streets. I could just make out the green trim of their storm shutters, the latticed windows tucked beneath overhanging porch roofs, the diminished whimsy of the pert finials. Small gates were built into the lichen-mottled stone walls that bordered the various wandering avenues of Windwardside; these opened into gardens that bristled with white and yellow flowers, declining now toward shades of violet and obsidian. Oleander and bougainvillea framed a succession of narrow cobbled paths that led up small flights of wooden stairs to the faintly lit parlors of homes with names like Bonnie Brae, Effie's Cottage and Sloterdijk's House. Occasional streetlamps

46

buzzed faint pools of light. I passed Maggie's cottage and could see through her lace-curtained windows the blue light of a television. In the old days before electricity arrived, oil lanterns were placed within the ornamental lampposts of the town by a local warden at sunset. I imagined an indefatigable old gentleman with a bristling Dutch mustache, dressed in a crisp khaki civil-service tunic and pith helmet, humming to himself some quaint *levenslied* and thinking quietly about a long-dead sweetheart whom he once courted in Haarlem. It was that sort of night. But I would not have found the imaginary old warden at work *every* evening; on those nights when the Caribbean moon was full, the streetlamps were allowed to remain empty.

Unfortunately, the Swinging Doors was closed, but just a few feet from the house where Josephus Lambert Hassell once lived (it is now a gift shop), I stumbled upon a small bar called Saba's Treasure. This turned out to be a memorable establishment, one owned, in fact, by the brother of the island's lieutenant-governor. The overall effect was of a tidy Cornish pub, fitted out with bric-a-brac and dropped incongruously into the eastern Caribbean. Old nautical charts were pressed into service as wallpaper, while a weathered cast-iron stove sat glumly and unused in the corner, surrounded by chipped bits of imitation Delft tile depicting various Dutch scenes: a view of Rotterdam, a windmill in Limburg, old fishing boats afloat in a much colder ocean, their crews straining to haul in catches of blue herring. There were photographs of nineteenth-century fishing folk on the walls, while from the ceiling were suspended some aged model boats: whalers, windjammers, old galleons, and sturdy ships of the line. Deadeyes blinked impassively down from the ceiling, an eerie parade of hovering and impassive skulls, while a few Japanese lanterns, pink and yellow, glimmered faintly from the corners of the room, framed here and there by faded long-line fishing floats, wrapped in rope netting. The floats looked as if they had served their time at sea, grasping the corners of nets and securing them atop teal waters that fell suddenly away into a sinister, impenetrable midnight. I wondered what sort of strange shapes these small satellites had glimpsed down below, darting shadows of dark, furtive dream creatures—silver scales like stars—as they navigated the edges of the fathomable world. Here was lesser work for them, suspended now above amber or green bottles of beer, and rooms brimming with a flotsam of tired, grinning patrons.

It was here that I met Pieter, a Dutchman with a shock of silver hair, and a dark, leathery complexion. He drank a glass of neat whisky (probably not his first), and spoke with a strange accent, more Portuguese than Dutch, it seemed to me. Pieter's blue eyes darted about the room from time to time, as if he sought to make sure that he hadn't been followed. It was difficult to guess at an exact age, for his disarming laugh and roguish grin belied the years that his weathered face and ghostly hair seemed, at first, to advertise. He claimed to have taken passage on a tanker that had put in at St. Eustatius earlier in the week, and to have flown into Saba for a few nights before returning to the former island and sailing out on another vessel headed north. It was not easy to tell if he was traveling in a professional capacity or out of a spirit of adventure. He reminded me of one of Kipling's gentlemen-at-large, and it was from Pieter that I first heard about the sunken cities. Nevis boasted a submerged village situated in the watery hollow north of Charlestown Bay, according to Pieter, while the stone foundations of private dwellings, factories and warehouses blinked up empty-eyed at the passing hulls scudding across Oranjestad harbor in St. Eustatius. The pirate-haunted neighborhoods of old Port Royal in Jamaica collapsed into the sea during the 1692 earthquake that struck the island; their remains might still be seen beneath the soupy waters there. Several contemporary pastors interpreted that disaster as an act of divine wrath. The Caribbean, I gathered, was full of such tales; indeed, the written accounts of the region begin at that fecund juncture of folklore and history, modern cartography and mediaeval fantasia, where cities and islands shimmer seductively in the offing, only to vanish just as seductively beneath the waves. The Portuguese speak of the Archbishop of Porto, who disappeared into the Atlantic with six other churchmen as Muslim invaders poured across the Iberian Peninsula in the eighth century, the clerics determined to establish a collection of autonomous Christian kingdoms somewhere across the Ocean Sea. According to legend, a young couple who arrived in Portugal aboard a merchantman several centuries later completed the tale of the Archbishop's adventures, claiming that the churchmen had discovered an island of vast beauty situated within summery, turquoise waters; here they had burned their ships, and established an ideal state where all men lived in peace. They called the place the Island of the Seven Cities, or Antilia (hence the name "Antilles"). More was almost certainly thinking of such tales when he sat down to write his *Utopia*, and Antilia still appears on Portuguese maps as late as 1455, four years after Columbus was born in Genoa. More recently, the wholly fanciful island of Fonseca was supposed to be somewhere in the Caribbean and was actually granted to the

Earl of Montgomery in 1628. If it ever existed, it is nowhere to be found in the twenty-first century. Such accounts stretch across the length and breadth of the pre-modern European imagination, from the Lyonesse of Cornish tradition to Plato's *Timaeus*, where the naval juggernaut of Atlantis sends its fleet against the European mainland before being lost for all time (except to various eccentrics) beneath the sea. Given his own predilection for the fantastical, one wonders if Columbus himself half-hoped to stumble upon the storied shores of Antilia (or those of Avalon, or the Blessed Isles) as he walked along the beaches of the Canary Islands, discovering strangely carved icons of wood that had floated east across the ocean: miraculous ambassadors from vanished and watery worlds. The sunken cities. 'You go and see,' said Pieter, his breath heavy with whisky and his eyes shining. 'You take a boat; you go and see. Look down. It was all dry land.'

A few mornings later I stood just outside the small airport terminal and gazed to the south. It was a startlingly clear day, and in the crisp early-morning light, I glimpsed the sharp silhouette of St. Eustatius, her northern peaks tacked abruptly onto a steel-blue sky. Beyond, the hazy mass of St. Kitts might be seen, as well as a fragment of her sister island, largely autonomous Nevis. Further south was the volcanic rock of Montserrat—active, unpredictable—and then the Windwards. I had determined that St. Eustatius, Saba's unassuming consort, would be my next destination. When the little aircraft materialized and began its rapid descent, I thought once more of Rémy de Haenen and his dramatic inaugural landing on this spot. The propeller from his plane still graces the interior of the airport terminal, a kind of talismanic testament to Saba's decisive encounter with modernity. In his 1952 article about the island, Alec Waugh speculated that—without a beach and with little in the way of lucrative employment—Saba would soon become depopulated and forgotten, its waters serving merely as a meritorious destination for adventuresome yachtsmen on their way to St. Maarten or St. Barthélemy. That this did not happen is a tribute to men like de Haenen and Josephus Hassel, to airstrips inaugurated and roads improbably built. It is just as much a tribute to the determination of the ordinary people of the island to 'man the soil and go down to the sea,' as William had put it. Indeed, *Remis Velisque* is Saba's motto, "With Oars and Sails," an utterance that carries with it something of the nautical proletariat, a sense that is not belied on this island by the presence of mass tourism and its various engines of luxury. 'Saba's still got a lot of character,' William had said from behind the wheel of his taxi, and I had to agree (though I wondered about the story of his chauffeuring the Crown Prince of Denmark). As I climbed aboard the plane I remembered my earlier conversation with Richard and was happy to see that the aircraft was empty.

ST. EUSTATIUS

You may find him depicted on the walls of Canterbury Cathedral and in stained glass at Chartres, but by far the most renowned representation of St. Eustace is the painting executed in egg tempera by the fifteenth-century Italian artist known as Pisanello. Proud astride his mount, bedecked in a gold hunting robe and trailed by pale blue streamers descending from the cloud, like a turban atop his head, the figure of the saint sits transfixed by a stag placed just before him, an image of the crucified Christ suspended between his antlers. In fact, Pisanello gives us a representation of the saint at the moment of his conversion to Christianity. According to *The Golden Legend*, that often-fantastical thirteenth-century catalogue of the lives of the saints and martyrs, St. Eustace (or St. Eustáthios, as he is known in the Orthodox Church) was once a pagan Roman general of the early second century named Placidius. While hunting in Tivoli one afternoon, he came upon the stag and the strange vision, was instantly converted, and had himself and his family baptized. Alas, his zeal for the new faith was not rewarded in the sub-lunar world: one legend has it that his sons were devoured by wolves or lions, another that the entire family was roasted alive in the belly of a bronze bull. During the Middle Ages, St. Eustace was widely venerated in the Roman Catholic Church, though today his powers of intercession are more likely to be called upon by the Orthodox faithful, who have ensured that his is a far-traveled name: churches dedicated to him may be found in regions as widely distant from one another as St. Paul, Minnesota and Melbourne, Australia. It was in his capacity as patron saint of Roman Catholic Madrid, however, that the name of Eustace was carried across the ocean and deployed to identify a small island of 11.8 square miles, situated at 63 degrees of longitude, about forty miles south of St. Maarten, part of the inner chain of the Leeward Islands, with a dormant volcano perched impressively at its southern tip and the smaller peaks of Boven and Gilboa to the north. This is the most likely account of the island's naming (and namesake), though some uncertainty exists, with a few early sources claiming that St. Eustatius was actually named for another early Christian martyr, St. Anastasia. What is certain, however, is the extent to which the island has been displaced from its earlier regional significance. Situated at the center of West Indian commerce and conflict throughout most of the seventeenth and eighteenth centuries, St. Eustatius now goes her own quiet way, a bit wistful, perhaps, in her solitary nonchalance and indifference to the demands of high-end luxury, the careful cultivation of tourist appeal. When you have ridden as many troughs and swells as this place, not much impresses you; as new economic engines replace older ones, perhaps you come to suspect that catastrophe and quietude will find their way as surely as a pirogue with a fair sky and a following sea, or the frigate of a bewigged, bellicose and blue-coated admiral stepped from a Gainsborough to take his revenge. Remote or half-remembered as they might be (and despite the fact that most travelers will disembark elsewhere), there is something disadvantageous and ungrateful in overlooking the timeworn tales of old saints and soldiers, old slaves and Levantine merchants, of passing over the storied shores of timeworn islands for trendier destinations.

*

Pressed on board a small aircraft without a single seat to spare and hurtling roughly through a thick night-time sky toward St. Eustatius, I wondered where I was to sleep that evening. Once more, I would be traveling alone; I had made online reservations through the island's tourist website several months earlier, but when I had tried to email my contact to confirm those reservations in the week before my departure, I had received no reply. As my airline tickets were already paid for, this was cause for some concern. Upon landing in St. Maarten, I made a series of hurried telephone calls to St. Eustatius' tourist office, calls from an airport payphone, as my cell received no signal there. With each call, I spoke to a different official at the tourist office, while my inquiries grew increasingly apprehensive. No one seemed to recognize my name and there was apparently no record of any reservation having been made "either online or in writing," as I was punctiliously informed. Each of my interlocutors was soft-spoken and unfailingly polite, but they were unsure what precisely could be done at this time. When I asked to speak to one of the more decisive-sounding officials whom I had talked with during my first call, I was told that he had stepped out of the office to drive his cousin up to Hearty, but that he would almost certainly return before the end of the afternoon. Realizing that I probably had no idea of what Hearty meant, the gentleman offered a clarification. 'That's near Round Hill,' he said. While not especially helpful at the moment, this further detail was offered quietly and earnestly, as if I was already comfortably ensconced in a small bungalow somewhere on the island, and had stopped to ask a constable for directions. The gentleman's name was Anthony, and his brief tutorial was a kind of premature welcome, an assertion that, despite my gathering alarm and uncertainty, somewhere nearby there was an island with streets and neighborhoods, houses and bedrooms, one of which (presumably) I would soon occupy. I gave Anthony the number of the payphone from which I was calling, but, having heard nothing further from the tourist board by the time my flight was to depart, I decided to climb aboard the aircraft, buckle myself in, and see what would happen upon landing.

Flying onto an unfamiliar island in the dark can be disorienting. Sea and sky are mingled in a skein of black that disables any sense of direction; silent bodies rock sleepily with each bounce of the aircraft, while far, far below there is nothing but a hypothetical ocean filled with weird, chimerical fish. Given the relatively late hour, I had expected an empty flight to St. Eustatius; instead, the plane was filled with what looked to be a mix of regular commuters and a handful of travelers who were returning home after extended sojourns farther afield. Young men with baggy blue jeans and heavy gold jewelry, baseball caps askew, sat beside older gentlemen in washed-out work clothes and tired-looking black shoes. A clutch of dark-skinned West Indian ladies sat together near the rear of the aircraft, hair pulled back handsomely and faces expertly (though softly) made-up, with bright, impeccable dresses of floral print design complemented by sets of smart high-heeled shoes. After we had hit a particularly wicked little bump, one of the ladies called out in an unhurried and somnolent tone, 'Don't worry. We in God's hands.' There was a trickle of laughter followed by further commentary, the women hurtling through space perfectly attired and engaged in a musical sort of point-and-counter-point dialogue, with all the ease and exquisite self-possession of a virtuoso chamber orchestra. Then all was silence. When the little orange lights of St. Eustatius suddenly appeared, blinking up from the diminutive, crooked streets of Oranjestad, I found myself scanning the horizon for that pair of straight, sharp blue lines that announce an airstrip. Had we been on our approach during daylight hours, I would have seen the green stump of Pilot Hill rising like a silent beacon to our left, fronted by the red rocks and white surf of Tumble Down Dick Bay. I was later to discover that the celebrated "Captain Pipe" was one of the first to land upon this airstrip, in November of 1946 (José Dormoy has not appeared in these pages for the last time). No sooner had I spotted the lights of the airfield, than the de Havilland thumped to the ground and grumbled to a stop beside a brightly lit terminal surrounded by fields of darkness.

Our arrival seemed to have burst the terminal building into a small frenzy. I passed through a narrow room where a crisply attired and scrupulous official stamped my passport with the careful attention of a painter of miniatures. "St. Eustatius. The Golden Rock," read the carefully applied imprimatur of the

Customs and Immigration Department. At the same time, the disciplined precision of the spectacled official was beset on all sides by a swirl of activity and good-natured volubility that belied the small size of the terminal. Travelers swarmed to collect their bulging suitcases and groaning cardboard boxes, the latter frayed at the edges and fracturing inconveniently, secured by rolls of duct tape and marked with names and addresses in big black letters. Luggage began to collect in little islands across the yellow terminal floor, as middle-aged wives in salmon kerchiefs and modest checked dresses greeted their red-eyed husbands, and a troop of younger arrivals whooped and hollered their jovial hellos and raillery. Amidst this raucous and generous homecoming, a rooster—the infamous and ubiquitous red jungle fowl, whose shriek has been said to recall even the dead themselves to waking consciousness—crowed shrilly and paced back and forth just beyond the doorway that opened onto the idling taxis and gasoline fumes: a finely plumed and virile threshold guardian. As I was clearly the only tourist to have arrived that evening, it was probably a simple matter for Beverley to identify me. She was from the tourist office, a tall, handsome black woman, with a soft voice and a languorous, sensual face. Quietly efficient and apologetic, she informed me that internet service had been down on the island for some time and had just been restored a few hours earlier; only then had she received the queries concerning my reservations. The confusion earlier in the day had arisen from the fact that my name had been misspelled in the official register (I never learned who Anthony thought I was supposed to have been). In any case, everything had been arranged and Beverley escorted me across the room, past the scurrying rooster, and outside to where the Daihatsu minivans huddled beside the curb. I was introduced to an elderly driver who shook my hand with old-world gallantry, and welcomed me to "Statia," as nearly everyone there calls the place. Beverley told him where I was to be taken and after offering me the passenger seat and climbing up behind the wheel we headed off through Oranjestad toward the neighborhood called Princess Garden.

There are one or two very small resorts on the island, but I had decided to forgo these places and instead made arrangements to lodge in the home of a Statian lady named Alma. Much has been written about the hidden costs of tourism in the Caribbean, particularly the ways in which all-inclusive resorts frequently serve to place the vacation industry into the hands of various off-island investors at the expense of local entrepreneurs. The elaborate nexus of airlines, tour operators and resorts managed by far-flung conglomerates has long meant that the all-inclusive hotels (with a more or less steady flow of tourists funneled into the pipeline) can often drive local competition out of business. To make matters worse, a sizable percentage of all monies spent at such resorts finds its way off-island to parent companies and international investors; such "leakages" sometimes running as high as 60%. The newfound ease with which individual travelers may research and book a vacation online could serve to alter this dynamic (only time will tell), but as of now it is still conceded by travel experts that vacationers who stay at an all-inclusive tend to spend less (and less usefully) relative to the overall island economies. Why hire a taxi and leave the hotel grounds for dinner when there are usually several restaurants at the resort, with meals often included in the overall cost of the booking? Instead, I decided on home-stay as the most equitable of travel options. While the cab negotiated a series of sharp turns through what appeared to be impossibly slender streets, I found myself musing upon the peculiar paradox confronting the contemporary traveler. The relative ease with which I may pass from here to there means that the very *raison d'être* of travel itself is called into question, just as my capacity to experience the evocative, particular difference of a place is gradually erased along with the ascendancy of a globalized space of familiarity and convenience, accessibility and cultural consensus. Travelers have always brought something of themselves to the encounter with their destinations (with more or less felicitous consequences), but at the dawn of the twenty-first century, the real *presence* of the destination is in danger of being overwhelmed and irremediably altered by the sheer quantitative heft of tourism and its various cultural and economic complexes. We travel further but get no farther, secular pilgrims from whom the holy places perpetually recede, even as we discover that we have already been there, regardless of the destination. This, no doubt, is something of what Albert Camus had in mind when he wrote that there are "no more deserts, no more islands," even though we need them.

It was impossible to obtain a clear sense of St. Eustatius in the dark. Occasionally, blue or electric-orange streetlights revealed a solitary pedestrian or a small collection of neighbors gathered quietly upon low-hanging balconies and within tiny, rusticated courtyards. There seemed to be no other vehicle on the road. Once or twice the minivan squeezed down cobbled alleyways so narrow that only a bare whisper of space separated the bruised vehicle from the clapboard or cement walls of Oranjestad. Fragments of domesticity were then briefly framed by half-opened windows and indolent shutters, shrugged casually aside. Disconnected blooms of architecture materialized suddenly and then vanished as our headlights quavered along small streets or spun lazily at various empty intersections: blank cement walls topped with strange crowns of cobwebbed rebar and roofs with red fish-scale shingles. Narrow balconies perched just above our heads, hemmed with spindly balustrades and crested by dissipated carved wooden spandrels. Seated behind me in the cab was a youngish man with sharp features, dark hair and a strangely orange complexion. He wore a cotton shirt, open at the neck, a pair of khakis and what appeared to be a set of greenish loafers (no socks); a heavy gold watch hung upon his left wrist and he would frequently turn the palm of his hand upward to check the time, glancing at the illuminated face through a pair of dark glasses. He seemed to belong to that species of nomadic corporate adventurer, half entrepreneur and half pirate, that one might often spy in air-conditioned airport lounges throughout the Caribbean: minding the main chance and dreaming outsized dreams of financial derring-do (and often dubious legality). I hadn't noticed him at first, but, having (apparently) made eye contact, he now seemed to feel the obligation to say something. As I shook my head uncomprehendingly in response to one or two Dutch interrogatives, he quickly turned to English, asking if I was involved with the refinery. 'What refinery?' I replied. He looked surprised and paused for a moment, glancing back over his shoulder for what seemed to be dramatic effect. 'You can see it when you climb to the top of the Quill,' he said, 'bunker fuel, for ships.' I nodded and he quickly fell silent. He seemed to feel that he had given away something vital to the uninitiated and a mild chagrin (conjoined with the effects of one tanning session too many) bloomed lividly upon his cheeks and colored the tip of his entrepreneurial nose. After a pause I asked the man if he worked at the refinery. He shook his head and grinned. 'Ever hear of the Orinoko Belt?' I hadn't. 'Largest petroleum deposit in the world not in the Middle East. You know where? Venezuela.' He raised a finger, as if asking for silence. After a pause he said, 'Chinese. Once they expand the Canal they're going to bring in the big boats, haul a hell of a load of petroleum back east: Japan, China, Vietnam. Beijing's throwing money around all over the place down here. There's a bridge in Dominica's got Chinese dragons at both ends.' Something outside the vehicle caught his attention and he quickly called out to the driver to stop. '*C'est le guerre,*' he added with a cryptic wink as he exited the cab and disappeared into the night. I noticed that he didn't pay the driver. Apparently arrangements had been made. There was something of the old playhouse villain about the man, I thought afterwards: a little sinister and faintly comic at the same time. I would see him once more before my departure.

I was to discover that securing a glimpse of the refinery was nearly impossible. A sliver of a view might be obtained from the rim of the Quill, but little else. Nevertheless, the facility—an important transshipment center with a storage capacity of five million barrels—generates a significant amount of revenue for St. Eustatius, serving as a link to the enormous refinery at Curaçao, which employs over a thousand people. A few months before my arrival, ownership had passed from Nu Star Energy to the Asian juggernaut Petro China. Royal Dutch Shell was among the first significant players in the processing, refining and transportation of South American petroleum, getting into the game around the time of the First World War. The refining of Venezuelan crude came along at a fortuitous moment for the West Indies: facilities on Aruba, Curaçao and Trinidad—as well as St. Eustatius—helped to employ a growing number of people who were left idle as the sugar industry continued its long decline and work wound down on the Panama Canal, which was completed in 1914. In particular, the large-scale migration of labor from the eastern Caribbean created an economically important but politically disenfranchised black population on the island of Curaçao. The unrest that followed when these laborers sought redress for their grievances may be said to have catapulted the Netherlands Antilles out of the doldrums and into the modern age. So, a digression.

Under the terms of the Charter which created the Netherlands Antilles in 1954, Curaçao served as the association's capital; on this island, however, a small non-black political elite ran the show and was largely indifferent to the plight of black migrant workers. Tensions finally erupted into outright violence in May 1969—whether the event was a riot, a strike or an insurrection depends upon who you ask—and the Hague was obliged to deploy a detachment of marines to restore order. The incident was deeply embarrassing for the Dutch government, which found itself accused internationally of harboring nefarious neo-colonial designs in the region. While this accusation was probably untrue, such violence did serve to demonstrate the limitations of the Charter and of the Netherlands Antilles as a workable political union. A growing sense of the Charter as fundamentally flawed was soon complemented by a challenge to its very *raison d'être.* The Charter had created three autonomous states as part of the Kingdom of the Netherlands: the Netherlands itself, the Antilles (consisting of St. Eustatius, Saba and the other islands), along with the former plantation colony of Suriname in South America. It had always been assumed that this arrangement existed as a temporary middle ground between the territories' colonial past and their inevitable future as sovereign states. Thus, when Suriname secured her independence in 1975, it was expected that the Caribbean islands would quickly follow along, an assumption that the tottering political and financial situation of the new South American nation quickly invalidated. Of particular concern to the little economies of the Antilles were those political realities which would come to pass upon full independence: the loss of the Hague's generous financial support, as well as gradually tightening controls on emigration from the Caribbean to the Netherlands (which would mean, among other things, fewer remittances). It thus became clear that, despite promises of Caribbean de-colonization that had been made by the Dutch monarchy as early as the 1940s, the six West Indian islands had little enthusiasm for independence. Thus, by the early 1980s the Charter could no longer be seen as a step toward full sovereignty, nor could it be understood as providing an effective model for open-ended, post-colonial Dutch administration. The sliver of a view from the top of the Quill thus calls to mind more than a sliver of the Dutch Caribbean past.

*

I arrived at Alma's house late in the evening but I was nevertheless quickly subject to the quietly assertive and bounteous hospitality for which the West Indies is justifiably famous. Alma herself was a large woman with big, powerful hands and broad, stoical features. Despite her size she moved with ease and grace, her soft voice occasionally exploding into unexpected barks of laughter and her still, phlegmatic demeanor suddenly dissolving into whirligigs of girlish delight. She habitually cleaned her glasses with a small handkerchief, the movements of her hands more meditative than fastidious. Removing her glasses from their red leather case, Alma would hold them up to the light and then produce her handkerchief with a quiet flourish, all amidst an extended silence that underscored the solemnity of the exercise. Such moments came to feel something akin to liturgical, the glasses and their case serving as domestic talismans. I thought that Alma was probably in her early fifties, but her face, ageless and imperturbable, kept this secret to itself. After I had deposited my bags in the rear bedroom, I suddenly found myself seated before a hearty bowl of pea soup, richly festooned with enormous dumplings, tasty-looking carrots and sapid hillocks of savory ham (this despite the fact that it was nearly eleven at night). I was to be the happy beneficiary of Alma's cooking throughout my stay. Often, as our conversations slowly circled to a halt amidst the torpor of a late Caribbean afternoon, a measured pause and a cleaning of glasses would be followed by my hostess' casual inquiry as to whether or not I would like something to eat. Whatever my response, I would soon find myself deliciously besieged by resplendent platoons of roasted chicken, flanked by battalions of pigeon peas and sticky brown rice, fresh papaya

64

and roasted breadfruit, or a full detachment of buttery eggs with warm biscuits and jelly. Nor do I ever remember dining alone. The fondness with which I recall these meals is thus no doubt colored by the delightful discussions that accompanied them, each exchange an admixture of modest formality and warm, unguarded sincerity. From Alma I learned that some "dude boys" were making a bit of innocuous mischief down in the lower town and that a new administrative superintendent had recently arrived from the Netherlands. I also discovered that a jeep had burst into flames quite mysteriously down near Mansion Pasture (a few people suspected foul play but it was difficult to credit such conjectures on an island of 3,500 souls, where people slept with the doors unlocked, often wide open). Through these conversations I was also familiarized with some of the *de facto* legal particulars of life on St. Eustatius. 'If a neighbor's cow wanders onto my property,' Alma informed me, 'I am required to tie him up and tell the man who own him.' On such a small island, the law apparently expected little confusion concerning the identity of the animal's owner. If, however, the cow was not claimed within ten days, 'Then he belong to me!' crowed Alma gleefully, and roared with laughter.

Alma's home was adorned with various photographs of her prodigious extended family, a welter of cousins, aunties, children and grandchildren. There was one very old studio image of a melancholy West Indian bride standing stiffly in a trim white dress and situated in a sepia landscape of European provenance, but nowhere could I discover intimations of a husband. Nothing happened in Princess Garden that Alma did not know about, often *before* it happened. She maintained a trim, genteel home that was open at all times to a variety of neighbors who often dropped in unannounced to enjoy a cool glass of iced tea upon her small shaded porch, exchanging news and gossip in tones that managed to be both cheerful and strangely solemn. I recall Alma presiding gracefully over these intimate gatherings in a light dress of modest length with a palm frond and leopard print pattern, eyeglasses perched in her right hand and a hymnal nearby. She was an active member of the local Methodist church, and sang (wonderfully well, I was told by several people) in the choir. She was also very much involved in the cultural life of the island: Ellis Lopes, St. Eustatius' resident playwright, was a close friend and Alma was preparing to perform the part of the Narrator in an upcoming performance of Lopes' *A Different Story* on the island of Antigua. This play, first produced on St. Eustatius in 2008 to commemorate World AIDS Day, tells the story of a young man called Timmothy who has inherited HIV/AIDS from his deceased mother and who has fallen in love with a girl named Carrie. Timmothy is urged by his uncle, Dr. Theopholis, to avoid sleeping with Carrie in order to spare her falling victim to the same disease. Theopholis tries everything to persuade his nephew, including a proposal of strategic masturbation ('Visit Mrs. Palmer and her five daughters'). Eventually the girl is sent away to school and Timmothy appears to affirm a celibate affection for her, although he is uncertain if he will live to see Carrie upon her return to the island. The playwright himself—son of St. Eustatius' first Island Council Deputy—worked for many years at the Lago Refinery on Aruba before serving a stint in the United States Army (improbably enough, he was stationed for some time in Anchorage, Alaska, where he learned ballet). Lopes inaugurated the St. Eustatius Action

66

Theatre in 1978 with an adaptation of George Bernard Shaw's *Mrs. Warren's Profession* and has gone on to pen more than twenty plays and skits. With his pensive face, trim mustache and piercing, attentive eyes, Lopes remains an institution on the island and is St. Eustatius' unofficial cultural ambassador to the world. I was very grateful when Alma presented me with a typed copy of Lopes' drama as a gift.

*

Despite the exhaustion I felt on the evening of my arrival, I arose early the next morning, anxious to see something of the island before everyone was awake. Having arrived in the dark, I was unaware of the situation of the house and of the landscape round about, but I soon discovered a small garden alongside my room, where wisps of bougainvillea were brushed by a faint morning sun into soft shades of coral and plum. Just beyond this garden, the land began to rise—gradually at first, then more dramatically—until it culminated in a half-broken crater rim, suspended nearly 2,000 feet above sea level. The mountain glowered in grayish-green shadow, the small white disk of the sun rising tentatively across the darkened, forested brim. This was the Quill, the cone of a dormant volcano that looms over the Statia landscape, and whose receding shadow announces the arrival of morning to the residents of the island, the majority of whom live on a narrow strip of relatively flat land situated between the Quill to the southeast, and a gathering of smaller peaks to the northwest. I had read about the Quill before my departure, but I had no idea that Alma's home was situated at the very point where the famous mountain began its ascent. I dressed quickly, passed quietly down the hallway and out into the small front garden where I might have a better glimpse of the peak. On the porch I was surprised to meet a young black man who was sitting quietly and sipping a cup of tea. He looked to be barely out of his teens but he was meticulously attired in a handsome charcoal suit and red tie, with a bulging satchel placed like a little terrier at his feet. His name was Bradley; a nephew of Alma's, he was currently in residence and was about to begin his rounds. He explained in a soft voice that he was enrolled in an expensive school off-island and that he secured a favorable adjustment of his tuition from the door-to-door sale of books during the summer months. 'Titles of an academic nature,' he offered gravely. I expressed curiosity about his cache of books, but he seemed to feel that hawking his titles to a guest was bad form, for, to my surprise, he made no attempt to do so. We sat together in silence and watched the sun climb over the mountain. 'It's a real panorama,' he said, and after a long pause he added, 'I've seen pictures of the Quill from outer space, on the internet.' Was it just as impressive? 'It looked small,' he said. Bradley spoke of the iguanas that lived inside the rim of the Quill: bright green and crested with a Mohawk fan along their backs, with cold reptilian eyes, undulating sandpaper skin and Jurassic claws that daggered the flanks of silk cotton and yellow plum trees down in the crater basin. 'But you won't see them,' he said, 'there are few of them these days. They eat birds' eggs.' A bookish and slightly funereal young man with big staring eyes and the whisper of a Van Dyke, he spoke with soft delight about the island, particularly as he had been given the chance to provide an introductory lecture on St. Eustatius to an older visitor. 'The Quill appears on the flag of St.

Eustatius,' he informed me. 'Aside from St. Lucia, St. Eustatius has the only flag in the world with a geographical feature as its primary device.' He seemed pleased to have imparted such expert information with such grave formality and went on to say that I must try and catch a glimpse of the White Wall, an impressive limestone formation on the far side of the Quill. 'It's a real panorama,' he said. We sat in silence; after a moment a large cow—eyes lolling and round udder shuddering with each step—moved slowly past the house and down the little street toward Cottage Pasture. I had yet to see a car drive past. My companion nodded and caught my eye as if to affirm the veracity of the odd and dreamlike interlude. 'Cows,' he said. Bradley took his teacup back into the kitchen and reappeared a moment later. 'My auntie is going to bring you breakfast on the porch,' he informed me with a solemn smile. I thanked Bradley for his company; he adjusted his jacket, gathered up his satchel, and headed down along the little front path. After stepping out onto the street he turned around to close the gate and glanced back at me. 'This island is my home,' he said in a dry, matter-of-fact tone that belied not a touch of sentiment. He nodded, secured the gate, and was gone.

*

The Quill takes its name from a Dutch word (*kuil*) meaning "pit," and the crater floor constitutes a unique micro-climate, full of flora and fauna that differ dramatically from what one finds upon the interior slopes of the mountain or along the rim. Dispersed across the floor of the crater is a thickly wooded tropical forest, with a canopy that towers as high as 130 feet;

here one may find red-skinned gum trees, as well as trumpet woods, with their strangely bulbous gray leaves. I also spotted bunches of wild bananas: smaller, greener and more tart than the store-bought variety. Yellow and fuchsia begonias also grow wild here, in small clusters of profligate delight, but one might also find cultivated crops at the bottom of the crater, particularly patches of cacao. Many of these plots have been cultivated by the same families for several generations, and while they are not noticeably demarcated, everyone seems to know which patch belongs to whom. Tending to the cacao plants is no easy task, requiring the growers to clamber up the sides of the Quill, across the rim, and then down along the interior slopes. There are many reports of broken limbs, but the stalwart farmers of St. Eustatius seem to regard this sort of thing as a rite of passage and no one is too awfully put out by the great difficulty. The interior slopes are quite steep and must be navigated carefully, although this landscape also provides an ideal habitat for a variety of birdlife: Red-necked pigeons and crested hummingbirds nest here, along with the stunning (and relatively uncommon) purple-throated carib, known as the *fou-fou* in the French Antilles. This creature grows to a size of about four or five inches, its hooked and extended beak an ideal instrument for securing nectar from the flowering plants that grow in Edenic profusion throughout the crater. The carib's wings are a jostled mix of cobalt blue and kelly green, its chest an electric lavender almost otherworldly in its brilliance. I was told that while the males tenaciously guard their favorite patches of flora from avian intruders, the females take a different approach, foraging across many miles in a process known as trap-lining. The highest point of the crater rim—known as Mazinga—affords a stunning view of St. Kitts and Nevis on clear days, and it is here that one may discover the small elfin forest that tufts the top of the mountain, punctuated by stands of wild balsam. The luxuriant and viridian picture of the Quill that one obtains from the Mazinga Trail belies a violent past, however—and one not so very remote—for the last volcanic eruption occurred only about 1,600 years ago. The Quill is unquestionably the most distinctive of Statia's natural features and seems to have always exerted an influence upon the aesthetic sensibilities of settlers as well as passers-by. In 1782, C. F. Bendorp executed a famous copperplate engraving of St. Eustatius, its harbor teeming with sloops and merchant vessels of various nationalities, as befitted one of the Caribbean's most thriving eighteenth-century ports. A number of dwellings cluster along the shore and atop the ridge that demarcates the upper town of Oranjestad, the entire scene executed deftly and tastefully, with a fine sense of proportion, until one glances upon the Quill at the right edge of the engraving. Here the ground rises too abruptly, the few homesteads situated along the outer slopes are perched disconcertingly at weird, impossible angles, while the rim of the mountain peeks through what might be either low clouds or ghostly plumes of hot ash, a lingering unconscious memory of earlier devastation. The bustling engine of Dutch commercial vigor is nicely fore-grounded by Bendorp, but his dizzying depiction of the Quill—monstrous, beautiful, alarming— situates the little world of men and merchants within the figurative penumbra of a natural realm that broods with an ominous indifference over such irrelevancies as markets, men and history.

Rather than attempt to scale the flanks of the mountain at the very beginning of my stay, I decided instead to explore the town of Oranjestad, a small settlement that one can investigate thoroughly on foot. The sun had risen higher in the sky, but it was still a delightfully cool Caribbean morning as I wandered past the trim medical center and down Queen Beatrix Road; once or twice another pedestrian would appear, and even more rarely a car would clatter past, but I spent the majority of the morning as a kind of solitary pilgrim passing quietly along empty streets, often beneath a canopy of feathery tamarind leaves or striking poinciana, carmine blooms turned to bright points of flame by sunlight that filtered street-ward through a warbled truss of branches and growth. One of the region's most striking trees, the poinciana (also known as the flamboyant tree) may put forth either red or orange blossoms; to me, it also seems to carry romance and history in its very name. Introduced into the region from Madagascar, it was christened in honor of Philippe de Poincy, a seventeenth-century governor of the French Antilles. De Poincy resided on St. Christophe, the same island which the British named St. Christopher, and which, for a number of uneasy decades, was shared (as well as contested) by both nations. Here de Poincy is said to have lived in outrageous Gallic splendor on his estate called La Fontaine, where he entertained visiting guests like the Swedish military engineer Peter Lindström within his four-story mansion, the structure surrounded by a walled courtyard and formal gardens which one approached by way of a soaring *allée* of trees. Maybe. No evidence of such magnificence survives on the grounds of the present Fountain Estate, though there is no doubt that this was the site of de Poincy's official residence. Rumor and fanciful imaginings apparently transformed a modest rural seat into something impossibly splendid; most of the habitations described by visitors to St. Christophe in the 1650s were built of boards arranged upon square posts. De Poincy's residence was probably built of similar stuff, and was probably not much grander than many of its neighbors. As a Knight of the Order of St. John of Jerusalem, however, de Poincy was entitled to wear a bright scarlet robe, so the tree which produced a similarly hued scarlet flower was subsequently named for him.

Continuing on my morning walk into town, I passed more and more houses situated alongside the road. These were unostentatious dwellings, comfortable but dignified, some assembled from clapboard (soft pinks and blues might be seen, though the Saba model of green trim on white was not uncommon), others from the distinctive yellow bricks manufactured in the Netherlands and shipped out to St. Eustatius many centuries ago. These narrow, peeling little blocks managed to impart to the various structures a sense of imperturbable privacy, impossible age and spry whimsy. They brought to mind Washington Irving's Sunnyside, that charming abode (built of the same stuff) on the banks of the Hudson River, a romantic testament to a bygone age of Pieter Stuyvesant and New Amsterdam, of farmwives with their linsey-woolsey right off the loom, and *myneers* with their plump paunches, pipes and ghost stories. The Dutch, often vague outliers in the American historical consciousness (outside of New York, at any rate), suddenly loomed large. I remembered that Stuyvesant passed this way in 1644 when he sought to retake nearby St. Maarten from the Spanish. It was in this failed attempt that he lost his leg and procured the wooden surrogate that Diedrich

Knickerbocker and Howard Pyle would make famous. I made a left on Breedeweg and passed a small park glittering with pink and white oleander. While my recollections of Saba are haunted by mists and twilight, Statia is always bright with sunshine and festooned with flowering plants: white stars of frangipani and swarms of yellow allamanda thronging the frames of old ruined houses, amber and apricot Barbados lilies run riot along a stone wall, flamingo flowers with their leaves like red-veined, synthetic salvers, even the odd St. Eustatius morning glory that was still blooming in early June, its mauve and cherry blossoms set off by the points of pertinacious white stamens. Nevertheless, such pleasant floral solitude was often only a street corner away from melancholy and moodiness. Some ghosts walk in the daylight, and are not frightening so much as vaguely (if amiably) sad. Such was the charm of this place, whether in the streets of Oranjestad or passing through those sparsely settled regions toward the windward side of the island: empty-looking scrub country dotted here and there with wonderfully lonesome homes carrying wonderfully lonesome names—Roots, Solitude, Mary's Glory—several of these lost amidst waves of purple corallita and sparkling oleander, the countryside as bedecked with blooms as a Botticelli springtime.

*

Breedeweg terminates at the point where it meets the Kerkweg, and to my right I saw the shell of the church which has given its name to the street. A low wall surrounds the cemetery, within which a number of old tombstones lie casually and quietly in the shadow of a tall tamarind tree, its dried, cast-off pods rasping faintly amongst the stones in a soft morning breeze, snapping now and then beneath my feet. The cemetery was spotted with hurricane graves: gray piles of stone topped with barrel vaults, they resemble small cisterns and are meant to withstand the terrible storm winds of August and September. Peculiarly, a single ancient-looking streetlamp is also situated within the cemetery grounds. Interred near the church is the body of Willem Crul, at one time something of a hero on St. Eustatius and thus afforded an enviable place amongst the departed of the Second Dutch Reformed Church. He was born in Haarlem in 1721 and was in command of the *Mars*, a ship of the line, when the British occupied St. Eustatius sixty years later. From my unquestionably imperfect translation of his tombstone, I gathered that Crul had organized a convoy to move men and materiel off the island (and thus out of the hands of the British), but that his vessel was overtaken by Royal Navy warships near Sombrero Island, possibly the same Sombrero that lies about thirty-five miles to the northwest of Anguilla. Crul was killed in the engagement and his body taken back to St. Eustatius for burial. At least I think that is the gist of the Dutch text. The church itself was erected in 1755, but all that remains today are the outer walls and the bell-tower; these are built of local gray-stone, volcanic in origin, specimens of which you might stumble upon even today in the more remote parts of the island. The timbered roof and flooring vanished long ago: a field of scrub grass carpets the nave of the church, while a ceiling of West Indian sky caps the weathered walls that once echoed with psalms and sermons. When was the last service held here, I wondered, and who was the man who fastened the door one Sunday afternoon upon what began—in that same moment—its career as a ruin, an artifact of devotion? Glancing through the eyeless window-frames arranged along the western wall, a cerulean ocean hung vividly in the morning calm. I recalled as I stood there D.H. Lawrence's claim that no church reaches its full perfection until it has become a ruin. In this place, a particular vocabulary of the sacred had run its course, even as the primary venerable things spoke once more and forever of themselves: earth and sky, light and decay, divinity and mortals and the sea.

The first place of Christian worship on the island was a small chapel erected within Fort Oranje, a fortification begun by the Dutch in 1629, razed and rebuilt on several occasions, and situated about 500 yards from the church I had just been exploring. One enters the fort through a sallyport on the landward side, passing beneath a mounted escutcheon, bearing a yellow field and five blue stars, topped by the Dutch crown. Beneath this device are the words LIBERTATE and VNANIMVS. The Dutch West India Company, overseen by the indefatigable Heren XIX, was less than ten years old when construction of the fort began, and while the first Dutch settlers apparently discovered a small French population that called the island home, there seems to have been little difficulty in securing their pledge of loyalty to the House of Orange. After passing through a narrow portal, one emerges onto a wide parade ground of flagstone and brick, the entire yard framed by a few small barracks, their stone foundations supporting yellowed clapboard walls capped by carpenter's lace and red-shingled roofs. A tall coconut palm stood near the barracks, where a magnificent blue and yellow parrot shrilled a sardonic commentary upon the faded martial glory of the place.

The perimeter of the fortification is defended by a number of small cannon mounted atop little green carriages and peeking out upon the sea through narrow cuts in the parapet, though such guns were of little use in 1781 when Sir George Brydges Rodney attacked and occupied the island, a campaign that still haunts St. Eustatius in many ways and which decisively lowered the curtain on its great age of prosperity. The current incarnation of Fort Oranje appears to date from the late nineteenth century, the main magazine and officers' quarters built of yellow brick (now a weathered gray and black), while at the center of the parade ground a plaque stands below the flag of the Netherlands, commemorating those who gave their lives in the service of the Dutch government-in-exile during World War II. As more than one Statian seemed rather proud to report, St. Eustatius (along with her sister islands) constituted the only free Dutch soil in the world after Germany occupied the Netherlands in the spring of 1940, and the Japanese took the East Indies archipelago (present-day Indonesia) in 1941. Just a few months before the beginning of the war, as the situation in Europe continued to deteriorate, and doubtless conscious of St. Eustatius' situation relative to the region's oil refineries, President Franklin D. Roosevelt visited the island and asserted the abiding good will of the United States toward the people of St. Eustatius. This visit is still commemorated on the island in at least two ways: the airport carries the name of the thirty-second president, while Statia and America Day continues to be celebrated on the sixteenth of every November. This date does not commemorate Roosevelt's stopover, however, but an even earlier event (largely forgotten in the United

States, though certainly not on St. Eustatius) that tied the fortunes of the nascent American republic inextricably to what was known as the Golden Rock of the Antilles. The first Dutch to arrive on the island sought to make their fortunes in tobacco, but it soon became clear that, in the days when other European powers severely restricted the trade of their own Caribbean possessions, vaster sums of money might be generated by developing tiny St. Eustatius as one of the region's only free ports. As far as London and Paris were concerned, any merchandise that changed hands in St. Eustatius and then found its way to Antigua or Martinique or Guadeloupe was contraband, while the activity of the Dutch merchants at Oranjestad was nothing more or less than smuggling. The mercantilist assumptions that underlay seventeenth- and eighteenth-century European colonialism presumed that overseas territories existed for the benefit of the mother country and that all goods purchased in those territories could only be brought to market courtesy of European merchants operating from French or British homeports. Frequently, finished goods manufactured from raw materials taken from the colonies themselves would then be shipped back to those same colonies from Europe, with a considerable mark-up. But such goods could be purchased much more cheaply from St. Eustatius than from the merchants and middlemen of Le Havre or Liverpool. Thus, the inhabitants of the French and British islands sought to dissuade their home governments from taking any action against St. Eustatius that might disrupt the status quo. In the fall of 1776, however, with the American colonies in open revolt, the governor of the Golden Rock was to go too far. On November 16th of that year a small two-masted brigantine called the *Andrew Doria* arrived just off Oranjestad. She had sailed secretly from Gloucester, New Jersey, just three weeks earlier. The ship was flying the red, white and blue colors approved by the Continental Congress in Philadelphia, and carrying a copy of the Declaration of Independence for the Dutch governor. Her mission was to purchase guns and powder for Washington's poorly supplied army and to transport these goods back to the pine-marshes and hidden passes of southern New Jersey. When the little ship fired its salute upon entering Statia's harbor, Governor de Graaff authorized a formal "return fire." With this salute, the American colors were formally recognized for the first time, St. Eustatius also becoming something of a lifeline for the rebellious American colonies throughout the war. It was this event that Roosevelt had celebrated in 1939, leaving behind a plaque at Fort Oranje that reads, in part:

> 'In commemoration of the salute of the flag of the United States fired in this fort November 16, 1776, by order of Johannes de Graaff, Governor of St. Eustatius… Here the sovereignty of the United States of America was first formally acknowledged to a national vessel by a foreign official.'

As I stood upon the empty parade ground, a red-plumed macaw joined his partner in the coconut tree; a wry, mournful shriek pulsed across the lonely paving stones and echoed back from the empty windows of the old barracks. Then, all was stillness.

*

'I not surprised you never heard a' "hippie,'" said Quentin as we each sipped a beer down at a little bar called Smoke Alley, 'but, you know, there's a statue out in front of Legislative Hall—the hippie band—it's the real Statia sound. It's the culture.' I had visited the West Indies enough to recognize the distinctive aura that informed this final word. In the United States, "culture" carries with it a whiff of the museum and of the obligatory, a collection of slightly effete pastimes indulged in and only vaguely enjoyed by a jejune cognoscenti. In the Caribbean, however, the term speaks of one's living heritage, one's patrimony, and is often colored by a populist, muscular mixture of swagger, pride and testosterone. Quentin was a high-spirited young man with serious eyes, a dark complexion and a face that frequently broke into a quizzical, almost derisive smile. Earlier in the day he had returned from St. Kitts, where he was helping a friend with a wholesale business in Basseterre. While he never played with a hippie band himself, Quentin sometimes composed little songs of his own, often on the spot. He was very knowledgeable about West Indian music in general and the music of St. Eustatius in particular. He remembered stories that his father had told him of a man named Peter John, who played the "African Drum" several decades back and who appears to have been a sort of beloved wandering minstrel on the island. Hippie itself is something else, however, and is usually performed by a band consisting of four or five musicians: a few guitars or ukuleles, a marimba, small flute and bahoe (a long tube-shaped instrument producing a low, metallic sound). 'My father says that around Christmas time the old rum shops used to be full of hippie for many nights,' said Quentin. 'You know, it must have been something, I think.' I discovered that his father had enjoyed a brief career as a musician, and I subsequently became the beneficiary of the musical knowledge that had been handed down from father to son. Quentin spoke about the history of calypso, Trinidadian music informed by West African *kaiso* and shaped by the experience of slaves on the old sugar plantations into a subversively cheerful diatribe against their masters and overseers, full of double entendre and musical horseplay. The earliest calypso recordings were made at about the time of the First World War, although by whom and precisely when remain points of contention. 'But hippie is part calypso *and* part reggae,' added Quentin. 'Reggae is Rastafarian music. The accent is always on the third beat of each bar—you know that?' I didn't. There was a brief pause, during which the young man sang quietly to himself from one of his own songs.

> 'Jah bless your hands.
> Jah bless your song.
> No more confusion.'

He was not a Rastafarian himself, he explained, but he enjoyed shaping these airs as little devotional exercises, 'keep me thinking right,' as he put it. The melodies were low and soft, impossibly gentle, I thought. We watched an enormous tanker glide silently northward toward the invisible refinery. 'There's music and there's *music*, you know?' asked Quentin. *Soca* remains something of a guilty pleasure for him. 'It's like calypso, but it's all party music—dancing music—nobody really talking about anything. That Arrow on Montserrat, he put it on the map. He grove good with it. Him I dig. But you wanna *hear* something you got to listen to Private. He's

Calypso and he lives here on Statia, comes down to Smoke Alley a lot. He like this place.' An Aruban with the poetical name of Leoncio Zhivago Lopes, Private is a fire-fighter as well as one of the island's most famous musical entertainers (I frequently heard of another celebrated vocalist and musician called the Mighty Fat, but neither he nor Private ever visited the bar while I was there, and I was never able to hear either of these musicians perform).

Smoke Alley sits on the leeward side of the island, on the way to the terminal and government dock. It is essentially an open deck beside the sea, built around a circular bar and small kitchen. I was a little surprised by the Caribbean kitsch of the place: plastic statues of fierce pirates and sensual mermaids, netting suspended along the rafters and wrapped round with small Heineken flags or red and yellow semaphore squares. My impression was that few tourists came to St. Eustatius, yet this place clearly seemed to be furnished with vacationers in mind. The reason soon became clear, as a boisterous congregation of American students from the medical college began to arrive for happy hour (two beers for three dollars). The sleepy mood of the place was quickly transformed, as a demonstrative, strident and bibulous fraternity party broke out before my eyes. I was reminded, after just a few days on soft-spoken St. Eustatius, of the *volume* of American life and American conversations. A clutch of young women with heavy eye-liner and honey-colored tank tops kicked off their shoes and danced together alongside the ersatz pirates (Red Stripes and cigarettes in place of plastic pistols and cutlasses), while several of their male companions gathered at the bar to talk basketball and residencies. I discovered that the college had been chartered in 1999, the same year that graduates became eligible to sit for the U.S. medical licensing exams; a number of the students specialized in undersea and hyperbaric medicine. While the medical college on nearby Saba was doing quite well, Statia's had often been viewed as its poor country cousin, much to the annoyance of my insistent drinking companions. Tonight, there was some additional concern amongst these young men that New York City might move to discontinue residency programs for graduates of medical schools in the Caribbean. 'That'd be a disaster for this place,' said one of them, neglecting to specify whether he was speaking about the school exclusively or the island as well. The music grew louder and the conversation more strident until finally it became almost impossible to talk. At one point Quentin leaned into me and asked if I had heard about the burning jeep up in Mansion Pasture. I nodded. 'It belong to him,' said Quentin, pointing to a man wearing a pair of dark sunglasses and greenish loafers with no socks. This seemed an odd coincidence. I told Quentin that I met the man when we shared a taxi on the evening of my arrival. He shrugged and said, 'Guess maybe the guy needed a ride.' The man seemed to be on friendly terms with one of the young women, although the precise nature of their relationship was unclear; he would have been close to twice her age. I raised my hand in greeting and he fired back a smart salute. 'Who is he?' I asked. Quentin paused. 'Some guy. Got something going down in Curaçao or someplace,' he said. A small pause followed, after which Quentin added, 'He don't belong here.' A little surprised by the bitterness of his retort, I let the matter rest.

Later that evening, as Quentin and I drove back up toward Princess Garden, the generator that provides electricity to the island shut down and St. Eustatius was plunged into darkness. For about thirty minutes, only the hospital, the police station, and the tiny airstrip were illuminated. 'Sometimes the lights go out,' said Quentin, stopping the car for a moment on the edge of a ramshackle little neighborhood called Benners. 'Look.' We watched as narrow doors were opened and darkened figures bearing hurricane lanterns stepped out into the night, the wavering threads of their lamps spinning soft saffron coils through the tapering streets. Silhouettes diminished their way down silent, cobblestoned back lanes, then passed into the light at various little gardens where young men had gathered with candles, lamps, and guitars, and where young women joined them, swaying and singing softly beneath a sky suddenly alive with an embarrassment of stars. This was an image of the Caribbean before electricity, in the days when kerosene was the latest innovation, displacing the dim-burning and malodorous oil harvested by whalers in the Grenadines. Two old men brought a pair of plastic chairs out onto a street corner, sat heavily and sipped lightly from a bottle of something potent and sweet. We watched as people passed in groups of twos and threes through shadowed arches into and out of the little pulses of apricot, salmon, and cream-colored light cast by ghostly lamps aglow within curtained windows. The chiaroscuro effects seemed to borrow something from the shadowed and smoke-colored frescoes of old churches, the people of Benners appearing for a few moments to be part of a procession of mystagogues or venerable old saints.

Someone was singing out in the dark. 'We need old Peter John or something with his drum,' Quentin laughed. Then he too sang, quietly and to himself,

> 'Jah bless your hand.
> Jah bless your song.
> No more confusion.'

*

The next morning I stopped by Legislative Hall and found the statue of the hippie band. Five slightly elongated figures performed a silent musical number, each on a different instrument: a guitar, ukulele and banjo, complemented by a small flute and bahoe. Surprisingly there was no real sense of movement in the piece, no flavor of the strut and swagger that usually accompany contemporary calypso or *soca*. These musicians stand with a loose, lanky attentiveness, playing their individual instruments with meditative grace and poised in hieratic charade like a congregation of casual, cigarette-smoking ecclesiastics. The hall itself is a two-story building with an outdoor stairway leading up to the second floor where the government offices and assembly chamber are located. The balcony looks down onto a pleasant courtyard and a few outbuildings, the entire diminutive assemblage enclosed within a tall rampart of chipped yellow brick, topped here and there by the tip of a frangipani tree, or awash in rivulets of red hibiscus. There is no need for the legislative building to be especially large, for the Island Council consists of only five elected members (joined by two commissioners and the governor). In the old days the government guesthouse was located here, and it was presumably on the second floor of this building that the inestimable Patrick Leigh Fermor settled in for the night with his copy of Kruythoff's *Netherlands Windward Islands* when he traveled through the region shortly after the Second World War. During the war, this most colorful and accomplished of travel writers had served in Greece. Secreted into the country, he worked to organize local peasants on the island of Crete in their opposition to the German occupiers. In 1942 he even managed to capture the German commandant, General Kreipe, in a daring raid. Several years before, during the early 1930s, Fermor had walked from the Netherlands all the way to Istanbul, a journey that he recounted many decades later in *A Time of Gifts* and *Between the Woods and the Water*; the third and final volume in the trilogy was published posthumously (Fermor died in 2011, at the age of ninety-six). Within the span of years separating the epic walk from the peerless writing, Fermor also published two books about his adopted home of Greece, *Mani* (recounting his explorations of the storied peninsula of the same name, jutting into the sea from the southern tip of the Peloponnese) and *Roumeli* (informed by his travels in an area of central Greece known in antiquity as Attica). Both of these books shimmer with exuberant prose and a deep love for the country, dense with history and impossibly sophisticated but earthy too, and full of an affinity for roughness and back-country places. *The Traveller's Tree*, an account of his journey through the post-war Antilles, was published in 1950, the first success in a long and accomplished career. In Fermor's description of St. Eustatius, the great writer tells of an island without automobiles, a place where every other house is a ruin, and where the population consists of barely a thousand people. He also suggests that the guesthouse was haunted, as Fermor's companion awoke the morning after their arrival complaining of ghosts who knocked over the furniture in his bedroom and chattered ominously amongst themselves all night. Perhaps the place is still haunted, with specters assembling during the dark evenings to enact various pieces of phantom legislation, ordinances that are stricken from ghostly ledgers with the coming of morning.

Kruythoff's unflattering description of the British occupation of St. Eustatius came once again to mind as I moved down a narrow street toward the Simon Doncker House, now the island's museum. The two-story house was built sometime around 1750 for one of the wealthiest of Statia's merchants. It was constructed of eighteenth-century Dutch brick at a time when nearly every other structure on the island was made of wood. The red gabled roof and the windows trimmed in green are complemented by an elegant, narrow balcony that imparts a sense of gracefulness to the building's façade. There is much of interest in the museum, an intimate collection of rooms filled with an assortment of artifacts ranging from the unsettling to the mundane. In the former category are a number of restraints and shackles, rusted thin and broken now, that were once fastened to the wrists or ankles of African slaves. Such objects serve as mute testimony to the brutality and exploitation upon which the vast wealth of the Sugar Islands was founded; amongst the French and the British, it was the Dutch slave-owner who enjoyed an especial reputation for cruelty and ruthlessness in the treatment of his human property. Caribbean slavery was brutal throughout the islands, however, even as the French, British and Dutch concocted various fictions that served to shed a humane light upon their own slave practices in contrast to those of their rivals. It is a peculiarity of history that while the Dutch were one of the most significant players in the slave trade (they built the infamous *Maison des Esclaves* on Gorée Island in Senegal, with its ominous "door of no return"), islands like St. Eustatius and Saba were simply not large enough to sustain the sort of plantation economy that created the financial incentive for the slave trade itself. Thus, the slaves of St. Eustatius were more likely to be pressed into service as carpenters, longshoremen, gardeners and household servants than were their brothers and sisters transported to places like Jamaica, Barbados or Martinique, islands where vast sugar estates drove the local economies. In fact, the number of slaves in the Dutch islands was always much smaller than in the British or French islands: when slavery was finally abolished in the Dutch Caribbean in 1863, only some 11,500 people were freed. By contrast, with the coming of emancipation to the British islands twenty-nine years earlier, 750,000 slaves had won their freedom.

The basement of the Simon Doncker House contains a number of startlingly well-preserved Amerindian skeletons exhumed during the excavation at nearby Golden Rock, while a first-floor parlor is stuffed with innumerable photographs of Queen Beatrix and her son, King Willem-Alexander. A formal family portrait of the House of Orange-Nassau hangs alongside a photograph of the Queen at her investiture, while childhood images of sisters Irene and Margriet are also plentiful (as are wedding photographs of the Queen beside her groom, the

initially unpopular but ultimately beloved Claus von Amsberg).
St. Eustatius feels more Dutch than Saba, and the sense here
is that one has been welcomed into a causal living room where
family portraits are presented with a mixture of quiet modesty
and genial pride. Island residents will often tell you that they
are "pleased to be a Dutch island," and perhaps remind you
of some of the tangible benefits that the Netherlands has
enjoyed thanks to her overseas colonies. In 1953, with the
Dutch just beginning their post-war recovery, massive flooding
took place in the southern part of the Netherlands, killing
some 1,800 people. The Antilles, at that time in a somewhat
stronger economic position than the mother country, provided
substantial aid in the wake of the disaster. There is even a 1953
photograph of dockside goods bound for the Netherlands that
may be seen as you approach a flight of stairs bringing the
visitor to the second floor. Here a genteel eighteenth-century
master bedroom has been recreated from an assortment of
authentic period furniture. A four-poster bed topped with a
canopy sits beneath a high ceiling of white beams and atop a
floor of mahogany planks aglow with honey-colored warmth;
the old dining room beneath is narrowly visible between the
strips of space that separate the floorboards. A period writing
desk sits in one corner, while a wonderful brass telescope peers
westward through a lace-bedecked window trimmed in powder
blue. This handsome, spacious room must have been the finest
on the island. It thus came as no surprise when I learned that Sir
George Brydges Rodney made this chamber his headquarters
when he took up residence in the Doncker house following
Governor de Graaff's capitulation to the British in February
1781.

Determined to neutralize an island that persisted in carrying on a robust trade with Britain's rebellious North American colonies—her merchants willfully deaf to repeated protests from His Majesty's Government—Rodney sailed from St. Lucia with a force of 3,000 men, once the Netherlands had officially entered the fray. According to several sources, when Rodney's fleet appeared in Oranjestad Bay, Governor de Graaff was unaware that the Netherlands and Great Britain were at war, news from home having not yet arrived on the island. Rodney offered de Graaff a chance to surrender the station and to avoid bloodshed, an offer to which the anxious governor acceded. Rodney was not only determined to seize the island for the Crown, but also to take his revenge upon the merchant community there, reducing prosperous St. Eustatius to a "mere desert," so that "this iniquitous island may be no longer [a] mart for clandestine commerce." He impounded cargoes carried in the hulls of over one hundred merchant vessels that were lying in the harbor at the time of his arrival, while he also ordered that the Dutch flag be kept flying from Fort Oranjestad, hoping to lure more ships into the bay where their cargoes might also be seized and the traders themselves taken prisoner. Some fifty British merchants from Antigua and St. Kitts who were thus apprehended earned Rodney's particular contempt. It has been estimated that Rodney confiscated some four million pounds' worth of merchandise; he destroyed the warehouses and factories in the lower town—"that nest of vipers," as he called it—and resolved to send the timber to St. Lucia, an island seized from the French less than three years before. According to contemporary accounts, slaves and horses were seized by the British, houses were ransacked and gardens (along with graves) were dug up as the military authorities searched for hidden treasure. For about three weeks all the shops on the island were shuttered as Rodney's men checked ledgers and inventories, and a number of those living in Oranjestad began to go hungry for want of provisions. No doubt Rodney was outraged by what he regarded as the perfidy of those merchants (a number of them Britons) who had grown rich through the sale of guns, ammunition, powder and rifles to North American rebels. His actions, however, provoked real anxiety in the British West Indies, as well as indignation at home. Britons in the Caribbean feared that Rodney's ruthlessness might encourage the French to behave similarly in those islands that they had recently taken from the British, while Whigs in Parliament noted that Rodney had disregarded his orders, which prohibited a general confiscation of goods and property. The admiral ordered that these be sold at a "military fair" a few weeks later and he was apparently willing to sell to all comers, as (astoundingly enough) French and even American ships purchased stores from his agents at Oranjestad. Rodney's military fair netted over £100,000, much of which appears to have gone into his own purse. Even the admiral's friends could not defend such behavior and he soon found it expeditious to return to London with his treasure in an attempt to plead his case to Parliament and King George (the latter refusing to receive him). It was well known to the admiral's foes—as well as to his allies—that Rodney's gambling debts had earlier led to his imprisonment in France and that he had barely escaped arrest when he returned to England to assume his naval command. It was common knowledge as well that Rodney was on the prowl for the sort of wartime prize money that might allow him to leave his family in a secure financial situation. St. Eustatius had provided him with an irresistible opportunity. Unfortunately for Rodney, while he was engaged in St. Eustatius' chastisement, a French fleet under the command of Admiral François de Grasse sailed freely past the Antilles astride the North Equatorial Current; it was this fleet that was to sweep up the Chesapeake and help lay siege to Cornwallis at Yorktown. Rodney's plundering of St. Eustatius may thus have significantly contributed to Great Britain's final, decisive defeat in North America.

In light of these events it might reasonably be supposed that the admiral's career ended ignominiously, but such was not the case. When word reached Britain that a combined Spanish and French fleet was soon to move against Jamaica, Rodney was once more dispatched to the West Indies. In April of 1782 he won a great victory against de Grasse at the Battle of the Saintes, a victory that contributed to a revolution in naval tactics when Rodney abandoned the traditional "line ahead" laid out in the *Permanent Fighting Instructions* of the Royal Navy and broke the French line in three places. Jamaica was spared and Rodney was rewarded with a peerage. While lawsuits pertaining to his conduct on St. Eustatius dogged him for the rest of his life, Rodney's great victory won him important friends at home: even MPs like Edmund Burke, particularly outraged by the naval commander's earlier behavior, now protected him. Preserving the British Empire in the West Indies had its advantages. Rodney's determination to turn St. Eustatius into Britain's Gibraltar in the Caribbean never materialized, however. The French recaptured the island in the fall of 1781 but found it virtually depopulated. St. Eustatius never recovered; even today's population of 3,500 falls far short of the nearly 20,000 souls that lived and prospered on the island in the heady days before Rodney's arrival.

I decided to head down to the lower town and observe what remained of the admiral's "nest of vipers." An old stone bypath called the Slave Trail descends from the little square just before the Roman Catholic Church, coming to a halt amidst low scrub and striking flamboyant trees some sixty-five feet below the upper town. By a peculiar coincidence of nature and human activity, St. Eustatius lacks a conventional "swimming beach." On the island's windward side, Zeelandia Bay offers an expansive and desolate shore, but dangerous currents and churning surf mean that swimming is forbidden there. On the leeward side, where the lower town ambles along a narrow stretch of land between Smoke Alley to the north and Gallows Bay to the south, the beach is strewn with a tumbled assortment of ruins: piles of gray stone and brick that recede seaward until they are lost to view in the belly of the ocean. As I wandered through the rock skeletons of old warehouses and stockrooms and factories, I recalled Pieter's excitement when he had spoken about the sunken cities of the West Indies. I appeared to have found one, for Rodney's revenge has been abetted by a rising tide that has since placed a good portion of the old lower town underwater. Coconut palms grew up through the shells of old sheds and stores, while here and there a narrow brick stairway climbed toward a terrace that had vanished more than two hundred years ago, the timbers long since hauled off into the shadow of the *pitons* of St. Lucia. Amidst a silence broken only by the light crash of wave upon stone, it was difficult to imagine the lower town at the peak of its eighteenth-century prosperity. These un-roomed and topless structures were packed then with casks of rum and molasses and heaps of dried tobacco piled alongside foodstuffs from the North American market (grain, salt fish and cured beef). The more terrible merchandise of guns and powder would also have been near at hand. It was hard to picture now the slaves from Gabon and Ghana, Benin and Angola—those who had survived the abominations of the Middle Passage—unburdening various hulls of comestibles, raw sugar and an assortment of finished goods, while a glistening admixture of guilders and doubloons, *kroner* and *louis d'or* jostled alongside shillings and pounds and promissory notes from Congress in Philadelphia. Quiet now, the lower town is a scene of agreeable desolation, a wilderness of stone having turned its back on the work of civilization and begun a slow but inexorable return to the sea. I watched from my seat atop a solitary stone as two young boys picked their way amongst the rocks and plunged into the water, swimming atop vanished gables and casting their shadows into sea-changed rooms whose secrets have long since been subsumed into an endless watery silence.

*

During my last afternoon on St. Eustatius, I decided to explore the ruins of the old synagogue before heading out to catch a glimpse of Zeelandia Bay. The imposing, lonesome structure sits along the Synagogue Pad (a path that runs between Fort Oranje and the ruins of the Dutch Reformed Church) and was built sometime around 1740 for the Congregation Honen Dalim: "The One Who is Merciful to the Poor." The Jews who worshipped here were mostly Sephardim, probably descendants of those merchants who left Recife in South America when the Dutch handed that settlement back to the Portuguese in 1654; presumably the commercial ambivalence of Dutch Protestants was preferable to the outright anti-Semitism and conversionary zeal of the returning Iberian Catholics. According to Yitzchok Levine, the Jewish community on St. Eustatius remained relatively small and was never especially well-off, even during the boom years of the mid-eighteenth century. Solomon de Leon had to petition the Jews of Curaçao for the funds required to build the synagogue, while the congregation seems never to have enjoyed the services of a rabbi, contenting itself instead with a simple *chazzan* (a cantor). The structure itself remains impressive—even handsome—if more than a little forlorn. Its walls form a closed square approximately twenty feet high which is perforated by sets of finely arched windows set smoothly into bricks whose exteriors have been burnt to a grayish-black, even as those within have maintained the creamy mustard tone of their original hue. The flooring of the synagogue has surrendered long ago to an ocean of grass that adorns the interior like a pale green carpet, while a narrow stairway clings tightly to one of the walls, climbing upwards to a long-vanished second story, its ghostly absence reinforced by the empty window arches that glance down from their marooned situation along the ramparts. An enormous tamarind hovers in mute guardianship over the structure, shadowing its lost voices with an abiding gentleness. It is generally acknowledged that the Jews of the island were singled out as particular victims of Rodney's wrath. Many were stripped of their goods and clothing in full view of their families, and sent into exile without any information as to where they were going; indeed, it was specifically the admiral's treatment of the Jews that Edmund Burke found so objectionable. In any case, Congregation Honen Dalim had been devastated; the synagogue fell into disuse by the beginning of the nineteenth century and was apparently already a ruin by the time that Anna Vieria Molina died in 1846, in all likelihood the last member of the old Jewish community of St. Eustatius.

Many peoples have prayed in many tongues on this tiny island: Dutch, Latin, Hebrew and even Arabic, for there is a small mosque in the upper town. Perhaps the most evocative peoples of all, however, are those who have vanished altogether. Late in the afternoon, as Quentin and I drove out beyond the airport on the way to Zeelandia, we passed Golden Rock. The site was closed, but we stopped for a moment to gaze through the fencing and out across the thick scrub beyond. Several archeological excavations were undertaken here during the 1980s and early 1990s; indeed, this site is considered one of the most important sources of information concerning the lives of the ancient Amerindian inhabitants of the Leeward Islands. A Taíno population appears to have dwelt here for more than 300 years, having arrived sometime around 600 AD. Little is known about the inhabitants but the site has yielded tantalizing fragments of information.

These people lived in small, round dwellings surrounding a central plaza: holes dug for strong vertical support posts tell us something about the dimensions of these homes. There were apparently six of them, three quite large, one possibly destroyed by fire. Curiously, they seem to resemble the large communal houses (called *maloccas*) constructed by the early inhabitants of the Amazon basin in South America, serving to reinforce additional anthropological evidence pointing to this region as the ancestral homeland of the Taíno. It has been estimated that the site probably supported between eighty to one hundred inhabitants, while a cache of quartz beads discovered in a child's grave attests to the possibility that the community engaged in some form of long-distance trade with other lands (there are no quartz deposits in the nearby Leeward Islands). This settlement certainly appears to have enjoyed a degree of prosperity, as mother-of-pearl pendants, shell plaques and a number of decorated bowls have also been discovered at Golden Rock. Suggestive of a complex ritual life, the upturned skeleton of a sea turtle was found at the lowest (that is, the earliest) level of the settlement's occupation, while one of the buildings, known as the Sea Turtle House, seems to have supported a roof in the shape of a hawksbill turtle shell. Surprisingly, only a small number of people were buried within the village compound, leading to some speculation that those so honored were particularly venerable citizens. Often it is Taíno pottery—characterized by distinctive zoomorphic images of fantastical creatures—that allows archeologists to definitively identify a site as having been inhabited by this people. It was the Taíno who introduced agriculture and a settled village life to the Leeward Islands, felling large trees with their very efficient stone tools and often constructing surprisingly large villages. While the Taíno of St. Eustatius may well have constituted an outlier community within a larger pattern of settlement, they behaved much like their brethren elsewhere: raising cassava on a series of slash-and-burn plots located near the settlement, while acquiring their protein by way of iguana flesh, sea turtle, conch, crab and fish. The native peoples of the Leeward

Islands probably consumed little fruit, however. Although the Caribbean has long been characterized by an exuberance of various fruits, nearly all of these (with the exception of guava) are imports: passion fruit from South America, breadfruit from the Pacific, bananas from Africa and oranges from China, to name just a few. This would suggest relatively low amounts of vitamin C in the diets of early Caribbean peoples, and perhaps somewhat compromised immune systems, as well. According to a number of scholars, however, the real problem was not dietary so much as the unhappy effects of a rather restricted gene-pool; the number of original Amerindian emigrants to the Antilles appears to have been quite small and nearly all seem to have derived from a homogenous population with relatively similar traits. The effects of exposure to European-borne diseases during the late fifteenth and early sixteenth centuries were thus disastrous. Historians continue to debate the number of native peoples inhabiting the Caribbean at the time of first contact with Europeans; figures range from 225,000 to six million, with most scholars these days tending toward the higher range. More certain is the fact that by 1550, with the exception of Kalinago settlements on St. Kitts, Dominica and St. Vincent, the native peoples of the Caribbean had virtually disappeared, including the Taíno of St. Eustatius. Perhaps the Amerindians of St. Eustatius simply moved on to other islands, but it is just as likely that they (along with their brethren on Saba) were deported by Spanish raiders and transplanted to Hispaniola to replace a decimated workforce.

As we stared through the fence and into the empty silence of the excavation site, Quentin, whose uncle had worked at the museum for a few years (and who thus felt a kind of proprietary concern for Golden Rock) posed an intriguing question. 'But where did their water come from?' I hadn't stopped to consider this puzzle. There are no streams on the island, nor, so far as I had heard, any freshwater springs. Quentin pointed off toward Boven Peak and Gilboa to the north. 'They gather water up in the mountains when it rain,' he said. 'They right in the middle of everything here.' Indeed, the site was marvelously situated astride the broad, flat "culture-zone" in the center of the island, equidistant from both coasts and close to the most reliable supply of fresh water. 'They wore lots of feathers; flamingoes and frigate birds,' said Quentin. Clouds began to gather to the east and the scene evoked in both of us an introspective moodiness, a sensibility no doubt reinforced by my own imminent departure the next morning. We had both quietly become aware—as travelers sometimes do—of the passage of time, the invisible yet unalterable accumulation of moments between one epoch and another, one people and another. I had read in Labat's *Memoirs* a charming account of a picnic organized by the priest and some friends on the island of Martinique. It was agreed that the guests would prepare their meal as if they had been buccaneers of an earlier and simpler day; the pig would be grilled on a traditional *boucan*, its belly filled with lime juice, salt and pimento in the old style, while wine would only be drunk from calabash cups, so as not to be at variance with what Labat calls "buccaneer simplicity." What astonished me was that this very self-conscious evocation of a more capacious and romantic Caribbean past took place in 1698. Even as early as the late seventeenth century the West Indies had grown old, while travelers had already begun to tell stories about a regional past that was equal parts willful fantasy and pre-Romantic yearning for a redemptive encounter with simplicity and nature. Many had passed through these islands; most have been forgotten. Indeed, travel reminds people that we are all transients, which is perhaps why there has traditionally been a strong connection between travel—in the form of pilgrimage—and notions of religious piety. An island named for a saint whose exploits exist somewhere in the space between myth and history, one who nevertheless wandered far to plant his name upon this quiet place, seemed to invite such musings.

Faint coral-lavender traces lightened an overcast sky as we arrived at Zeelandia Bay about an hour before sunset. The beach was desolate and the sand cold underfoot; the surf was furious, more of the Atlantic than the Caribbean in its wild spray. The ocean had grappled angrily with the windward coast, forming a sharp precipice of about twenty feet where the earth had been clawed away along the southern stretch of the beach, its gray sand awash with dried seagrass and debris from lost ships. 'If you come back late in winter,' said Quentin, 'you might see the turtles here when they come ashore to lay their eggs: hawksbill, green turtle, loggerhead turtle—very rare now; endangered. I not seen a leatherback in a long time.' Quentin stretched out his arms to suggest something of their size. 'They real monsters, man.' He paused. 'Not in a long time.'

NEVIS

Throughout my brief stay Nevis seemed to me a place of contradictions. There is a simplicity about the island—an unself-conscious and quiet sincerity—that is often belied by Nevis' carefully cultivated, slickly marketed image as the "Spa of the Caribbean": favored destination of royals and celebrities, fully equipped with the sort of high-end tourist infrastructure that might make even the most privileged of vacationers blush. At the ultra-exclusive Four Seasons Resort near Pinney's Beach, one might enjoy a mango sea salt scrub and sugar cane exfoliant, followed by a rum, ginger, and honey-glaze chaser. The par 70 Robert Trent Jones golf course skirting the slopes of Nevis Peak is one of the finest in the Caribbean, winning a place on *Condè Nast*'s prestigious gold list. The hotel itself contains 196 rooms and suites, as well as ten tennis courts, a biomorphic pool and a fitness center. The more rough-hewn yet equally elegant Golden Rock offers its guests the option of bedding down in an actual sugar mill overlooking the grounds of a former estate, with a luxurious hot stone massage available upon request. With the notable exception of the Four Seasons, Nevis' principal resorts are locally- and family-owned affairs.

Thus, even the most strenuously splendid of these comports itself with an easy and casual grace that is worlds away from the half-desperate and insistent high-octane joviality one tends to find amidst the clutter of the mass tourism market. Hotel operators on Nevis speak of their establishments as "heritage inns," a term that only half-acknowledges the historical complexities that inevitably underlie the Caribbean tourism industry. While there is something a little self-serving about the term, it is nevertheless true that the model of the heritage inn has helped to preserve a good deal of Nevis' past; the material remains of an elegant yet terrible before that would otherwise have been lost amidst omnivorous tropical forests. Nor has the determined gentility of the island's tourism culture been subject to the damage sometimes wrought by overwhelming numbers; any cruise ships in the vicinity will certainly bypass Charlestown, for its harbor can only accommodate shallow-draught vessels. Thus, Nevis' capital is free of the catchpenny waterfront shops that one sees in some of the larger islands. Air service from the United States is likewise limited, and connecting flights from Antigua or St. Maarten are occasional. Thus unsuited to the relative advantages of mass tourism, this island of thirty-six square miles and about 15,000 persons has appealed instead to a leisured elite, an entourage of well-heeled travelers who often arrive as guests and return as expatriates.

Oprah Winfrey has visited Nevis often and Princess Diana fled to the posh Montpelier Plantation as her marriage to Prince Charles began to come apart, William and Harry in tow. After the humbler and less ostentatious islands of St. Eustatius and Saba, it was a bit jarring to find in Nevis a fully mature and ably managed culture of *haute* tourism; professional, precise and informed by a carefully calibrated amiability. There is, of course, something faintly troubling about all of this exquisitely packaged (if easy-going) luxury. Late one evening I sat on the elegant stone veranda at Golden Rock, surrounded by a playful network of little lakes and fountains, a soft southeasterly blowing in from Montserrat under an electric sea of stars. It was off-season and the bar was empty, the resort's few guests having turned in early; two or three waitresses giggled somewhere in the dark, gathering up silverware and folding cloth napkins with small, ghostly flourishes. A middle-aged *maître d'hôtel* in a red vest and with a face like dark, chiseled stone stood behind a small bar in the dining room, hunched over a copy of *Popular Mechanics*. From time to time during the last few days I had felt ill at ease as Erin and I visited one or another of the island's resorts. On this particular evening the cause of my vague disquiet at last became clear. This constellation of magnificent hotels—Montpelier, Golden Rock, Hermitage Inn—had once served as a network of sugar plantations, each managed by one or another of Nevis' most prestigious (and often infamous) families. Even today one encounters the old names everywhere, Prentice and Huggins and Pinney echoing like a kind of unsettling litany into the new century, their old estates situated as decisively as ever at the heart of the Nevisian economy. Where field slaves once cleared and dunged the land, where the tall cane was attacked with cutlasses and stripped by hand, carefully landscaped orchid terraces, poinciana and splendid wax-flowers coil about stone paths and half-opened, vine-clad gates; where once the newly cut cane was ground and pressed, the extract skimmed and boiled in large copper pots within simmering stone walls, wealthy (and overwhelmingly white) tourists enjoy a supper of braised pork shoulder or spiny lobster with a lemongrass consommé, ordering a second rum punch from a black waiter who caters smilingly to their every need. One cannot help but feel that old patterns continue to discover subtle ways of replicating themselves, that the line between service and servitude must often strike the sensitive resort worker as peculiarly thin. It is an odd thing to plant a pleasure garden atop and within the ruins of those estates that consumed so many souls so brutally, and the exquisite beauty of these places cannot but sit uncomfortably beside the ghosts that manifest themselves so easily to those with long memories.

*

The airport was still when Erin and I arrived late on a Saturday evening. It was June and the wetter part of the year was in the offing, a heavy downpour having pummeled the tarmac shortly before our arrival. Clouds of steam drifted across the runway and out into the thick tropical night as we disembarked and shuffled with our bags like silent penitents into the darkened Vance Amory Airport. As we entered the terminal a large sign blared a warning that it was illegal to wear camouflage clothing on the island. This seemed strange, but the building was nearly empty and the one or two tired personnel who stood about in an official capacity appeared disinclined to offer clarification. We did learn, however, that the airport was named for a former premier, leader of the Concerned Citizens Movement and very much in the running for reappointment to his position should the C.C.M. make a strong showing in the next month's contest. Amory had served for some fourteen years (the longest tenure of any Nevisian premier), and had been at the helm when the island nearly seceded from St. Kitts in 1998. We were processed through customs by a somnolent official who stamped our passports with a disappointingly bureaucratic imprint that sat with some envy alongside the more self-dramatizing contribution of St. Eustatius' customs and immigration department. On the way out from St. Maarten, I had caught a glimpse of tiny congregations of little pink lights gathered atop the black ocean. The streetlamps of St. Eustatius blinked up at us with the faint glimmer of vigil candles ranged along the apse of a darkened church. It had been over a year since I visited the island and I thought of Alma and Quentin, of the desolate ruins of the Dutch Reformed Church and of the silent stone parade ground of Fort Oranje as the aircraft banked to the right and passed above St. Kitts with its network of brightly illuminated neighborhoods, scurrying avenues, and bustling quays. Across the Narrows I caught my first glimpse of Nevis, a solitary beacon light blinking atop Round Hill. Erin had discovered a small house that we might rent for a few days; a charming, unsophisticated and slightly frayed little bungalow tucked into the corner of the rainforest that edged the small community of Fothergills. A jade and coffee-brown ghaut runs through the district and down to the sea, its fringes laced by a low mist of witch alders, each cluster of flowers a silent galaxy of diminutive starbursts. As the airport is situated at the northern tip of Nevis, our taxi headed south along the narrow two-lane road that rings the island, the gentle sweep of Long Haul Bay drifting to windward and out into the black, breathing ocean as we drove beyond the lights of Newcastle and passed into open scrubland. A collection of half-forlorn and sleepy hamlets stared back at us from the dark, although occasionally we caught a glimpse of Saturday night festivities; in Butlers a handful of young men and women had gathered outside a rum shop while a pair of musicians performed atop a wooden platform situated beneath tall coconut palms. The smell of fresh ganja was in the air. Across the street two old men in dungarees and shirtsleeves sat barefoot along a cement retaining wall; they attended the comings and goings at the rum shop with impassive faces and red, tired eyes. One of the men raised his hand in an enervated salute, as our driver shouted out a greeting. South of Butlers, he nodded out toward the dark. 'There's an old estate out that way, up in the bush. People say it's haunted. There's a lady who cries in the dark.' There was a long pause; the tires atop the wet roadway and the persistent whistle of innumerable small frogs were the only sounds. We were passing, he explained, through St. James Parish, largest of the island's five parishes but sparsely settled and by far the most desolate and lonesome. A few cracked cement houses and shops clustered around the narrow highway while occasionally I glimpsed a small wooden domicile somewhere far beyond and up above the road, a home set back into thick scrubland with a soft blue light aglow within and a dog howling in the yard.

Our driver pointed out the power station and the new Drag Raceway, its empty asphalt lanes a strange lambent indigo under tall electric lights; nearly in the shadow of the raceway, the stone tools and broken shells of an old Amerindian settlement continued to while away the centuries, presumably unperturbed by the roar of the engines, the charred smell of exhaust. After another pause we asked the driver about the sign we had seen at the airport. 'Only the Defense Force is allowed to wear camouflage fatigue,' he replied, 'for we don't want hell and devil and all kind a confusion with people wearing this and that.' 'The Defense Force is the army?' I asked. 'Right. You know that some of them went to Grenada way back in them days.' It took me a moment to realize that he was referring to the 1983 United States invasion of that country, known at home by its military sobriquet: "Operation Urgent Fury." The St. Kitts and Nevis Defense Force is part of the Eastern Caribbean Regional Security System, which was formed in 1982, just a few months before the sister islands themselves obtained full independence from Great Britain. Consisting of an infantry and a maritime unit, the Defense Force works in conjunction with the police and is largely responsible for internal security and drug interdiction. As for the Grenada operation, Regional Security troops did not take part in the invasion itself, but did work to provide security on Grenada in the aftermath of the U.S. action, guarding prisoners mostly, and accompanying American troops on patrol (the Regional Security forces wearing blue armbands so that they would not be mistaken for hostile Grenadian soldiers by American troops). The Defense Force enjoys the prestige attendant upon a relatively long past; founded as a volunteer unit in 1896—primarily to counter growing unrest on the sugar estates—its recruits marched in the London parade of colonial and imperial troops that was organized in 1911 to celebrate the coronation of King George V. The Defense Force was reconstituted as a regular standing army during the 1960s and was called into action during the tumultuous year of 1994, when unrest in the wake of a contested election led to a ten-day state of emergency, followed by a prison riot and breakout that further disrupted life on the island. 'Joint exercises every year with the other islands,' said the driver. 'When I was younger I wanted to join the reserve, but...' His voice trailed off and he shrugged. In the darkness and silence I recalled images I had seen of the Coronation Parade. There was the royal carriage ornamented like a four-wheeled Versailles and accompanied by be-whiskered, black-hatted Beefeaters (halberds a-shoulder); there was the bearded monarch with the piercing, empire-enraptured gaze, the heavy epaulettes and high collar, the frogging and sash and the Star of India; and then the troops themselves, the Life Guards astride their mounts with cuirasses at the ready, the turbaned lancers overtopped by fairy-tale pennants, the Jamaican Zoaves with their sleeveless scarlet jackets and breeches as blue and billowing as the sea, and finally the polished black boots and smart tunics of the St. Kitts and Nevis Defense Force. 'We coming into Gingerland now,' said the driver, as the clouds of empire dispersed. 'Almost there.'

*

The house was situated at the end of a rough trail that rambled along through darkened scrubland like some reckless and reclusive sleepwalker; as the vehicle idled astride a set of narrow cement tracks, I stepped out and pulled aside a creaking iron gate that served to sequester the house from a scattering of other small homes belonging to the quiet community of River Path. The car pulled forward onto a low, rolling lawn that terminated abruptly in a wall of night and vegetation. A muscular black gentleman with graying hair and a shy, girlish grin met us beside the stone path that led up to the house through a narrow garden tucked beneath spreading mango trees. We paid the driver and were ushered into the house, where the man who presented himself as Spenser quietly introduced us to the worn little building where we were to make ourselves "right at home," an invitation that felt less like a rehearsed welcome than a tentative, genteel suggestion. Spenser moved through the house with surprising suppleness, gesturing like a Sotheby's auctioneer to the low wicker furniture and humble galley kitchen, the high West Indian ceiling with its odd angles and dark corners, the bedrooms with their spectral, diaphanous curtains and their windows secured with peeling, wrought-iron grilles. In the simplicity of its furnishings, the dilapidated charm of its worn clapboard and lattices—as well as in its general isolation— the house reminded me of a nineteenth-century tea planter's bungalow somewhere in Ceylon; tasteful yet unadorned and simply but warmly appointed. 'You in the skirts of the rainforest here,' Spenser said softly, 'and you must keep an eye out for the monkeys. They look around for the mangoes when the sun come up, first thing.' By the time we were settled in it was too late for dinner; Erin and I decided to compensate for our empty stomachs with a big breakfast the next morning. Lying in the dark on the edge of sleep, we watched the bats at play beneath the eves while an invisible chorus of frogs chirped a loose and generous accompaniment. Juan de la Cosa was the chief cartographer of Columbus' second voyage to the West Indies in 1493, the only one of the mariner's four journeys that brought him through the archipelago that would come to be known as the Leeward Islands. A map created by de la Cosa in 1500 thus offers the earliest representation of Spain's island possessions in what would soon be called the Americas. A world map, its picture of Asia was taken from the accounts of Marco Polo and its depiction of the African coast based upon the charts created by Portuguese navigators. With its proliferation of beasts and kings, its glittering, fanciful medieval cities spread beneath unfurled scarlet banners and arranged alongside gardens of spiraling wind-roses—blue and gold and green— the map is also a luminous work of art. De la Cosa himself was an adventurer of uncommon ambition and ruthlessness. Part-owner of Columbus' flagship *Santa Maria* in 1492, he would later be among the first Europeans to set foot upon the islands of Curaçao and Aruba, after which he and the leader of this latter expedition, Alonso de Ojeda, explored and laid claim to the South American mainland, including the territory they named Venezuela ("Little Venice"). De la Cosa's map appears in this narrative because of the ways in which it speaks to the vagaries attendant upon any attempt to discover decisively who it was who gave what name to which island, and when. The map clearly identifies Guadeloupe, Montserrat and Redonda, situating these islands in roughly the correct configuration (and reinforcing the generally accepted claim that Columbus himself christened them). The waters grow murkier, however, when the eye travels toward the northwest. The island that came to be known as *San Cristobal* to the Spanish—St. Christophe and St. Kitts to the French and British, respectively—was apparently called *La Gorda* ("The Fat One") by Columbus in 1493, while its sister island of Nevis was originally given the name *San Martin*. Not until several years later does the island begin to appear as "Las Nieves" on maps of the Caribbean, although some charts drawn up as late as 1570 continue to identify her as *San Martin*. "Las Nieves" is an abbreviation of "Nuestra Senora de las Nieves" (Our Lady of the Snows), given no doubt in testament to the heavy white clouds that perpetually gather about the summit of Nevis Peak, dressing the forest canopy in a Caribbean evocation of winter in the Sierra Nevada. Perhaps it would be more appropriate to say "an evocation of a snowfall in Rome," as this was the improbable and delightful event that brought Our of Lady of the Snows into the lexicon of Catholic legend. The Church of Santa Maria Maggiore was constructed on Rome's Esquiline Hill sometime during the papacy of Liberius (352–66); apparently a childless patrician couple was looking for an appropriately pious way to dispense with a vast fortune, praying to Mary for clear guidance on this point. Miraculously, on the evening of August the fifth, amidst a blazing Roman summer, snow fell on a single spot atop the Esquiline, and thus the Blessed Mother decreed to the elderly couple the preferred location for her new, generously endowed church. According to Père Breton, the Kalinago name for the island was *Oualie*, an appellation commemorated in Oualie Bay and Beach Resort on Nevis' leeward coast. De la Cosa's chart thus serves to illustrate an early moment in the watery world of sixteenth-century Caribbean nomenclature. The cartographer himself would come to a dark end about ten years after he made his most enduring contribution to the history of mapmaking and European exploration. Traveling once more with Ojeda, de la Cosa was surrounded by hostile Indians following the Spanish defeat at Turbaco (near Cartagena); here he was killed in a shower of poisoned arrows. He never lived to see the rechristening of *San Martin*, but he probably would not have cared much. The Spanish were largely indifferent toward the Lesser Antilles, particularly after the conquistadors began to open up Mexico and Peru to colonization. Vast caches of precious metals soon discovered on the mainland turned Spain away from the Caribbean, with the exception of Cuba and the walled town of Santo Domingo on Hispaniola (the former providing a jumping-off point for the Silver Fleet, the latter a somnolent preserve for bureaucrats and lawyers filling out the paperwork of empire). The Leeward Islands, for their part, were depopulated and transformed into grazing land for Spanish livestock, the pigs and cattle themselves soon forgotten and left to wander the lonesome shores of lands whose peoples were gone and whose names were lost.

*

Early the following morning we found the monkeys. Below the bungalow and tucked beneath a stately mango tree, a small stone bench seemed the ideal place to perch in anticipation of the creatures' appearance. I rose in the morning twilight and dressed quietly, took my copy of St.-Johnston's *From a Colonial Governor's Note-Book* from the nightstand, and padded carefully down to the bench. Sensibly enough, Erin preferred to sleep. I had read that monkeys might be found virtually everywhere on the islands of Nevis and St. Kitts (though nowhere else in the Leeward Islands), that they were the tropical equivalent of North American squirrels or rodents, and that I would very quickly lose any sense of wonder I might have felt relative to such pesky, aggressive and noisome creatures. All of this seemed impossible as I approached the bench with feline stealth and sat with monkish patience amidst the crepuscular haze cast by the soaring, shadowy trees, their upper branches a highway for the formidable and mysterious simian beasts. I felt a little like Beowulf in the sleepy mead-hall, although in this case it was a collection of half-eaten mangoes scattered around the bench that alerted me to the fact that my quarry was near. After about ten minutes, a faint rustle in the canopy announced the arrival of the most curious (or hungry) of the monkeys, and I glanced up in time to behold a gangly, white-bellied creature reaching awkwardly for a lone mango, wrenching the fruit from its branch as the leaves grumbled dryly, then scurrying up and out of sight, the prize clutched greedily in its skeletal black fingers. I couldn't decide whether to wake Erin or remain seated in anticipation of further visitors. Shortly afterwards, however, what appeared to be the same piece of fruit fell with an unceremonious plop onto the be-mangoed earth beneath the trees, only one or two bites having been taken. This was surprising, as the mango appeared to be perfectly ripe, but I was later to learn that of all the nettlesome things that these creatures get up to, the monkeys' profligacy with fruit drives the Nevisians most decisively to the point of distraction. Perhaps this is simply a manifestation of traditional West Indian probity and economy, but whenever anyone from Nevis complained about the animals, the list of grievances—foraging parties tearing up entire gardens and upsetting rubbish bins, a soaring population that creates real driving hazards but which the government refuses to address because "the tourists like the monkeys"—almost always culminated with that most violent of criticisms: 'And the damn things don't even finish the mangoes, they just take a bite and leave them lying around.'

Within a moment of this first encounter, I spotted three other monkeys clambering through the canopy, their dorsal fur ranging from chestnut to a grayish-green color, their eyes an uncanny yellow-red blinking out from a leathery, obsidian mask. These creatures are only semi-arboreal, feeding and sleeping in the trees at night, while remaining largely earthbound during the day. Once while we were exploring the grounds of nearby Golden Rock on an overcast afternoon, Erin and I ran across a much larger troop of about ten to fifteen monkeys; as the resort was nearly empty, they had the place to themselves, clambering through the small saffron cottages and tentatively exploring an abandoned swimming pool. One of them—perhaps an aspiring politician—clambered atop a small cistern and kept lookout, baring, from time to time, a prodigious set of fangs in a languid but impressive display of primate authority. Finding little in the way of food, the troop moved on quickly into the bush. As any Nevisian will tell you, the animals are aggressively omnivorous, devouring everything from eggs and the birds that lay them, to rodents, lizards, and small household pets; they have also developed a fondness for the brightly colored alcoholic drinks left half-finished at beach establishments like Chevy's and Sunshine's. As is true of nearly all West Indian flora and fauna, these creatures are not indigenous island dwellers. Ancestors of today's green vervet monkeys (*Cercopithecus aethiops sabaeus*) were brought from West Africa by slavers during the first years of British settlement. It is believed that by about 1670, a small number of these pets had escaped and began themselves to undertake their own sort of colonization. The population on St. Kitts is larger than that on Nevis, and some researchers have even begun to speculate that the monkeys on the latter island constitute a distinct sub-species. It is sometimes claimed that these creatures also reside on Anguilla and St. Martin; this is untrue, and strangely, no one seems to know how the story spread in the first place. Another colony of green monkeys may be found on Barbados, where a rumor abounds that an infamous eight-hour power failure on Halloween night in 2006 was caused when one of the animals clambered up a power line and bit into a cable carrying some 20,000 volts of electricity. No monkeys are willing to speak on the record, however, and it would thus seem unlikely that this explanation of events will ever be officially corroborated. As the islanders themselves (whether on Barbados or St. Kitts-Nevis) feel little in the way of affection for the creatures, one suspects that—in the case of the Halloween blackout—the monkey was made something of a scapegoat.

There is no doubt that these creatures constitute a driving hazard on Nevis, but then driving itself is a hazardous activity here. Climbing behind the wheel on Nevis is one of the most vivid and distinctive ways to experience the élan, the characteristic style of the place, and not simply because you will almost certainly have to dodge a monkey or two. The drivers here have a peculiar habit of parking their cars directly in the road, thus effectively shutting down an entire lane of traffic. As the roads that cut through St. George's Parish are particularly sinuous and narrow, this tendency has the effect of transforming even the most casual of excursions through the southern reaches of the island into a series of adrenaline-fueled maneuvers that rely at least as much upon blind faith as the skill of the various drivers. In defense of the local motorists, it should be pointed out that there is most often nowhere else to park one's car but in the street, particularly outside of Charlestown or away from the island's resorts and restaurants. In the event of a jump-up (a house-party) or some large religious gathering, five or six parked cars will often line the road bumper to bumper, while the approaching motorist will have to quickly estimate how much time he or she must spend in the oncoming lane in order to pass the pack of vehicles. On Sunday mornings such hazards increase exponentially. The Methodists who gather at Gingerland Church with admirable, perhaps even alarming, frequency are joined across the street by the parishioners of St. John de La Salle Roman Catholic Church; together these congregations effectively blockade the Beach Road where it turns to the west just beyond the high school. As religious services in the West Indies tend to be a good deal longer than those celebrated in northern climes, this stretch of road thus constitutes a driving adventure well into the afternoon. Such developments are less common in the north of the island, where the land is less populous, the main road less circuitous and the country more open. Nevertheless, aggressive driving remains a problem, not just on Nevis but throughout the West Indies, where overtaxed (and often treacherous) roadways are frequently compelled to accommodate far too many vehicles. A lingering culture of machismo behind the wheel has compelled the Nevisian government to erect a number of road signs warning particularly against the dangers of passing slower vehicles without taking a good look at oncoming traffic. While direct, these markers speak with a kind of charm that does nothing to undercut their earnestness. The most grimly poetical was a sign on the way to Cottle Church that read simply: "Undertakers Love Overtakers." For those unwilling or unable to climb behind the wheel themselves there are always the buses; more properly speaking, the minivan taxis. The southbound buses are most likely to be found idling near the government dock in Charlestown before the arrival of the ferry from St. Kitts, or perhaps slumbering in Memorial Square beside the old courthouse, the drivers insouciant and jocund with their bright shirts and rock-star swagger, music from various car stereos joined in a fractious yet satisfying cacophony. A classic by Bunny Wailer mixes exuberantly with a smooth *Soca* refrain or even some local Big Drum offering to produce a kind of Caribbean evensong in the sidling cream-lemon light of late afternoon. There is something ritualized about the scene: the practiced poses, the variegated and lively vestments of the drivers, the aura of solemn ceremony touched with a vivid and buoyant flummery. Far too serene to bother with petty solicitation, the drivers wait to be approached by prospective passengers. Placing one after another into their minivans, the drivers arrange the passengers according to an obscure seating plan that allows them to organize their routes most efficiently while requiring the fewest readjustments to the overall configuration of the travelers. This sort of thing is apparently a point of pride, as is the appearance of a full bus. Unfortunately, this means that the earliest arrivals might have quite a long wait before the vehicle is adequately occupied and the driver says his final farewells to the assembly gathered in Memorial Square. Once underway, however, the driver fulfills his obligation not simply to transport a collection of passengers from one destination to another, but also to put on a show—his boldness and gallantry inspiring accolades and voluble exhortations on the part of the travelers, but also running the risk of provoking their wrath should the driver's audacity cross the hazy line into recklessness. The individual traveler may not know precisely when he or she will be deposited at their final station, but the discovery of the specific route is part of the pleasure of the ride. The experience of traveling in these vehicles is considered to be so authentic a part of island life that the Nevis Museum includes a small installation celebrating the culture of the buses. It is most certainly a culture of preen and swagger and testosterone. The drivers christen their vehicles with impish monikers like The Energizer, Smile Orange, and (easily my favorite) The Juggler. Hurtling down the road with a peacock's self-conscious flash, a devil-may-care grin and a highly subjective schedule of arrivals and departures somewhere in mind, these are the buccaneers of the Nevis asphalt, celebrated in tall stories and much admired by the young ladies.

*

Charlestown, the capital of Nevis, is an amiable and antique little city that manages to combine a somnolent and frayed seaside allure with bursts of bustling modernity. Like many Caribbean towns it is best viewed from the sea, where its unpretentious and ambling façade of low buildings—pink and yellow and pastel-blue—glances over a handsome seawall toward the western ocean. The capital's graceful allure belies an early history not quite as felicitous as its contemporary fortunes. In 1689 the little town of bustling docks and wattle-and-daub, timber-frame structures was filled to bursting by refugees fleeing a French invasion of the recently settled island of Anguilla. A few months after their arrival a severe earthquake struck Nevis, causing landslides on the Peak that swept away most of Charlestown; the tsunami that followed dragged what was left into the sea. What made the disaster even more alarming was the fact that, small as it was, Charlestown was by this time the capital not just of Nevis but also of the newly minted colony of the Leeward Islands. With King William's War having spread from New England into the Caribbean, an alarmed Governor-General Codrington struggled to keep Nevis from collapse even as he led the fight to secure all the English Leeward Isles from French predation. Long vanished from the waterfront is the spacious seventeenth-century warehouse with its distinctive red roof; it was alongside this structure that local merchants watched in horror as American privateers made off with a cargo of sugar and molasses during the War of Independence, in open defiance of both British customs officials and a severely overtaxed Royal Navy. Wandering from the fishermen's pier and past the outdoor market along Prince William Street, traditional West Indian architecture, with its hipped roofs and clapboard upper stories perched atop solid stone foundations, mixes with a more utilitarian, nineteenth-century municipal style; the solemn, unadorned, whitewashed exteriors of public buildings, their windows shuttered against the heat while behind their rounded arcades old men and women gather within the cool, tiled shade of roofed passageways and narrow halls. This sort of functional public works construction inevitably marks a town or territory as an erstwhile corner of the British Empire (which Nevis and her sister island were for more than 350 years). Earlier English visitors to the Caribbean—men like the historian James Anthony Froude—were often horrified to report that, while Spain's architectural legacy in the region included the grand cathedrals and palaces of Old Havana, or impressive fortresses like San Juan's *El Morro*, Great Britain's brick-and-mortar patrimony would consist merely of an assortment of depressingly functional and decidedly unspectacular public buildings. 'We English have built in those islands as if we were but passing visitors,' wrote Froude in 1887, 'wanting only tenements to be occupied for a time.' Despite some impressive work on the larger islands of Trinidad and Jamaica, it is true that many of the most spectacular examples of imperial architecture tend to be found East of Suez and engage most dramatically with Asian architectural precedents (the work of Edwin Luytens, for example). Nevertheless, the functional style that Froude found so unsatisfying and so unworthy of a great empire has settled into itself in places like Charlestown. Amidst the bustle and clamor of the city—as commuters disembark at Government Dock after a squall and automobiles worry their way through narrow rain-washed streets, as harried customers queue outside Windwatt Power with their rumpled utility bills or gather more pleasantly beside the little bookstore tucked into the Cotton Ginnery, as vendors hawk their yams and papaya and mangoes beneath the blue awnings of the Charlestown Market, and fishermen hurl jack and snapper onto cakes of ice spread upon the splintered platforms there—these stalwart, dilapidated old buildings grumble a bit but remain fixedly and quietly present, redolent in a thoroughly unsentimental way of things past. Indeed, now that the sun and time and political independence have done their work, there seems to me something reassuring about such structures and what they represent. It has been said that no colonial-era Briton went to the Indies (East or West) with good intentions. Far more true than not in the seventeenth and eighteenth centuries, this becomes a much less assured assertion relative to the Victorian epoch, and the decades after. During these years the faults were more likely to be ignorance and paternalistic self-rightousness than barbarism and naked exploitation. Certain it is that the rebellious slaves of Jamaica's Baptist War put the nail in the coffin of slavery, and certain too that when emancipation came it was the slave owners who were compensated for their lost "property" rather than the slaves who had themselves been reduced to mere chattels. Yet slavery had become an affront as well to the parliamentary managers of Britain's overseas holdings. Such men (Wilberforce, Clarkson), along with the increasingly recalcitrant slaves of these islands, bequeathed to the new century a new idea of British suzerainty. What finally emerged was an empire that, albeit with shameful belatedness and unflattering ambivalence, felt itself morally obliged to abolish slavery and managed (finally) to do so with some moral decisiveness; an empire that, paradoxically and often against its will, bequeathed to its West Indian subjects a tradition of stable, parliamentary democracy; an empire that, despite the handwringing of men like Froude, largely eschewed architectural grandiloquence and was content instead to leave as its own memorial a simple schoolhouse or a medical clinic or an utterly practicable customs building in a cordial blue and white seaside town.

*

Nevis was first settled by Europeans in 1628, when a planter from St. Kitts named Anthony Hilton arrived on the island's leeward coast in July and began clearing land in the vicinity of what would become Charlestown. Almost immediately there was trouble; Deputy-Governor Henry Ashton of St. Kitts, resentful of Hilton's success in recruiting some 150 settlers away from that island, tried to have Hilton murdered when the latter returned to St. Kitts to check on his tobacco holdings. The mistrust and suspicion that would long characterize the relationship between Nevis and St. Kitts was thus established within the first few years of their respective settlements (St. Kitts was Britain's first Caribbean colony, Sir Thomas Warner having arrived with his "gentlemen adventurers" in 1624). Repeated attempts by increasingly frustrated British authorities to integrate the governments of the two islands were unsuccessful, Nevis and St. Kitts each insisting upon maintaining their own individual governors, assemblies, councils, and laws. This despite the fact that the sister islands are just about two miles apart (when Britain finally placed Nevis and St. Kitts under a single administration in 1882, this was only accomplished in the face of bitter opposition on both islands). Shortly after the settlement of Charlestown, Spain roused herself from the torpor of her traditional indifference toward the Leeward Islands and launched an attack upon the settlers of St. Kitts and Nevis. In 1629, Don Fadrique de Toledo led the outward-bound Spanish treasure fleet in an attack upon Nevis that the settlers could only answer by firing a single large gun that had been placed upon Pelican Point. After their ammunition ran out, the Nevisians were compelled to surrender when, according to tradition, a number of Irish indentured laborers swam out to the Spanish ships and told their fellow Catholics where the islanders had hidden their provisions. St. Kitts and Nevis were briefly occupied by Spanish soldiers, but the treasure fleet (with its cargo of precious silver) soon disembarked for Spain and British colonists quickly returned to Nevis. This island soon outpaced St. Kitts as a source of tobacco and other crops, thus making Nevis a perpetual target in a long series of regional and global struggles—from King William's War to Napoleon's Caribbean adventures—some more disastrous than others for the people of Nevis. In March 1706, during the War of the Spanish Succession, the island was once again attacked; this time the French led the assault. By the early eighteenth century, sugar had displaced tobacco as the island's most important cash crop. The planters on Nevis were apparently so determined to save their valuable estates from depredation that they capitulated to Admiral Pierre le Moyne d'Iberville virtually without a fight. Scandalized by what he perceived to be the inhabitants' cowardice and base self-interest, d'Iberville demanded an even higher indemnity from the Nevisians than he had originally proposed. The ignominious conduct of the plantation owners was thrown into stark relief by the bravery of their slaves; many of the latter retreated to Nevis Peak and held out for some time against the invaders, thus earning for themselves the grudging approbation of the French. Such esteem did not save them from further humiliation, however, for the soldiers of Louis XIV would transport over 3,000 Nevisian slaves into servitude on the French islands of Martinique, Guadeloupe, and Grenada.

*

Nevis Peak dominates the profile of this island as decisively as the Quill overtops nearby St. Eustatius; regardless of where you find yourself on Nevis, the Peak is inescapably visible, nodding overhead like some ravishing, temperamental Olympian, at once severe and exuberant, guarded and expansive. The mountain towers some 3,200 feet above the shoreline and in many parts of the island (given an often remarkable lack of development) it is still possible to trace the undulations, crests and curls of the peak as it unfurls on all sides toward the ocean, rolling in largely unbroken scrub and savanna down to the beaches and bays. Toward the south, a number of smaller crests thrust skyward in plaintive imitation of the towering crag. Saddle Hill offers a particularly generous view of Nevis' southern coast, with nearby Redonda and distant Montserrat in the offing. Great waves of green pivot from the Peak in diminishing billows out toward the leeward coast, softening ripples that are gradually subsumed into the sea at Pinney's Beach (with its superb view of St. Kitts just across the Narrows). The beach is named for one of the island's most storied families. Azariah Pinney had been involved in the Duke of Monmouth's rebellion against King James II in 1685; the uprising had failed and Azariah found himself charged with treason. Seizing the opportunity presented to him by Judge George Jefferies to emigrate rather than face execution, Pinney was shipped to Nevis where he made a fortune in sugar and purchased a prosperous estate called Montravers. Eventually nearly nine hundred slaves would be put to work there. Located just above the beach, the ruins of Montravers' Great House still stand, an enormous baobab tree hovering like a spectral sentry just beyond the sea-gazing, tumbled wreck. The beach below stretches for some seven miles, its pepper and gray sands (testament to Nevis' volcanic past) holding the warmth of the Caribbean sun until early evening. When the sun begins to redden and falls behind the rim of ocean, young black

124

men and women gather in small, clamorous groups beside a rustling, lavender sea. The women laugh and whisper to one another while the men wrestle good-naturedly or backflip with violent grace into the foamy, celebratory surf. Swifts with their black collars scatter overhead in cruciform benediction, catching the last light like anxious sparks flayed skyward from a fanned coal-pot. The restless liberty of the birds and of the ocean seems to find its complement in the brash good humor and vigorous self-display of the young men and women along the shore. Sometimes it is just possible to conceive that everything past and burdensome might finally be left at the water's edge, wherever there are islands, and young people, and generous sunsets like scarlet wounds. Nevis Peak has not erupted in historical time but powerful subterranean forces are nevertheless at work; the famous hot spring just outside of Charlestown testifies to this fact, as does the fumarole that has been belching sulfur and other gases near Cades Bay since 1953. Earlier eruptions must have been massive, for no matter where you travel on Nevis inevitably you will find volcanic rocks and boulders of various sizes littering the island's bays and savannas, villages, and dense rainforests, a fiery detritus hurled with indiscriminate ferocity from the once-smoldering mouth of the giant mountain. Planters had long complained that the profusion of big stones scattered throughout the island made growing and harvesting their crops extremely difficult; indentured laborers and slaves had to work by hand to negotiate these ubiquitous rocks. Despite such challenges, Nevis' tobacco and sugar plantations quickly became some of the most prosperous in the Caribbean; a pyrrhic prosperity, to be sure, as the island was essentially reduced to a tropical desert by relentless deforestation on the part of its early settlers, combined with a set of ultimately unsustainable agricultural practices. The same fields were often worked year after year until the earth became exhausted and the soil utterly depleted. Complicating the agricultural picture still further, Nevis Peak tends to deflect the rain-bearing winds, which means that precipitation on the island is especially capricious and hard to predict. While heavy rains fall regularly on the mountaintop (one hundred inches annually), the lowlands often suffer periodic droughts. One or two lost seasons was often enough to ruin a planter family or to drive absentee property owners to sell cheaply and invest in more reliably lucrative corners of the empire. Planting and harvesting constituted only one part of the equation. For many centuries Nevis was subject to the, often dramatic, fluctuations of the European sugar market. A volatile, boom-and-bust economy thus came to characterize the island, with fortunes made and quickly unmade; seasons of wild prosperity followed by sudden collapse, foreclosure and abandoned properties. The abolition of slavery in 1834 virtually ended the successful cultivation of sugar on Nevis, despite a brief renaissance in the 1860s and 70s. It was at about this time that sugar was superseded by cotton as the island's most important export crop and the cultivation of Nevis cotton would continue well into the twentieth century. The conclusion of the First World War, however, brought an abrupt end to the island's cotton boom, just as sugar had been toppled some eighty years earlier. The evidence of collapse is ubiquitous, for abandoned estates dot the landscape; some converted to heritage inns, others moldering and forgotten on the edge of the forest, disconsolate and sinister and slumbering dumbly in the strange, greenish Caribbean twilight. Everywhere the old windmills lurch upward in a series of ghostly, despondent salutations—sinister monoliths, the fabric of their arms having vanished long ago—while the impassive and solemn Peak looks on.

*

One morning Erin and I decided to hike into the area known as Herbert's Heights, where the land begins to rise toward the summit of Nevis Peak. We stopped at a nearby inn where Lisa, the manager, lent us some walking sticks and suggested that we head toward the Source, following a path that bisects an old pipeline bringing water from a mountain stream down into Stony Hill Reservoir. We had gone to the inn for breakfast our first morning on Nevis and as the place was nearly empty we had been invited to join Lisa at her table on the upper terrace. An affably casual, generous and loquacious hostess, she informed us that she counted members of the Huggins family among her ancestors; the same family that had operated the place during the early nineteenth century, when the inn had been given over to sugar production.

'Everywhere you looked there was a Huggins,' she told us, referring to the days of the plantations, but the same might also be said of Nevis today, for the surname remains ubiquitous. We would later discover the infamous role that the Huggins family, particularly Edward, played in the history of the island; on this particular morning we were simply told that Edward Huggins had made many enemies on Nevis because he had been unwilling to lend his money to any feckless adventurer who came to him with a proposition. While a reputation for miserliness must have spread very quickly within the small community of Regency-era Nevis planters (many of them besieged and desperate for cash), Edward Huggins' recalcitrance and purported sadism would make his name as familiar in the halls of Westminster as on the island of Nevis. On the morning of our hike Lisa was engaged in a battle of wills with a narcissistic lorikeet who had stolen into the women's restroom and apparently fallen madly in love with its own reflection in the mirror above the sink. Understandably frustrated at his inability to make amorous contact with his double, the befuddled bird would occasionally go mad: shrieking wildly, fluttering about in a shower of feathers and making a mess of the bathroom tissue. 'Be careful in there,' Lisa advised one of her guests who was about to enter, 'the bird seems a bit disturbed.' As several hikers had just departed along the path leading up to the Source, we asked if there wasn't another, more isolated trail we might explore. 'Oh yes,' remarked Lisa, 'you might head up toward Hard Times. You'll find a snackette out there that's usually open. Just go 'round toward the road if you get hungry.' Snackettes, we discovered, are little roadside food stands that might be found in even the most isolated parts of the island, selling anything from fresh mangoes and fried plantains to grilled fish, barbecued ribs, and savory oxtail soup. Along the busier roads it is not uncommon for commuters to order their meals to go, but in quieter places the snackette serves as an informal community center where villagers pause for an hour or so to exchange gossip, play a game of dominoes, and talk politics. As Erin and I moved off toward the trail, we passed an older woman in an orange sundress and expensive shoes who was waiting for a ride to the airport. We recognized her from the morning we had come for breakfast, when she informed Lisa that she would be taking a private charter to Martinique, where she would board her Air France flight to Paris, arriving in that city with enough time to catch her breath before a Saturday wedding that would no doubt prove to be "a very smart affair" (I hadn't realized that people still spoke this way). On Monday she would return to Nevis. More than a few times on this island Erin and I experienced the sensation of having strayed onto a preserve of sorts, an informal but exclusive sanctuary for the casually privileged and the transient well-to-do. There are still enough quiet corners on Nevis to make room for less affluent travelers, particularly if they are willing to strike out on their own, pick up after themselves, and do their own shopping. The breezy nonchalance of the restaurants and resorts means that occasionally even these frugal travelers might come into contact with the sort of person who weekends in Paris and socializes with film stars, politicians, and other members of the international elite. You might not recognize them, but there is little doubt they recognize you, as well as the fact that you don't quite belong. Given the holiday atmosphere and the generally pleasant manners of the privileged, the anomaly of your presence will be tolerated with good humor. However, for me there remained a kind of thrill in negotiating what felt like a delicate deception, as if I had been dropped behind enemy lines and was managing to pass as one of them, as if I was the clever servant of Roman comedy who gets to enjoy the privileges of being king for a day, or as though I was carrying on a clandestine affair with the king's daughter.

As we followed the trail into the foothills, scrub woodland began to give way to patches of tropical forest. A towering banyan tree stood sentinel, a maze of thick roots wrapped around its base like the grappling mahogany tentacles of some subterranean beast. Above our heads sprays of bougainvillea blazed momentarily within those fractured shafts of sunlight that managed to pierce the wild gloom, lianas clambering upwards like the long fingers of ambitious monkeys grasping for the canopy. Amidst the deep silence of the path strange flying insects colored an iridescent blue lighted our way through the darkness and swirled about our heads—playful signifiers of enchantment—while an enormous boulder topped by roots and vines broke the trail into several scurrying rivulets. Beside a nutmeg tree Erin spotted a dry ghaut and we decided to follow this to wherever it brought us. Within about ten minutes a broad, soggy path appeared, looking as if it had been hacked out of the jungle by a machete, but generous enough to accommodate a small automobile. Traveling a bit further, we came to a collection of what seemed to be derelict houses; single-story structures with damp, concave roofs, darkened windows and small yards littered with debris, old boots, a toppled chair with three legs, a child's doll, armless, naked and abandoned. After passing into a declivity along the side of a rocky esker, we saw the rest of what revealed itself to be a small village, at the center of which stood a battered pile of wood and tarpaulin siding which at one time was probably a small rum shop and general store. On the far side of the street the carcass of an old car, burned and harvested of its valuables, stranded atop four gray blocks, leaned unsteadily in the direction of a muddy crossroad that leapt crazily down toward the lowlands. Chickens, along with a few hungry-looking dogs, ambled about and had apparently come to some sort of truce. We saw no one and thought that it might be best to retrace our steps when suddenly a voice broke the macabre stillness. An old toothless woman was sitting in the shade beside one of the houses, waving her arms. 'No, no,' she said, as some of the dogs looked up from the scrubland beside the road, 'that way, the path is that way,' gesticulating with her right hand in the direction of a low rise. Another of the residents appeared at a nearby window while three dark-eyed faces peered from the door of the erstwhile rum shop, one of the men stepping out onto the road. 'You looking for the Source,' he mumbled. 'That's the other way.' It felt like some sort of deep and unhappy truth when he said it. We had come to a small village just outside of Rawlins, an area that was once known as the breadbasket of Nevis but which has since suffered significant economic distress. The hard times seem to have been unequally and arbitrarily distributed, however, for while some villages are able to situate themselves as cultural sites along the trails that clamber upwards from inns like Golden Rock and the Hermitage Estate, others have nearly collapsed into a welter of poverty and neglect. When the infrequent traveler happens to stumble onto this place, the locals politely inform him that he has obviously taken a wrong turn, stare for a few moments, then return to their routine. Oddly for people who must live further from the sea than most Nevisians, many of the villagers here traditionally specialized in the making of nets and lobster traps. There wouldn't seem to be very much work for them these days. Erin and I stood awkwardly in the road while two children clambered up into the stripped automobile and stared at us absently. The few residents we met were cordial but guarded, a bit suspicious, perhaps, of what had brought us there. 'Down that way,' one of the older men reiterated, jutting out his chin and scratching vacantly behind his ear. Somewhere one of the dogs began barking excitedly. At first, no one moved. Then three of the villagers gathered silently in the road and watched as we withdrew back into the forest.

According to the Foundation for the Development of Caribbean Children, the poverty rate for St. Kitts-Nevis continues to hover somewhere in the neighborhood of 20%, this despite the fact that unemployment on Nevis remains rather low, perhaps a little over 5%. This would seem to suggest a sizable number of working poor, people who are employed but who cannot earn enough to pull themselves out of poverty. Such unhappy realities are not limited to Nevis, for each of the islands faces a considerable challenge in preparing its population to compete in an increasingly unforgiving economic environment where only a highly skilled workforce with diverse expertise is likely to enjoy real prosperity. A disproportionate number of the world's microstates are found in the West Indies and despite the creation of various institutions like the Organization of Eastern Caribbean States and the Caribbean Central Bank, centuries of political parochialism and (often quite justifiable) self-interest have continued to hamper regional cooperation well into the post-colonial era. Throughout the Caribbean, tourism has fostered the emergence of an economic monoculture every bit as pervasive as that which existed in the era of sugar's primacy. Many economists argue that as long as most of the capital driving the tourist industry remains largely in North American and European hands, the local populations of these islands will find themselves limited to relatively low-paying, service-sector jobs within an economic system that feels little incentive to diversify and little flexibility to do so. Those governments that have sought to facilitate different avenues for growth have repeatedly been frustrated by such hard economic realities, though sometimes government itself *is* the problem, for politicians in the eastern Caribbean have often secured power merely as a means of gaining control of the agricultural and tourism sectors (thus generating jobs and securing patronage, while expatriating profits and clamping down on the opposition). The Labor government of Robert Bradshaw on St. Kitts evidenced a decidedly authoritarian strain during the late 1960s and early 1970s—just ask the people of Nevis and Anguilla, both of whom sought to cut ties with Bradshaw and St. Kitts, the former unsuccessfully—while the Bird family in Antigua dominated that island for many decades (there is more to come on this topic). Further to the south, amidst the sulfurous mountains and dense jungles of Dominica, Patrick John—the nation's first prime minister—used the army to crack down on his political opponents and worked to severely restrict freedom of speech; in this case, such heavy-handedness backfired, leading to John's imprisonment and to the founding of the Dominica Freedom Party. Its landslide victory in 1980 saw the party's leader, Eugenia Charles, become the Caribbean's first female prime minister. Each of the islands of the Eastern Caribbean thus confronts a similar set of economic challenges and institutional constraints. Which is not to say that opportunities for a more stable and prosperous future do not exist. Tourism, with its many contours and permutations, is the one, inescapable economic reality; how the various islands choose to accommodate or perhaps re-imagine what has been variously called the "experience economy" or the "tourist-industrial complex" will be a decisive issue in the coming century. One hopes that these islands may always remain places for people to live and work rather than places for visitors to consume. I wonder how our own presence as tourists—and the inevitable ambivalence it inspires—serves to bedevil and injure (as well as to fund and secure) the things and people we have come to see.

*

Nevis' two most famous residents belong to the second half of the eighteenth century, and each speaks in a different way to the complex ties that bound the West Indies to the United States during the early years of the Republic. Sometime around 1755, Alexander Hamilton was born in Charlestown to a woman named Rachel Faucette; his father, James, was a British aristocrat who had been raised in a twelfth-century castle in Ayrshire, Scotland. With three elder brothers, James could be fairly certain that little of the family fortune would ever come into his hands, so he left home and sailed for the Caribbean to make his fortune in sugar. These plans apparently came to naught and he seems to have vanished from the picture by the time Alexander was about ten years old. Rachel and James were unable to marry in any case because she had never technically been divorced from her legal spouse, one Johann Michael Levine, a merchant from the Virgin Islands who was apparently much older than Rachel and something of a brute. According to tradition, Levine once had his young wife sent to prison for refusing to sleep with him. No doubt Rachel was pleased to have escaped from such a marriage, but her particular circumstances meant that as far as the Church of England was concerned the union of Rachel and James was unlawful: Alexander and his brother were bastards. The boys would thus have been barred from attending the island school which was operated under the auspices of the Anglican Church. Intriguingly, Alexander seems to have received his earliest education at a small Jewish school instead, run by an elderly Charlestown lady who taught the boy not only the rudiments of reading and writing but also a smattering of Hebrew; enough, in any case, to have permitted Alexander to recite the Ten Commandments in that language (by the middle of the eighteenth century, Nevis was home to the largest Jewish community in the British Leeward Islands). When Hamilton was born on Nevis, the population of the island approached 9,000—black slaves outnumbering free whites by about eight to one. From a young age, he would thus have been exposed to an especially brutal system of slavery, one that consumed far more lives than even the plantations of North America. Hamilton himself remained opposed to the "peculiar institution" throughout his political life and one might imagine that this antipathy was rooted partly in his early memories of Nevis and the British Caribbean, where island assemblies rigorously defended their own prerogatives from a meddlesome Crown even while stridently espousing the legitimacy of slavery. When Hamilton observed similar behavior in the assemblies of the fledging United States, he was deeply aware of the fundamental and troubling irony. 'Who talks most about liberty and equality?' Hamilton asked rhetorically in 1791. 'Is it not those who hold the Bill of Rights in one hand and a whip for affrighted slaves in the other?'

At the same time, Hamilton's determination to create an economic model for the United States founded upon responsible finance and vigorous manufacturing was no doubt informed by his awareness of the dangers attendant upon the sort of plantation-based economic model that had emerged in the West Indies, where the interests of powerful planters trumped all others. The Museum of Nevis History is housed on the first floor of a two-story stone structure built upon what is believed to be the site of Hamilton's birth. In testament to a lingering association of Hamilton (and his birthplace) with the principle of self-determination, the Nevis Assembly gathers on the building's second floor. It is here that legislation is enacted for an island that is essentially autonomous in terms of its domestic affairs (while laws pertaining to St. Kitts-Nevis as a whole are the prerogative of the legislature that sits in Basseterre, capital of the Federation).

A second museum is dedicated to Nevis' other historical luminary, Horatio Nelson. Here one will find a reproduction of the vice-admiral's blue undress coat worn at the Battle of Trafalgar in 1805, done up nicely by Henry Poole and Company, 15 Savile Row, London. Preserved behind glass and faintly aglow in the chamber's solemn half-light, the garment hangs like a churchman's cope or like the ceremonial vestment of some distant and peculiar tribe lost to time. Nelson's victory against a combined Spanish and French fleet at Trafalgar confirmed British hegemony at sea, frustrated Napoleon's hopes for an invasion of England, and permanently transformed the character of naval warfare when Nelson (very much like Rodney a quarter of a century before) abandoned the traditional "line ahead" and instead attacked the enemy fleet at right angles, breaking the flotilla into isolated pockets which the British warships could then engage in a series of individual melees. Nelson's Prayer Before Battle and his celebrated "England expects that every man shall do his duty" have become the stuff of legend, just as his death at the hands of a French sharpshooter at Trafalgar served to make him one of Albion's Immortals. His body famously preserved in brandy, the vice-admiral's remains were returned to London for a spectacular state funeral at St. Paul's. As one contemplates the museum's assortment of Nelson memorabilia—nineteenth-century cameos and dolls, plate-ware and standing plaques, Toby jugs and porcelain figurines—along with an antique model of his flagship, HMS *Victory*, one is reminded that Nelson's career coincided with the beginnings of the industrial revolution and its culture of mass production. Indeed, these various objects serve to reinforce the fact that the hero of Trafalgar—Viscount and Baron Nelson, Vice-Admiral of the White Squadron of the Fleet, Baron of the Nile, Duke of Bronté in the Kingdom of Sicily and Member of the Ottoman Order of the Crescent– was also his country's first modern celebrity. The museum's artifacts were lovingly gathered by Robert D. Abrahams, a Philadelphia lawyer and author of children's books who for years displayed the collection in his Nevis home. Very much interested in securing Nevis' past for future generations, Abrahams also worked to preserve the remains of the old Jewish cemetery located on Charlestown's Government Road (where nineteen grave markers remain, bearing carved inscriptions written in English, Portuguese, and Hebrew).

Nelson may have become Britain's greatest naval hero but he was not especially beloved when he arrived at Nevis in command of HMS *Boreas* in 1785. Despite being courted by their rebellious North American brethren, merchants and planters in the British West Indies had remained loyal to the Crown during the American War of Independence. While the markets of Philadelphia and Boston were at least as important to them as those of faraway London or Liverpool, the buyers and brokers and agents of the English Caribbean refused to trade openly with the rebels during the war and turned their backs upon the principles of independence and self-governance. The hope was that such fidelity would be requited after the war by Parliament's setting aside the Navigation Acts that limited island commerce exclusively to trade with Britain and her Empire. This would allow for a resumption of the lucrative commercial traffic between the Leeward Islands and His Majesty's former colonies in North America. Instead, the Navigation Acts were reaffirmed, and as Nevis had sometimes defied the provisions of Parliament in the past, Nelson was sent from English Harbor in Antigua to patrol Nevisian waters. When four American ships that had anchored off the coast refused to depart within forty-eight hours, Nelson seized them, infuriating the inhabitants of Nevis. The island's planters lent money to the ships' owners so that they could undertake legal action against Nelson, who was compelled to remain aboard the *Boreas* in order to avoid being arrested. 'The West Indians hate me,' he wrote, '[as] they will every officer who does his duty.' While this dispute was finally settled in Nelson's favor, he remained very unpopular on Nevis; it has long been suggested that his marriage in 1787 to the widowed niece of the island's Council President had more to do with allaying the hostility of Nevis' planters than with any deep affection that Nelson may have felt for his bride, Fanny Nisbet. The register of their marriage is still on display at St. John's Fig Tree Church; the couple was not married there, however, but at nearby Montpelier House. Nelson's good friend and the captain of HMS *Pegasus*, Prince William Henry, gave the bride away. Forty-three years later he would be crowned King William IV, the so-called "Sailor King," who presided over the abolition of slavery and the passage of the Reform Act of 1832 (he would also be the last British monarch to appoint a prime minister contrary to the will of Parliament). While Montpelier House itself no longer stands, a small plaque along a narrow dirt track commemorates this most celebrated of the island's weddings.

*

Nevis is full of the past. Given the small size and relative economic unimportance of Saba historically, there are few structures of great age on that island. On St. Eustatius a cluster of old buildings may be found in the Upper Town, but there is little in the surrounding settlements or the countryside that does not belong to the later decades of the twentieth century, few ruins to excite the imagination or (as the case may be) to make one's blood run cold. Contrarily, on Nevis you are always passing into or out of the long shadow cast by what had been a thoroughly mature, brutally efficient slave society. Ruins abound. One of the more significant of these may be found along a rough road that ambles off the main thoroughfare near the northernmost tip of the island, running through empty savanna and low hills on the edge of the jungle. Gradually out of the green and gloom a tumble-down pile of rock will creep toward you on the right, the remains of a stone church like something out of Wordsworth, except for the nodding beach morning glory that ornaments the stones, the dangling red caterpillars of bottlebrush blooms that shadow them. One approaches the roofless church through an *allée* of serrated aloes leading up to the rounded arch of an empty doorway; a few despondent knolls lurk to one side of this path like refractory parishioners, while further away looms the perimeter of the forest. Cottle Church was built between 1822 and 1824 by slaves who belonged to one Thomas Cottle, son-in-law to Edward Huggins, owner of the Golden Rock Estate. For more than a century this isolated ruin was in the process of being consumed by the encroaching jungle until an effort to clear the ground and preserve the structure was undertaken, spearheaded by Cecil Huggins and Mike Mills, two local stonemasons. The site is important in the history of the Caribbean, for this was the first Anglican church in the British West Indies where blacks and whites were permitted to worship together. Constructed from local volcanic rock, the stones of the church range in color from chalky ash to faint ochre, and a moody greenish-gray; grass has grown in to replace the absent floorboards. While parts of the small structure have been reassembled, the church has not been "restored" in the conventional sense; the interior is vacant and gloomy, the walls somber, while the two tumbled transept peaks have been disarranged into a mournful profile, dimming with the languor of a drowsy archbishop into the shade of late afternoon. We were told that monkeys sometimes congregate here; their scurrying silhouettes and strange cries—combined with the general isolation of the place—have apparently unsettled more than a few travelers.

One of the most compelling aspects of the site is undoubtedly the list of those slaves who lived and worked in the area when the church was being erected: a small plaque is affixed to an interior wall of the structure, cataloging their names and ages. A recent archeological survey has revealed that many of these slaves are buried nearby. Some, like Isaac (thirty-four years old) and Monday (seventy-two years old) were born in Africa, while others—presumably including the slave named Nevis— were born on the island. In many cases the names appear to have been taken from popular fiction, drama, or classical mythology—Clarissa, Cordelia, Ulysses—while names like Quasheba and Bunda reverberate with echoes of Africa. The list of names peoples this desolate site with the shades of those who constructed the church and who lived and died here nearly two centuries ago. Yet even as the inventory brings these men and women within the space of conscious memory, such a list also places them further and further away from us. What made them laugh? What made them angry? What did those with a memory of Africa think of this strange place? Was building the church undertaken in an attitude of piety, as an act of devotion to the God who promised them atonement and salvation? Or was this deity a stranger, an unwelcome interloper in the domain of axe-wielding Ogun or watery Olokun (upon whose domain they had passed when wrenched from home and into the global economy of capital and flesh and bone)? The names remind us that all we have are the names.

I sometimes think of Nevis as an island of ghosts. After visiting Cottle Church, Erin and I recalled our cab driver's unsettling remark about the old woman who cries in the dark somewhere near Butlers. The next afternoon, we decided to explore further. Across from the St. James Raceway and just beyond Manning's Seventh Day Adventist Church lies the shadow of a great stone house where a particularly unhappy event occurred long ago, again involving a member of the Huggins family. Constructed in 1740 and finally abandoned about two hundred years later, the once-proud hall has diminished to a forlorn pile of rock. It was here at the Eden Brown Estate in 1822 that Julia (Edward's niece) became engaged to a young man by the name of Walter Maynard. Unfortunately, this match met with the strong disapproval of Julia's brother, John, who challenged his sister's fiancé to a duel and shot him and killed him. Brokenhearted, Julia lived alone for the rest of her life, even as her brother found it impossible to take a wife, for his fellow planters regarded him as a murderer and forbade him the company of their daughters. After her demise, Julia is said to have continued her mourning. Many claim to have seen her ghost hovering about the tumbled stone ramparts on warm moonlit nights, bedecked in a moldering bridal gown and wailing wildly as her unbound tresses fall and flail in the wind.

Erin and I came upon a roofless and overgrown two-story structure—mournful and primitive-looking—with an outdoor stairwell clambering upward toward a vacant porcelain sky. Beneath the stairs a wooden door with rusted iron hinges hung half-open, grasping tendrils of covetous weeds having scurried up the planks and pried the door open in search of some treasure hidden away in the dark basement. Grown up within the walls of the vanishing house and thus shielded from the heavy gales that often lash the windward coast, lush tall trees towered above the ruined enclosure. The bloom of jungle growth there was sprinkled with small pink wildflowers—with frangipani-like flakes of warm snow and clusters of ebullient yellow bells—all abuzz with various insects and a-rustle with the activities of small invisible things. There has been no effort to restore this place or to rescue it from the encroaching jungle, yet it seems to me that the structure exists at this moment in precisely the right condition to inspire those strange and funereal moods that toppled towers and abandoned estates have always evoked in sensitive and solitary travelers. Because the path is not especially well-marked and because there are no interpretative displays or glossy flourishes of historical annotation, in coming upon these ruins one truly experiences the hushed surprise and sense of solemn wonder that is most often associated with the explorations of a bygone age; one feels that one has found something along the way, and that the proper attitude is one of rueful reflection. All too often (though with the very best of intentions) ruins like these are mediated for us until they become mere historical "sites," overfull of information, diminished and emptied of mood and metaphor. There is a certain dismal honesty about all of this too, for at Eden Brown time has not been called to heel and continues to do its sad, entropic work. The sense that we are "all becoming shades" has not been attenuated by scholarly text or colorful brochures, and lonesome wayfarers like ourselves are permitted the sort of sad, introspective wonder that bald facts and mere information might compromise. We can, should we choose, do our reading afterwards.

*

There was a bat in the house. Erin was showering and I had just finished dressing for our dinner at Montpelier Plantation. It was around dusk. Coming out onto the little screened-in sitting room toward the front of our cottage, I spotted a dangling, leathery-looking creature suspended upside down from a plank of wood on the outside of the screen. Intriguing. With the screen between us, this seemed a rare opportunity to get a very close look at one of the several kinds of tree bats for which the island is famous (there are some nine or ten different species of bat on Nevis; these apparently the only native mammals known to occur here). As I moved closer, I could make out the tiny, slightly sinister rodent face. A wizened devil, wings sheathing its body in dark mockery of Isaiah's seraphim, the creature glanced back and shuffled its inverted, claw-like feet, grasping the screen now and taking two small steps to the left. I realized only at this point that the bat was not suspended from the outside of the screen, but upon the inside: indeed, mere inches away from my face. Apparently the creature made a similarly startling discovery at about the same moment, for suddenly he was airborne. So was I. The bat buzzed past my ear and headed up toward the ceiling. I screeched and tumbled toward the nearest of the two bedrooms, slamming the door behind me and abandoning whatever claim I may still have had to masculine self-possession. 'What?' Erin called from the adjoining bedroom. 'Bat!' I cried. 'Don't come out.' It is not an especially flattering story, but one which must be told. Separated from one another by a single clapboard wall, neither Erin nor I dared to enter the common room, which was now the domain of the children of the night. Or one of them, anyway. 'What should we do?' asked Erin, once several

144

minutes had elapsed. It was a reasonable question. How were we to know whether the creature was still caroming through the sitting room or whether it had departed for greener pastures? I cracked the door, stood very still, breathed deeply, and stepped out into the chamber. All was quiet. Night was falling fast. Then—like some squeaking dormouse that had been secured to a mini leather hang glider and catapulted skyward—there it was! Hurtling from one end of the room to the other about eight feet above the floorboards, the creature sent me leaping backward into the bedroom. Clearly the bat wasn't going anywhere. After about a half-hour of this—a ballet of mutual panic, and slamming doors, and fraying tempers—the bat withdrew far enough into one of the dark corners of the high ceiling that Erin and I could persuade ourselves he had left. Now more than a little late for our dinner—glancing carefully first in one direction and then another—we darted through the sitting room, hurtled through the front door and down the stairs to where our rental car awaited; a space of asylum and refuge from the be-fanged intruder who now held illimitable sway over our cottage. Upon our return there was no sign of the bat, but the following afternoon he reappeared and once more lurched in skittering flight just inches above our heads. By this time, however, we had come to an understanding. There were worse things, after all, than a hungry bat clearing our rooms of tropical mosquitoes and whatever nastiness they might be inclined to inflict on us. Just so long as he stayed out of the bedroom when we slept, the bat was welcome. We actually came to look forward to his "flitting at close of eve," to his sudden appearances and his gliding repasts. I'd like to think that somewhere—all clicks and whistles and whirrs—the bat is working up his own account of the episode. Good luck to him, I say.

*

'They got the eighty-four million, and that's no small thing,' said Pauline, a dark-skinned lady in her late thirties who stepped outside the Nelson Museum to chat with us about the upcoming elections. She was dressed smartly in a crisp white blouse and long blue skirt, her hair pulled back tightly and fixed in a bun. Pauline's sharp eyes bespoke an intensity of political feeling, even as the earnestness of her engagement was occasionally belied by a touch of lightness and vague irony. She had dropped by the museum to deliver a package to the woman working at the front desk, and she spoke nostalgically about the place, telling us that she had taken an especially memorable field trip to the museum as a young girl. 'My mother had bought me a new dress and new shoes. I was so excited to put them on that I dressed up like I was coming to church,' she told us softly. Pauline's wistfulness vanished, however, when the subject turned to politics. Just before Erin and I had arrived on Nevis it was announced that Prime Minister Denzil Douglas had secured a promise of \$84 million in a Stand By Arrangement with the International Monetary Fund. The global recession that began in the fall of 2008 had dealt harshly with the West Indies generally and with St. Kitts-Nevis in particular; there were sharp declines in tourism and construction as well as a concomitant rise in public debt. In the light of these circumstances, strong financial support from the IMF was indeed "no small thing." Most of the money was earmarked for the improvement of financial oversight and

Customs Department reforms. 2011 was an election year, however, and Douglas' success with the IMF did not translate into Pauline's support for his Labor Party allies at the ballot box. Instead she supported the Concerned Citizens' Movement, a conservative party founded by Vance Amory (for whom the island's airport is named) in 1987. Nevis takes its politics seriously; partly a function, perhaps, of full independence having been accomplished so recently (1983), and partly a function of a relatively small political landscape. Adversaries for high office are sometimes next-door neighbors and legislative decisions often have immediate, tangible consequences.

In terms of actual territory, St. Kitts-Nevis is the smallest sovereign state in the Western hemisphere (had Anguilla been the third island of the federation—as Great Britain had initially intended—Grenada would probably have enjoyed this distinction, but that is a story for a later chapter). The political intimacy that characterizes the life of St. Kitts-Nevis is rendered even more palpable when we recall the latter island's relative autonomy; Nevis and St. Kitts often conduct their affairs apart from one another, though the premier of Nevis, should it prove expedient, may form an alliance with the prime minister of St. Kitts. This was the situation going into the elections of 2011, with Douglas' Labor Party having partnered with the Nevis Reformation Party (N.R.P.), led by Premier Joseph Parry (despite full independence from Great Britain, Her Majesty Queen Elizabeth II remains head of state, with St. Kitts-Nevis a full member of the British Commonwealth).

'A couple years back the N.R.P. began telling tales about the C.C.M. and the premier. They say that eighty acres of government land was given illegal to the brother of the housing minister. Nobody ever prove a thing, but the C.C.M. lost the Assembly.' Pauline shook her head. The Nevis Assembly consists of five seats; in 2006 the Concerned Citizen's Movement lost three of them and thus the majority. Joseph Parry replaced Vance Amory as the island's premier. I mentioned that Erin and I had seen several signs throughout Nevis commanding the voters to "Remember 80 Acres." 'Yes,' said Pauline, 'that's what we talking about.' She may have had little good to say about the Nevis Reformation Party, but it seems true that (at least initially) the N.R.P. had a certain aura about it, in part because of the unfortunate events that inspired its founding in 1970.

On August 1st of that year, a ferry named *Christena* left St. Kitts for Charlestown on her second run of the day. This twenty-two-ton vessel was built to carry no more than 150 passengers but on this day she held above 300 persons. It was also subsequently revealed that the careless crew had set sail with a critical deck opening left uncovered. Just before the craft entered the Narrows—the two-mile passage between St. Kitts and Nevis—she encountered a small swell and began rolling dangerously; within just a few minutes, the *Christena* capsized and sank in about sixty feet of water. So quickly was she lost that no distress signal was sent and no life rafts deployed; 239 people were drowned and relatively few of the bodies were ever recovered. The fact that most of the passengers were from Nevis while the boat was operated by the government of St. Kitts meant that old animosities were once again rekindled, particularly when a commission of inquiry created by St. Kitts issued what many Nevisians found to be a wholly inadequate report that neglected to assign any responsibility for the disaster. Within a few days of the report's publication, the Nevis

Reformation Party was formed: its ultimate goal was secession from St. Kitts. 'The N.R.P. done some good in the past,' Pauline admitted grudgingly, 'but what since they win back in 2006? Secret contracts,' she answered, 'a 17% VAT tax… 17%! They talking a lot of nonsense.' A small pause followed, during which the dark mood seemed to pass from Pauline's face. She smiled wanly and shrugged as my Italian grandmother used to when she meant to say, 'What's the use?' 'The whole place nearly come apart back in the 90s, you know… when the drugs was everywhere passing through; I mean, the whole thing,' she thrust her hands apart and splayed her fingers to suggest a cataclysmic blast, 'boom!' Did she support full independence for Nevis? Pauline looked slyly at us and shifted her feet. 'Lots of people do,' she said, and shrugged again.

*

During the 1920s, a dashing, handsome gentleman named Sir Reginald St.-Johnston—administrator, essayist, poet, and author of several short stories—served as governor of St. Kitts-Nevis and eventually of the Leeward Islands. In period photographs he stands proudly in his ceremonial whites, an ostrich-plumed pith helmet tucked beneath his left arm, high forehead and pink complexion complemented by a pencil-thin mustache and a grin that is half-Edwardian conceit, half-roughish good humor. He assumed the administration of the Leeward Islands in September 1929, just a few weeks before the Wall Street Crash and the onset of a worldwide depression that plunged the islands into desperate waters. Fortunately, he seems to have been adept at securing loans from the Colonial

Development Fund during these difficult years and it was St.-Johnston who first brought electricity, hurricane-proof concrete housing, and a modern system of water catchments to Basseterre, the sister island's capital on drought-prone St. Kitts. He was also among the first individuals who worked to develop a regular commercial air service for the British Caribbean. On the other side of the ledger, St.-Johnston has been criticized for his heavy-handed response to labor agitation on St. Kitts during the tumultuous years of the 1930s; likewise, an initial enthusiasm for Benito Mussolini and for fascism in general cannot but discomfit us a little (though to be sure St.-Johnston's attitudes largely reflected those of his class; he was not the first to be taken in nor was he the last to stand corrected). He clearly seems to have felt a particular regard for Nevis, the island whose "pale ghosts" he famously celebrated in a poem that exhibits a good deal of nostalgic affection for the days when the island "reigned West India's Queen." St.-Johnston's 1928 *West Indian Pepper Pot* contains a handful of mildly engaging (if mostly conventional) short stories; his personal reminiscences, however, are something else altogether, really a kind of literary marvel. Crisp, humane, and often humorous—sentimental while never quite succumbing to mere sentimentality—*From a Colonial Governor's Note-Book* makes for delightful reading, particularly when St.-Johnston reminds us that, throughout much of the eighteenth and early nineteenth centuries, Nevis sat at the center of West Indian taste, fashion, and recreation. Tales concerning the restorative powers of Charlestown's hot spring had long circulated throughout the Caribbean, turning Nevis and its capital into a spa resort many centuries before the modern tourist industry caught on. In Great Britain, the precise nature of the island's curative mineral waters was initially misunderstood, and St.-Johnston recalls discovering an early stamp showing two ladies "taking the waters" at Charlestown, apparently quaffing enormous draughts of what would appear to be sparkling tonic (rather than *bathing* in the healing waters, as was more typically the wont of visitors). Nevertheless, St.-Johnston reminds us that as late eighteenth-century travelers returned from Nevis to Jamaica, Antigua, and even to Britain itself—the symptoms of their gout and rheumatism having vanished—invalided majors and colonels, aging sea captains and bewigged planters (along with their finely attired wives and daughters) arrived in greater and greater numbers, the island becoming a place of frantic gaiety and bacchanal, of hushed liaisons amidst the shadows of tropical gardens. Healthy waters (and health generally) was a great magnet for many residents of the Caribbean, until the late nineteenth century, yellow fever and malaria killed one-third of all European emigrants within three years of their arrival, thus the West Indies' infamous sobriquet: the White Man's Graveyard (an outrageous misnomer, as in the bad old days of King Sugar a far greater percentage of blacks than whites died of disease). As interest in the island grew, a wealthy merchant named John Huggins (yes, another one) decided to build a hotel which could accommodate some fifty guests at any one time. The establishment would include a large ballroom and a dining hall filled with mahogany furniture situated atop heavy rugs and gleaming floors. Built around 1787, many believe that the Bath House (as it was known) constituted the Caribbean's first resort hotel; its many distinguished guests are said to have included the poet Samuel Taylor Coleridge and Sir

Frederick Treves, the physician who treated John Merrick, the "Elephant Man." According to Gertrude Atherton, who wrote about the hotel in her novel, *The Gorgeous Isle* (1908), the Bath House suggested an "[e]astern palace with hanging gardens," galleries and balconies festooned with teak and mahogany, gilt mirrors and chandeliers aglitter like conventions of fireflies in the gloaming. There were wide-terraced gardens in those days filled with orchids and lilies and bougainvillea. There were narrow stone paths where young girls and their eager admirers walked alongside quiet pools of dark water, the young men doffing a Wellington or a D'Orsay in greeting to passing swains as the genteel masquerade was replicated in dim shadow on the blackening surface of manicured lawns and atop discreet lagoons. The hotel did not long survive the collapse of the island's sugar estates, however, and by the time William Paton visited Nevis around 1890, the Bath House was derelict, a "picture of desolation and decay," as he tells us in *Down the Islands*, its verandas collapsed, its windows and casements long since used as firewood, its wide empty chambers the "abode of bats and owls." During the Second World War the structure was partially rehabilitated and was used to house West Indian soldiers preparing for combat support overseas; following political independence, the space was again improved, this time to house government offices, certainly the most bureaucratic of the Bath House's many colorful incarnations. Today the Bath House has been restored as a tourist site, its façade graced by three stories of fine balcony trimmed in blue and white. And you can still take the waters there, at a little fenced-off spring with descending steps and a tiled floor. It is a quiet place. Sir Reginald St.-Johnston returned to Britain and became a barrister. The celebrated artist Evan Charlton painted his portrait in 1936. St.-Johnston died in 1950. Among his several additional tales are *A History of Dancing* and *Dogs of Every Kind*. The latter may be accounted for by the fact that St.-Johnston was, after all, an English gentleman; the former resists simple explanation.

*

'Yes, everywhere you look there's a Huggins,' Lisa repeated with a touch of satisfaction. 'John built the Bath House and Edward, the one who ran this place, he was John's brother. That's what some people think; maybe a nephew. There were a lot of Johns in the family at that time. It's hard to know exactly who was who.' Erin and I had returned to the nearby heritage inn for our final breakfast on Nevis and Lisa had stopped by our table to say her farewells. As our bungalow was so closely situated to the hotel we had become regular morning visitors, lured as much by our hostess' tales of old Nevis as by the menu and the view. Nevis Peak was wrapped in clouds and the sea to the south looked gray and unsettled. There had been some rain earlier in the morning and the veranda was cool and empty. The troop of monkeys had vanished, probably moving back into the upland forest. 'They say that Edward died when he fell out of his carriage,' Lisa added. 'He was the one who made it into the history books.' She shook her head as if to say that her forbear's infamous reputation told only part of the family's story. That may be true, but it is nevertheless a savage and disturbing tale. In January 1810, Edward brought thirty-two of his slaves—men and women—to the marketplace at

Charlestown and publicly flogged them. Precisely why (setting aside simple sadism) remains a bit of a mystery, though Huggins had sometimes accused his slaves of insubordination. According to later court testimony, one male slave received 365 lashes while a female slave endured 292. Although Huggins was within his legal rights to administer such punishment, the Nevis Assembly was so troubled by his conduct that the body adopted a resolution describing the floggings as 'cruel and illegal act[s] of barbarity altogether unprecedented in this [i]sland'. When the case came to trial in May of that year, however, Huggins was acquitted by a jury of his peers, some of the jurors being the very same men who had earlier claimed to find his conduct so dastardly and deplorable. Such hypocrisy was not the end of the story, for seven years later Edward was once again brought before an island court to defend himself against charges of brutality. This time he was acting as attorney to his son-in-law, Thomas Cottle, overseeing affairs at the latter's Round Hill Estate while Cottle himself was in England. After being informed by the estate manager that one of the slaves had stolen some stockings, Huggins ordered his driver to administer a hundred lashes to a slave who was found to be in possession of a pair of socks, as well as another eighty to a second slave (named David) who was also suspected of involvement in the theft. When the victims' sisters began to cry out, Huggins had both women –Thisbe and Cressy—pulled out of the crowd and saw that each was given a minimum of twenty lashes. Edward was charged with cruelty under Westminster's recently enacted Amelioration Act and was brought to trial; once again he was acquitted. In 1818, however, when the case came up for debate in the House of Commons, the body's abolitionist members were incensed, horrified as much by Huggins' barbarity as by the indifference of the island's judiciary. The West Indian planters were clearly determined to subvert any attempt made by Parliament to improve the situation of the slaves or to safeguard even those meager rights that had been afforded them. Full emancipation, argued the abolitionists, was thus the only possible way forward. Unbeknownst to him, Huggins' cruelty had helped set the stage for the most radical transformation of Caribbean civilization since the arrival of the first Europeans: the abolition of slavery, and the inevitable demise of the planter class to which Huggins himself belonged.

On Nevis, Emancipation Day is commemorated as part of the island's Culturama Festival. There are boat rides and street jams and a Grand Cultural Parade where participants from across the Caribbean perform their cakewalks and quadrilles to the accompaniment of string bands and big drum music, tatterdemalion masked performers spinning like parti-colored whirlpools along the route and stilt-walking Moko Jumbies gliding stiffly above the fray. Someone will be installed as Calypso King, his partner crowned Miss Culture Queen. And all night long little coral-hued bonfires will light the fringe of ocean at Pinney's Beach—here where the waves murmur at the lace margins of sleep and where the swifts race the stars in their courses.

ANGUILLA

The sill that separates Anguilla from St. Martin is a narrow one: a ferry rolling out of the French town of Marigot will negotiate the channel and deposit you onto the dock at Blowing Point in about twenty minutes. This is not to say that the passage is devoid of drama, however, for the British island is situated to the north of its neighbor, with the prevailing winds and currents frequently driving large swells and generous gusts through the channel, following the general rule in the West Indies that weather begins in the southeast and blows toward the northwest. As the ferry chugs and shudders its way out of the anchorage, the gray little town begins to drop away behind the breakwater, while high and sparsely settled hills roll skyward and the expanse of Nettle Bay opens up to the lee, festooned with white sails and quick cloud shadows. While Marigot often seems a bit ashen and dingy in the tropical heat, the town nevertheless maintains a raffish charm. Tourists regularly arrive from the Dutch side of the island where many of the cruise ships reach their furthest and final port of call, where the resorts and high-rises are glossier and the Guyanese jewelry merchants of

Philipsburg open their doors to a largely American, bathing suit-clad clientele. The Princess Juliana airport is also located on the Dutch side, just beyond the vast lagoon through which runs the administrative boundary that divides the Kingdom of the Netherlands from the Republic of France. As Anguilla's airport is too small to accommodate the fleet of big, high-flying jet aircraft that do most of the aviation industry's heavy lifting (and as her harbors are too small and shallow to make room for the increasingly vast Carnival or Royal Caribbean vessels), visitors headed to Anguilla from Europe and North America must first put in at St. Maarten, pass from the Dutch to the French side (St. Martin), and climb aboard one of the ferries that depart every half-hour from Marigot. There is no visible border between the two nations, no fence or customs house with blue-coated gendarmes standing at attention beneath a fluttering *tricolor*. Instead, a certain *je ne sais quoi* marks the passage from one side to the other: more open scrubland, no Kentucky Fried Chicken franchises, road signs in French rather than in English (you will see or hear very little Dutch on the Dutch side). As the taxis scuttle toward Marigot Bay, the town itself appears by turns deserted and bustling. A crumbling and vaguely sinister alley will suddenly give way to a street packed tightly with small shops and ramshackle restaurants, crowded tenements sharing the street with elegant townhouses peering from behind whitewashed walls topped with sprawling bougainvillea or elegant citrus trees. Nearby, in the open plaza which bustles with merchants and merchandise, an old wrought-iron bandstand looks out to sea. Finely worked and filigreed, topped with a genteel cap of white and blue and conjuring up the pressed tunics, the imperial swagger, of Napoleon III, the gazebo stands a bit forlorn amidst the bustle and baggage, the idling taxis and diesel exhaust of the waterfront.

Rolling out of the bay, the ruins of Fort St. Louis glance down from atop a promontory to starboard. Given the proximity of British Anguilla to the French settlements on St. Martin, each island was regularly pillaged by the other throughout the wars of the eighteenth century. Fort St. Louis was built in 1767, as a defense against raids like the one launched by the Anguillians twenty-three years earlier, when the French settlements on St. Martin, as well as those on nearby St. Barthélemy, were overrun. In 1789, in an attempt to forestall the spread of French revolutionary fervor, the Dutch militia crossed the frontier and briefly occupied the redoubt (their concerns were not unreasonable, for the Revolution did come to the Leeward Islands a few years later, Victor Hugues bringing his guillotine to the public square in nearby Guadeloupe, beheading royalist planters and abolishing slavery on that island before cooler, more commercially minded heads prevailed). As the ferry rolls languorously forward, her engine still undemonstrative under the careful hand of the ship's captain, Friar's Bay lounges past and quietly falls behind; here the mild but impressive hills begin to fall away sharply, descending from an amiable green to barbed and rugged rock before terminating in a trough of deep blue and angry spray. Only the edge of demure and graceful Grand Case may be glimpsed as the ferry pulls past the Petites Cayes, the town an exquisite collection of low, whitewashed structures that hug the rim of the bay beneath a press of rolling bluffs. Here the ship will finally roar awake, the full thrust of the engine propelling her forward into the wide and exuberant swells that roll like sliding turquoise hillocks down the length of the sill.

The captain had better be a skilled pilot, for acknowledging his competence (or lack of competence) is a characteristic part of the crossing for local passengers. Commendation must be inferred; chastisement is clearly articulated. Anguillian sailors have long enjoyed a reputation as some of the finest boatmen in the Leeward Islands and it is an unfortunate pilot who lets down the side. As long as they are conversing amongst themselves upon general topics, it may be assumed that the ferry passengers approve of the handling of the boat. After one or two heavy thuds as the ship bottoms out in the belly of a deep trough, however, an ominous silence begins to reign, the men scowling and the ladies clicking their tongues. Any more of this sort of thing, and unpleasant criticisms begin to fly. 'Someone tell him he carrying people back here, not goats!' Worst of all is laughter, the passengers chortling to one another as if to say, 'This one is hopeless. Best to leave him on dry land.' All of this has its serious side, however. The island's boatmen had acquired their renown at least as early as the 1890s, when a severely depressed local economy compelled a large number of Anguillian males to begin their annual migration to the Dominican Republic, there to find work on the island's sugar plantations. In January, at the beginning of the cane season, some 300 men would crowd aboard the schooners gathered in Road Bay, after which the ships would race one another westward toward the Dominican ports of San Pedro de Macoris or La Romana, sometimes making the trek in a mere two days. A similar contest would take place in June, when the migrants would race back home with ten or fifteen dollars in their pockets, received with much fanfare by the women who gathered ashore to await the return of their husbands, sons, and fathers. Stories are told that the schools were empty on the days when the schooners returned. Sadder tales are part of this history as well, tales involving grim days of sailing home against the wind, of exhaustion, and death and burial at sea. A number of the ships that ferried the cane workers between the islands survived into the late twentieth century, including a beautiful old black-hulled schooner called the *Warspite*; originally a sloop purchased by Arthur Romney Clark in 1916, the ship saw service as a transport vessel in the wake of sugar's long mid-century decline, even for a time acting as the supply ship for the Sombrero lighthouse, situated on a barren piece of rock some thirty-five miles to the northwest of Anguilla. The *Warspite* continued to ply local waters until her demise at the hands of Hurricane Klaus in 1984. Even today, the boat races held at various times throughout the year serve in part to commemorate the gallant spirit of Anguilla's mariner forefathers. During the festivities associated with Carnival in August or Anguilla Day (May 30th), an entire fleet of ships might be discovered pulled up onto the wide beach at Mead's Bay or Sandy Ground, a host of exotic and handsomely contoured sea creatures momentarily beached upon the sand, their turquoise and lemon and coral-hued hulls every bit as colorful as the banded butterfly and corpulent parrot fish that glide about nearby in the shallow reefs. Along the bay, sails pierce the blue sky like a story-book landscape of steeples and towers beneath which gather the sailing crews, each bounded by a host of grinning acolytes churning and promenading along the bay in giddy expectation of the imminent competition.

There is always music somewhere: imperious calypso kings and smooth reggae crooners, complemented occasionally by a driving *soca* beat. Calypso in particular has long provided the preferred soundtrack on Anguilla; from Lord Suprisum in the 1960s to the more contemporary sounds of Exodus or the Musical Brothers, the island's rich cultural and political life has long taken its color and rhythm from the sounds of calypso kings and queens, while the first draft of history is usually as much the work of the calypso performer as of the journalist. The first plane crash on Anguilla was commemorated in song by the Mighty Duggie—a performer from George Hill, where the incident took place—and when Queen Elizabeth II visited the island with Prince Philip in 1994, the Mighty Upsetter performed a song especially composed for the occasion. But in many ways the grandest of occasions are the boat races. From East End and Island Harbor, from the Valley and the Farrington, from Old Ta and Crocus Bay and Road Bay, everyone is there to watch the vessels put out to sea, their proud sails snapping into a myriad of right triangles, a blizzard of white blazing with the wind across sapphire waters and indigo skies.

Traditionally, the larger craft carry some ten men (although it is not unheard of that one of the crew might be hurled overboard if it looks as if his boat is about to be surpassed in a close race); these vessels have no decks, and employ rocks or bags of sand in place of conventional ballast. Usually the ships first race away from shore to a stake boat set a few miles out, then turn back toward land, the crew hoping to be the first to make contact with the finishing post, which is a buoy placed a few yards from the beach. Cricket may be a popular pastime in the British West Indies, but make no mistake: the national sport of Anguilla is boat racing. *Da Wizard*, one of the most celebrated of these vessels, even graced the front lawn of the island's Heritage Museum for a number of years. Along with an abiding enthusiasm for the ballot box (turnout in 2010's legislative elections was 82%, which is typical of voter turnout generally), skillful sailing and the thrill of contests at sea remain some of the most characteristic aspects of island culture. 'Votin' and boatin',' as an especially poetical old gentleman at Crocus Bay once put it to me, 'it's what we Anguillians do.'

Although situated a mere six miles from St. Martin, Anguilla is often barely visible until well into the crossing, being a remarkably flat island whose highest point rises only some 200 feet above sea level. At one time, when the climate was cooler and drier, Anguilla and St. Martin—along with St. Barthélemy—were joined together to form one large island, the watery channels between them an expanse of graceful, low-lying plains and lagoons. In those days creatures like the long-extinct *Amblyrhiza*—an enormous rodent the size of a small deer—wandered the scrublands spread between the islands before finding themselves marooned at the higher elevations as sea levels rose (one of these animals apparently met its demise in a cave just above Katouche Bay, for that is where its fossilized remains were discovered in the middle of the nineteenth century). The Leeward Islands consist of two parallel arcs that run along the edge of the highly unstable Caribbean tectonic plate. The inner arc is the younger of the two, its islands having been formed within the last twenty million years; these include Saba and St. Eustatius, St. Kitts and Nevis, as well as the more southerly islands of Montserrat and the western portion of Guadeloupe. The islands that constitute the outer arc, St.

Martin and St. Barthélemy, Antigua and Barbuda, are twice as old as their younger sisters and are thus more significantly eroded: while the islands of the inner ring are still dominated by sharp and impressive peaks that have been built up around volcanic cones, the outer islands—subjected to some forty million years of weather and wind—are comparatively flat, lying low above the water. Anguilla sits at the northern edge of this latter arc, an island of thirty-five square miles built upon a base of volcanic rock and overlaid by coralline limestone. This highly porous material allows the island to capture very little of whatever rainwater might fall (less than forty inches annually, on average); the soil itself is thus thin and poor in nutrients, while the absence of freshwater streams has rendered most attempts at cultivation extraordinarily difficult. Indeed, the descendants of those English settlers who came ashore in 1650 soon found the island so inhospitable that they conjured various schemes of moving on to greener pastures, going so far as to launch an invasion of nearby Crab Island in 1717. Repulsed and captured by the Spanish, most of these invaders escaped and limped back to their arid, unhappy home. Indeed, drought conditions have often prevailed on Anguilla, at times rendering the place nearly unlivable. During the 1830s and 1840s the situation became so desperate that Lord John Russell, Britain's Secretary of State for War and Colonies, proposed to the Governor-in-Chief of the Leeward Islands that the entire population of Anguilla should be relocated to the colony of Guiana, in South America; there the erstwhile Anguillians might be put to work on the sugar plantations. Getting wind of this scheme, the administrator of Dominica even offered free passage and free housing to those emigrants who chose to take up residence upon that island. Despite this offer—and despite the extraordinarily difficult living conditions that prevailed on Anguilla during the middle of the nineteenth century—hardly any of the island's 1,500 residents chose to leave. Eventually, Secretary Russell's plan to effectively terminate the colony was shelved. Their forbears' refusal to abandon Anguilla has remained a point of pride for the people of this island down to the present.

Amidst the low growl of the engine and the crash of spray upon the ferry's starboard windows (thoughtfully closed by a young attendant as we passed into the channel), I glanced around at the other passengers. Toward the stern was a gaggle of well-heeled American tourists bound for those high-end resorts for which Anguilla is famous; these range from the casual-chic ostentation of Viceroy on the island's leeward coast, to the breezy nonchalance of Cap Juluca with its Moorish-inspired buildings situated along Maundy's Bay. There is the Spanish-style, pink coral effusiveness of the Frangipani Beach Club on Mead's Bay and there is CuisinArt, too, with its hydroponic farm, its Venus Spa and its signature Greg Norman golf course. One of the most interesting of these destinations is the remarkable assemblage of individual units scattered about Shoal Bay West, comprising the Cove Castles Resort. Designed by the renowned American architect Myron Goldfinger, these sleek two-story structures—startlingly white in the Caribbean sun, with their strong geometric forms and elegant curves—rise along the rim of the bay like so many impetuous windjammers, sails unfurled and anxious to put out to sea. In *Villages in the Sun*, Goldfinger writes of his enthusiasm for traditional Mediterranean architecture and of its importance as a model for him in his own work; this legacy is not immediately obvious at Cove Castles, but gradually the compelling, finely integrated organic design—a sense of privacy conjoined with an agreeable openness—begins to clarify the little villages of the Greek Isles as the source of the architect's inspiration.

Tourism came relatively late to Anguilla and its coming changed everything. Cove Castles was amongst the island's first luxury resorts, opening its doors in 1985, followed closely by Cap Juluca, in 1988. In one sense, the timing could not have been more fortuitous; Anguilla's salt industry had collapsed at about the same time and the island was surviving economically much as it had always done, through remittances from abroad. Unemployment at the time hovered at 40%. Daily life was a struggle and the advent of tourism offered a solution to the hard realities of existence on a desert island that had always asked much of those who chose to live on it. But the sudden turn toward high-end tourism brought with it many challenges, particularly for a people who had always espoused a generous, practicable communalism in their everyday lives. If no one was very rich, at least no one was living in utter and abject poverty. The inauguration of a tourist economy sparked a land rush and real estate frenzy; it is said that some people became very rich while many lost what little they had. In his exciting thriller called *What You Sow*, set in the 1970s but first performed by the Gold Tones in 1983, island dramatist Colonel Harrigan speaks to the anxiety that many Anguillians felt as the drive to create a legally established land registry worked to prepare the island for the high-stakes game of high-end tourism. In this play, a deceitful businessman named Blakey dupes a poor farmer into selling him his land for a mere four hundred dollars;

when an American tourist later offers him $1,000 for a single acre, the farmer discovers how much his land had actually been worth, and how much money Blakey stands to make as a result of his duplicity and sharp practices. As the drama unfolds, it becomes increasingly clear that speculators like Blakey represent a value system that is inimical to traditional Anguillian notions of decency, cooperation and social cohesion. Infidelity and murder are in the wind. On the island today, tourism generates close to $100 million annually, according to the United Nations Commission for Latin America, with 60% of all jobs either directly or indirectly tied to the tourist industry. Nevertheless, something of the play's ambivalence toward tourism and speculation remains, even as the threat of overdevelopment becomes more and more of a concern to many; a contemporary song advises the island's citizens to resist the temptation to part with their holdings in exchange for money down, no matter how badly they might seem to need those dollars in the short term. 'They may promise you money like sand,' warns the refrain, 'but hold on to your land.' It is worth noting that the people of Anguilla reserve the right to become indignant even if they themselves are not the ones being duped. During the construction of the Viceroy resort, amidst growing accusations that the laborers recruited from South Asia were being poorly treated (paid less than $200 a month, and held as virtual hostages by their employer), the islanders quickly and forcefully expressed their disapprobation. In the summer of 2006 a series of protests occurred in The Valley, with demonstrators carrying signs reading "Enough is Enough" and "Slavery is in our Past, Let's Keep it that Way." When the Indian laborers themselves marched from the West

End to the capital, I recall the Roman Catholic priest who celebrated mass at St. Gerard's exhorting the congregation in no uncertain terms to support the marchers by providing them with food and water. The relatively recent gap that has opened between the island's most prosperous and its least fortunate has no doubt contributed to the suspicion that mechanisms of exploitation have contributed to such a gap. Sometimes, suspicions are well-founded.

The customs station through which arrivals are processed is located at the small (and aptly named) village of Blowing Point, situated on a low peninsula lodged between Little Harbor and Rendezvous Bay. All is handled with quiet efficiency: passports are stamped and most bags given a cursory glance while visitors are assigned to taxis which will transport them to the appropriate villa or resort. Until the fall of 2017 a proper customs building stood at Blowing Point, but Hurricane Irma obliterated the structure in September of that year; the fragments that remained were dismantled as part of the recovery (a military-style tent stood in its place when I visited several months later, giving the appearance of some sort of field hospital having been erected quayside). Until quite recently locals as well as visitors might step across the street from the former customs station and duck into Pear's for a few drinks. It was one of my favorite stops. Taking shelter from the blaze of high noon with its shortened shadows and silent streets, I stepped into the unadorned little canteen upon my first arrival on Anguilla and sipped a rum and coke, listening to reggae music pulse across the cement floor then down the worn steps and grassy macadam that constituted the bar's makeshift veranda. Twice I heard a recording of "Just Cool," the second followed by "Busted in Barbados," both performed by local musician and impresario Bankie Banx. A young man with a Cleveland Indians baseball cap sat in a corner mouthing some of the lyrics over a bottle of Presidente, nodding to an older man in a plaid shirt and dungarees who popped the lid off his second Carib and stepped back outside to join some friends who laughed quietly and saluted him upon his return. It was the man's birthday as I discovered and he was soon being serenaded by his companions who proceeded to sing several verses of the "Happy Birthday Song," including a few I had never heard ("May the Good Lord Bless You," "May the Future Bring Joy"). They leaned back in their white resin chairs beside explosions of frangipani and the sign that read "Government Officials Parking Only." The older man grinned and cleaned his glasses with a handkerchief he pulled from his breast pocket. Then he blew his nose and daubed his eyes and forehead. Across the parking lot uniformed constables passed with crisp competence into and out of the police station. Diesel fumes lingered in the air, mixing with the scents of dirt and sand and the inescapable smell of the sea. A rooster called loudly while he paraded through the irregular arrangement of parked cars and idling taxis, the shrill bleat of wandering goats, the grind and chatter of outboard motors completing the sound-scape of Blowing Point. All of these noises are gathered and dispersed by the perpetual winds that whirl from the land and from the ocean: whirl across the low roofs of the small houses (coral and blue and cream) through the ambling branches of the little gardens—down the main street toward the brightly painted Roti House and the little grocery store, across the roofs of homes whose projecting fingers of rebar presage second stories (whenever time and money allow)—whirling as well into the slumberous, darkened windows of the seaside homes and out again to where the fishermen's boats nod their intermittent greetings as the ferries come and go.

I climbed aboard a taxi and asked the driver to head for Little Harbor. I would have the good fortune of staying at a villa called Mainstay, at Elsie Bay. Famous for its coral-colored roof tiles which may be seen from a distance as you approach the house, it combines a spacious, high-ceilinged gracefulness with quiet simplicity and a lack of pretension. Its view of St. Martin is probably the finest on Anguilla while the property itself (located just up the road from a mangrove swamp in a corner of the island that is still largely undeveloped) retains the feel of a nature preserve. Mourning doves and sharp-shrilled bananaquits have been regular visitors (the latter persistently building nests in the outdoor light fixtures), while cattle egrets occasionally perch upon the low rock walls of the gardens and once or twice a wandering goat has poked his head into the living room before moving on to tastier pastures. There are gulls always—frigate birds occasionally—and often a yellow warbler who enjoys pestering his reflection in the passenger's side mirror of whatever car may be parked in the driveway. Until recently a land crab lived in a little hole beneath the frangipani bushes and would snap at you when you returned to the house late at night, a weird alien creature gliding atop its armored spider's legs and enforcing a strict curfew. Just beyond the colonnaded veranda lies Elsie Bay with its labyrinth of coral canyons and its strong tides that send the fish there hurtling and tumbling through patches of floating seagrass like scaly acrobats and finned funambulists. Sometimes before bed you may still see the lobstermen submerged in the bay and checking their traps, or rather you will see the lights they carry skimming just below the surface of the water like sunken, wandering will-o-the-wisps (a full West Indian moon looking down like some pale porcelain salver and awaiting an imminent supper).

As the taxi pulled out of the parking lot and headed for Mainstay, the flag of Anguilla fluttered overhead, a blue ensign with a Union Jack in the canton and a shield to the right bearing the beloved image of three orange dolphins at play above a turquoise sea. This banner was first flown on May 30th, 1990, after having been approved by Queen Elizabeth II. The three dolphins (representing strength, endurance and unity) were first depicted on a flag that was flown shortly after what is known here as the Revolution, when Anguilla defied Great Britain herself in an attempt to thwart a deeply unpopular union with St. Kitts during the late 1960s. Since 2002, the island exists officially as a British Overseas Territory, autonomous in its domestic affairs yet with a governor who serves at the pleasure of Her Majesty the Queen and who answers directly to the Foreign and Commonwealth Office in London. While his Full White Dress, plumed tropical headgear and ceremonial sword might seem to bespeak responsibilities that are largely symbolic, the governor does possess some very real power (though the extent to which he exercises such authority is largely left to the careful judgment of the governor himself, informed by a determination not to overstep and an unwillingness to alienate the elected government). Anguilla's is a parliamentary (or ministerial) system of government organized along the lines of the Westminster Model; there is a small, multi-party assembly and a chief minister who acts as the head of government. The governor, however, in addition to his management of the island's national parks, is also responsible for internal security, foreign affairs and oversight of the judiciary. In the event of an emergency, he even reserves the right to dissolve the government and to administer the island directly (which happened as recently as 2009 on the nearby British Territory of Turks and Caicos). I have been using the third person masculine pronoun somewhat carelessly, as it turns out: in 2013 Anguilla received its first female governor, the energetic and popular Christina Scott. Although the Revolutionary Flag was flown only briefly and unofficially, its three dolphins have since found their way onto the state banner, and even onto the governor's official ensign, where they swirl whimsically at the center of a spirited Union Jack. A largely autonomous island which also sits amongst the final outposts of that Empire upon which the sun never set—a defiant and proud people who have nevertheless maintained a spirit of *politesse* and an amiable commitment to Elizabeth II— these are some of the rich contradictions that the blue banner of Anguilla both celebrates and seeks to reconcile.

*

When Erin and I returned to Anguilla in the summer of 2018 we discovered that nearly everyone had an Irma story to tell. It is no wonder. This behemoth was the strongest Atlantic storm on record and the first Category 5 hurricane to strike the Leeward Islands in recorded history. Official wind speeds topped out at 180 miles per hour, but the anemometer installed at the Juliana Airport in St. Maarten

literally went to pieces as wind-gusts reached this velocity...
so who knows? The storm is believed to have caused some
$65 billion worth of damage throughout the region and to
have resulted in something like eighty fatalities. Anguilla was
hit especially hard, although somehow the island suffered
only a single casualty. Photographs of Sandy Ground showed
a village that looked as if it had been blasted by a battery of
howitzers, Blowing Point fared not much better. Those who
had experienced their first serious hurricane told hair-raising
tales, while the understatement of older residents belied
what must have been a harrowing several hours (fortunately,
Irma moved quickly). 'The wind was blowing so hard the
rain didn't touch the ground,' said one young man, 'there
were cyclones—water spouts—I see them come ashore. It
feel like an earthquake, man. Cars rolling over and blowing
down the street.' Out at the East End, Mrs. Hodge was a
bit more restrained in her description, though the image she
presented was perhaps even more chilling. 'Irma came early
in the morning. It was still dark. We lost power, so we moved
to the far room. Then we heard a terrible noise. We had lost a
storm window somewhere. The hurricane was in the house.'
As if some malevolent being from your worst nightmares had
gained egress. On one hand the island recovered quickly—
schools reopened in a matter of weeks and electrical power
was restored before Christmas—on the other, Erin and I saw
evidence of terrific damage nearly a year afterwards: both
Ebenezer Baptist Church in the Lower Valley and Bethel
Methodist at South Hill remained roofless, while houses
outside of Blowing Point sat gutted and despondent. The
week we arrived the British Government had just dispersed

some £60 million. For those who live elsewhere it is easy to forget the volatility of this region; those who live here are unlikely to do so.

*

It is hardly remarkable that tourists come to Anguilla for its beaches; what *is* remarkable is that the little island is fringed with such a fine and various assortment of them. I write with some reluctance about these beaches, partly because it is difficult not to feel that one is peddling something, partly because of an apparent monotony in appearance. The suspects are the usual ones—sunsets, sand, pellucid waters—and banal modifiers gather upon the page like nettlesome gulls prepared simply to squawk the familiar observations and to fly off. The monotony is *only* apparent, however, and at the end of the day one might just find a booby or a pelican instead of gull. My latest encounter with a pelican occurred at Little Bay, an amiable gap on the island's leeward coast where the water's surface is always impossibly still and where the only landward approach involves a delicate descent by rope through a maze of cactus and aloe. On the north side of the bay an imposing yellow-gray limestone cliff grapples skyward to a height of some thirty feet, occasionally sloughing off rounded rocks and shards of coral stone down onto the ocean floor. Here caves and small crevices gape with broken teeth and nets of seagrass like baleen curtains, dark and melancholy with their shadows and squares of diffused light. Laughing gulls build their nests atop the tall cliffs, along with red-billed tropic birds and brown pelicans, while the large stones that have tumbled from the summit into the shallows have done their own remarkable work, shaping a generous habitat for a variety of swimming or lumbering creatures. Caribbean spiny lobsters, with their creeping legs and antennae eyes, clamber carefully across the rocky bottom like armored ambassadors from a seascape arranged by Hieronymus Bosch. The underwater cliff face exhales brigades of sergeant majors and small clouds of spade-shaped blue tang as well as rarer residents: a juvenile yellow-tailed damselfish (its most remarkable feature not its eponymous tail but small, impossibly luminous flashes of turquoise that blink and shimmer all across its flanks), or the strange pink cylinders of shy trumpet fish that hide themselves in the shade, floating perpendicularly amidst tufts of seagrass and swaying slightly with ghostly, musical grace. Undulating, polarized clouds of herring or silversides roll and separate, surrounding the curious diver on all sides like a sudden submerged lightning storm before vanishing just as quickly down toward the depths or up toward the surface of the bay. It is there that the pelicans make short work of them. As I was walking from the water late one afternoon I heard a sudden and very loud splash close behind, a particular surprise, as on this day I had the bay to myself. Turning quickly, I saw an enormous brown pelican floating only ten feet from where I stood, the rubbery pouch beneath his bill shuddering with all the desperate tumult of a fishy meal. After a moment the pelican took again to the air, wheeling, banking silently, then turning sharply into a steep dive. Its wings collapsed in toward its body, the bird drove once more with explosive power into the ocean. The force with which the brown pelican strikes the water is critical to the success of its endeavor: momentarily stunned by the shock of its arrival, the fish are easy targets for its long bill. However, the bird requires a few moments to shuttle its supper down, during which time it is not unheard of that the pelican's scavenger brethren (the gulls and terns) strike quickly and pluck the wriggling fish from out of its very pouch. No such sortie was launched this afternoon, and after a second serving of silversides the creature was gone, suddenly airborne, sated and indifferent, vanishing over the edge of the cliff. The rasp of small ground lizards across dry leaves was now the only sound that disturbed the perfect silence of the bay.

Each cove and beach—each inlet and small harbor—possesses its own distinct mood and character. Lonely, majestic Little Bay is situated just to the north of Crocus Bay: it is from this latter location that you might hail a boat to bring you up the coast to Little Bay should the rope descent not appeal to you. Broad and hospitable, Crocus Bay sits at the foot of Crocus Hill, only some 213 feet above sea level but the highest point on the island, and across which runs a steep road that links this bay to the Valley, Anguilla's shambling and unpretentious capital. Easily as attractive as Mead's or Shoal Bay—two of the more popular tourist spots—Crocus Bay is most often bypassed by visitors, thus remaining an hospitable rendezvous for the Anguillians themselves; fishermen's boats fanned in shifting constellations across the smooth sea with all the sleepy satisfaction born of hulls heavy with grouper or triggerfish. It was here that several hundred French invaders stormed ashore in May of 1745, an attack launched in retaliation for raids against St. Martin and St. Barthélemy that had been carried out by Anguilla a few months earlier. Unfortunately for the French, the heights of Crocus Hill proved an ideal defensive position for the 150 men of the island militia under the command of Governor Arthur Hodge. Within fifteen minutes the French suffered about a hundred casualties, while the remaining attackers quickly withdrew. This was the time when the Caribbean was earning another of its infamous sobriquets, "the Cockpit of Europe." There is no ruined fortification, plaque or marker of any kind at Crocus Bay to commemorate this engagement; few such may be found anywhere in the Leeward Islands in remembrance of the days when there was "no peace beyond the line" (the grim stone edifice at Brimstone Hill on St. Kitts is the exceptional World Heritage Site that proves the rule). Doubtless this is in part because very little was affirmed in these various struggles beyond the most sordid of motives: avarice and sheer restlessness, along with a mutineer's contempt for settled ways and civilization. The grand and terrible engagements were most often fought at sea while battles fought on land were generally nasty small and brief, quickly resolved and quickly forgotten. It is equally true that the current inhabitants of the West Indies feel a certain distance from the struggles waged by those white Europeans whose descendants chose long ago to abandon the Caribbean for England or France. This sense of distance is further exacerbated by the fact that the spoils of victory in these various conflicts often included additional caches of slaves; no doubt the stakes of war appear different to those whose forbears were taken as prizes. There is a fine beach at Crocus Bay and just beyond there is a little gathering spot with tables and benches laid in the tree-shade beside an old stone wall. Local entrepreneur David Lloyd has recently opened a restaurant here, elegant, casual, vaguely Balinese in its décor (with the broad steps leading up to its grand dining-porch carefully arranged around the proud trunk of what was once the village's celebrated old tamarind tree). With the coming of twilight the profile of the cliffs at Katouche Bay diminishes into a chiaroscuro haze to the southwest. The young boys who had been diving and splashing in the bay at sunset have left for home. The stars are out. There is something meditative and soft at Crocus Bay; there is nothing that remembers either the glories or the meanness of men and history.

One of Anguilla's most popular beaches may be found at Mead's Bay, located on the leeward coast at that point where the island begins to narrow quite perceptibly, rapidly diminishing in the direction of West End Village and finally dissolving into those coral-gray outliers—Anguillita and tiny Blowing Rock—that mark the terminal point of Anguilla's westward reach. An expansive mile-and-a-half crescent of white sand unfurled between a cerulean sea and a thin tree-tousled barrier of scrub, Mead's Bay is punctuated by a number of beach villas and resorts: Carimar, Frangipani, Viceroy. Looking toward the ocean you may just glimpse what appear to be flat, ghostly agglomerations of rocks and slivered cays. These are the islands of Dog and Prickly Pear, hanging in the offing like *fata morgana*, the work of mischievous, West Indian water sprites. On clear afternoons the sharp outlines of their flinty profiles seem to suggest that these islands lie within reach of a casual swimmer, just beyond the bend of the bay. This is not the case and I would not recommend an attempt. While Mead's is a bit more developed and beset by tourists than some of the smaller or wilder bays, the natural world exhibits its regular, predatory work in full view of the beach's strolling, sunning clientele. Swimming some forty yards from shore early one afternoon, I suddenly found myself beset by schools of tiny, sleek silver fish, leaping in sputtering, staccato arcs across the surface of the sea, generating wave upon wave of small, pearl-splashed bows. I was surprised that none of these myriads of fish bounced unceremoniously off my head as they passed by. Rather quickly, however, events took a more gustatory turn. Chortling and swooping suddenly down upon the fish—snapping, wheeling, diving and skimming the waves—quick-winged least terns and royal terns devoured any number of the little herring who nevertheless continued to hurl themselves out of the water and often down the gullet of one of these careening predators. Situated squarely in the midst of this savage meal, I noticed that similar pockets of feasting terns bloomed and faded across the surface of the bay for what seemed to be about fifteen minutes. I was later informed that this was something of a regular occurrence at Mead's Bay during the summer months, precipitated by periodic and sudden blooms of small jellyfish. These creatures are apparently irresistible to the herring and silversides that swoop in to devour them, only to be swallowed up themselves by flocks of hungry birds. My richest recollection of Mead's Bay is not associated with the sunshine, however, but with the night-time. Shortly before midnight, with a full moon recumbent overhead, I slipped into the still water with a few friends and swam out to a depth of some twenty feet. The only sound was the soft wash of the surf upon the sand, while the curve of the shore and the silhouettes of the tall trees were bathed in bone-white and powder-blue moonlight. The few faint stars that were visible shimmered their likenesses upon the dark rise and fall of the water's surface while far below us our shadows fanned and shuttled across the ivory sand of the bay's bottom. I thought—amidst the strange, quiet mood there—of those lost to the warm sea of the Antilles, of their shadowy and water-bedded wraiths awash beneath our skimming arms and legs. Anguilla is ringed by wrecks, as it turns out, and something in the pale light—in the black water—brought those earlier mariners to mind. The ocean lathed our limbs and buoyed us like a benediction in the wet dark; awash in a strange and indeterminate space between the sea and the sky, the graying moon swam at my elbow.

Just beyond the road running behind Mead's—separated from the beach by a narrow border of trees and wayward tufts of dry grass—lies one of Anguilla's several salt ponds. Brown and brackish, smelling of chlorine and damp earth, it is not an especially impressive sight, particularly in such proximity to the postcard image of the nearby bay. A second look, however, reveals a remarkable diversity of birds and water fowl: willets and white-cheeked pintails, teals and black-necked stilts, occasionally a great egret—snowy white with its rapier beak and sharp, reptilian eyes poised atop a serpentine and sinister neck—or (more rarely, around dusk) a yellow-crested night heron, orange eyes glaring from within its mask of black and white. The island is marked by twenty salt ponds, critical habitats for some 130 species of birds; in fact, 80% of the region's birds depend upon such ponds at some point in their lives. And that is not all. Whether as a buffer against storm surges or as a trap for the sort of sedimentary run-off that might otherwise damage seagrass and coral reefs, these salt ponds play a critical role in maintaining the ecological health of the Caribbean archipelago. They have also decisively shaped the history of settlement in the Leeward Islands, particularly on Anguilla.

Formerly such ponds represented some of the very real stakes of transatlantic commerce and regional warfare. Until the industry collapsed in the 1980s, salt remained central to Anguilla's economy, though in later years little of it ended up on the kitchen table. Most of the salt extracted on Anguilla in the late 70s was shipped to Trinidad, where it was used in the refining of jet fuel. At Road Bay, where the most profitable of these ponds was located, salt was traditionally harvested by hand, small parties of workers wading out into the shallow basin alongside a tiny skiff (called a flat), upon which cakes of salt would be placed. This process of harvesting was known as "picking" and usually resulted in dried, lacerated hands. When the flat was full it would be returned to shore, the salt taken to the nearby factory (later a popular bar) where it would be ground into fine crystals and piled along the beach in towering heaps awaiting export. In another of his plays, *The Hard Days*, Colonel Harrigan allows one of his characters to describe how Anguillians from the Valley would traditionally depart for the pond at Road Bay before dawn, calling out to those who were still tarrying in their homes so that the laborers might walk to work together. One of the earliest references to salt production on the island dates from 1769 when the brigantine *Elizabeth*, sailing from Grenada, was wrecked on a reef beyond Road Bay just before she could take on her anticipated cargo of salt. In fact, while Britons from St. Kitts were the first Europeans to permanently settle on Anguilla, it seems likely that Dutch entrepreneurs from St. Maarten had begun to visit the island as early as 1631, extracting salt from the pond at Road Bay as well as from those at Mead's and Sandy Hill Bay. Lured to the Caribbean largely because of its various salt deposits, early

Dutch corsairs and privateers initially fought the Spanish for control of those pans along the South American coast. As these engagements became increasingly bloody (and indecisive), the Dutch turned instead to the salt ponds of the Leeward Islands, a region concerning which the Spanish displayed a general apathy. What most interested the Dutch was the Baltic, however, and the ships of the herring fleet that plied those cold, unsettled waters. Rising imports of West Indian salt would allow the fishermen of the herring fleet to dry, preserve, and sell greater numbers of fish, a development that served to increase the size of that fleet dramatically. While 150 ships coursed the Baltic fishing grounds in 1550, a century later that number had risen to four thousand. A relatively brief period of cooperation between the Dutch and the English during the early years of Leeward settlement is reflected in some of the Dutch surnames (like Van Buren and Vanterpool) that survive on Anguilla down to the present, as well as in one or two place names. A small declivity behind Little Harbor, for example, is still sometimes referred to as Statia Valley, commemorating those smugglers and traders who traveled back and forth between this part of Anguilla and the nearby Dutch island of St. Eustatius. If you travel to Anguilla and happen upon one of its ponds on a windy day you might yet glimpse frothy spheres of meandering salt-foam trundling about the edges of the water like small snowy tumbleweeds, while squadrons of sandpipers and yellowlegs race their reflections down and back beside a muddy shore.

*

I had heard that Windward Point was not to be missed by visitors, that the landscape was untamed and desolate, the surf explosive and fierce, the view of neighboring Scrub Island especially impressive. I rented a car and—as an ascent of Windward Point sounded like hot work—I determined to get an early start. The road from Little Harbor took me through the Valley and the Quarter, out beyond Sandy Hill—its slave burial ground hidden in the bush—and past the scattered settlement that constitutes East End Village, site of the old primary school. Beyond the village the land became wilder and more sparsely peopled. The road lost its macadam finish, growing rougher, generously holed and veiled in more frequent clouds of drifting loam. Several isolated and abandoned homes were in the process of being reclaimed by colonizing vines and sinuous creeper while gnarled and skeletal trees clambered strangely through shutterless window frames. Here and there I was surprised by large, fenced-in pieces of cultivated ground: rich red soil respiring beneath overspreading thick green leaves, each leaf eyed hungrily by small herds of passing goats. Sometimes a brightly painted home stood close by, ringed by a perimeter of tall palms. Just as often, however, no structure appeared as claimant to the tilled earth, and I passed once more through stands of bedraggled and empty scrub forest. Finally I turned right and proceeded down a thoroughly rutted track that seemed to disappear into the woods. Fractured and fissured, with jagged tusks of exposed stone clawing at the tires, I was pleased when my car finally passed beyond this steep, burrowed trail and onto a small plain of smooth, brick-colored earth. Turning eastward, I left the track that runs toward the beach at Junk's Hole, and hoped that I was headed in the direction of Windward Point. I soon discovered that the trails here cross and re-cross one another, passing through thickets of prickly shrub, low nettles and knots of loblolly into labyrinths of sequestered clearings and piles of broken rock. Surrounded and overtopped by dense scrub, each of these gaps looked very much like any other, so that it was some time before I was able to find my way onto a second sharp-toothed track that led out of the low plain and toward the eastern tip of the island.

The tires groaned atop stabbing coral and it quickly became clear that taking the car any further would probably result in four flats so I pulled over (insofar as this was possible), removed the key from the ignition, cracked the windows and began walking. As I wandered further through the dry and deserted landscape of the East End, the bones of the island came into view: exposed and shattered coral fragments growing more and more visible along the path. I passed beneath an electric cable borne aloft by a series of sagging, wayward wooden poles that diminished into the distance and wavered in the rising heat; somewhere in this forlorn place there was a lonely house at the end of the line. The rusted hull of an abandoned backhoe sat glumly just beside the trail, as if some quixotic developer had once tried and failed to civilize this place, the steel skeleton a kind of threshold marker signifying entry into a more primary and primitive corner of the island. As I came to the top of a low rise a gray and forbidding valley fell away before me, broken by razor-sharp clusters of dead coral and sinister-looking cactus. Beyond this valley and rising into the air was the large rock acclivity that was my destination: Windward Point. It was now about ten o'clock in the morning and the blue of the sky had blanched to white; beneath this paling void the earth was a lifeless gray-green broken, from time to time, by stunted flowering mahogany trees, each of their tiny blooms a faint white, a fainter pink. As I moved into the valley and threaded my way carefully across the dry wash of coral and cactus, the breeze which had been my companion since I left the car and began walking quickly died away; the sea was also lost to view, though from time to time I could still hear the ghostly exhalation of thudding surf. The coral plain was dangerously holed and fissured, the various apertures home to concealed batteries of prickly pear whose spines invited unpleasant thoughts as I picked my way through the desolate terrain. The day grew hotter, the sky paler; the ground leaden, barren and bleached. I had been walking for about an hour when I came across the twisted wreck of a desiccated tree in the middle of the valley; the strange spirals of its roots and branches seemed still to strain for nourishment in this utterly parched and empty earth. The faint, petulant wailing of invisible goats only reinforced the sense of isolation and the obdurate indifference of the land to all living things. The first sign that I had passed through the valley and begun the ascent of Windward Point was the return of the sea breeze, initially fitful and hesitant but rising into a full-throated wail as I climbed slowly up the side of the escarpment. I chose each foothold with care, as every stone support might just as easily give way beneath me as provide a firm foundation for the ascent. Apparently solid arrangements of blackened rock often rolled apart and tumbled down the steep surface of the rise, the rattling, sibilant sound of their descent diminishing and finally lost amidst the bark and clamor of the wind. At last—with the treacherous trail of cactus and teetering stone steps behind me—I lurched

184

upward onto a dry table of earth and broken rock; the rust-orange scaffold of a beacon placed here by the Royal Engineers in the 1970s served to signal that I had finally arrived at the summit of Windward Point.

The dry and featureless landscape through which I had passed spread out below and behind me. Forlorn clusters of Turk's head cactus were tumbled across a low plain of nearly lunar appearance. Dead-gray agglomerations of pitted coral-stone were spread out upon an arid surface crisscrossed by ragged goat trails. Crabbed mounds of mummified scrub fretted the landscape which was fringed on the ocean's edge by tracts of black-hued bladder-wrack. Oleander and the occasional splash of white-flowering yucca were the only fulgent colors to be seen in the valley. Above my head several frigate birds sailed upon the updrafts of air that whirled toward the top of the cliff from the wave-washed shore many feet below, while hundreds of little white butterflies blinked and bustled about the summit in the driving wind. To the southeast the high surf of the Atlantic rushed in endless, white-flecked ranks against Anguilla's windward coast, battering, exposing and reducing its crumbling, coralline profile. Here hangs a tale, for it was along this stretch of coastline that *El Buen Consejo*, a Spanish Royal Merchant vessel, came to grief in the early morning hours of July 8th, 1772. Traveling with a flotilla of fifteen additional ships that was headed for the Mexican port of Vera Cruz, the 980-ton *Consejo* (along with a sister ship) became separated from the main body of the fleet and was driven upon the submerged crags of the island's inhospitable eastern tip. The currents that writhe and pivot through the narrow channel separating Windward Point from Scrub Island are still infamous today, discouraging even Anguilla's most assured sailors from attempting a passage through this watercourse and down the coast, except under ideal conditions. According to the ship's log, the *Consejo* was carrying a rich cargo of books, medicines, cinnamon and wire, as well as eighteen cannon and at least one hundred religious medallions (these last presumably belonging to some of the fifty-two Franciscan missionaries who were on board). No lives were lost but at the time of the wreck Anguilla's population barely exceeded three thousand, thus there was some difficulty in making room for the many sailors, officers and passengers who found themselves cast ashore and dependent for their maintenance upon the hospitality of those English settlers who had traditionally been some of Spain's greatest regional foes. Tensions apparently increased during the Spaniards' sojourn, as Lieutenant-Governor Roberts was compelled to call upon the British 68th Regiment to be dispatched to the island in order to keep the peace. Eventually, the castaways were safely repatriated to Puerto Rico. The story of the *Consejo* does not end in the eighteenth century, however. While the tale of the lost ship remained very much alive in Anguilla lore, the site of the wreck had been largely forgotten until 1987 when it was rediscovered by a local fisherman named Leander Bryan. Unfortunately, because the vessel had sunk in such shallow waters, once the remains of the wreck had been rediscovered they proved nearly impossible to protect and were thus thoroughly pillaged, even following the designation of the *Consejo* site an Underwater Archeological Preserve in 1994. Then, in the fall of 2008, some of the religious medallions identified with the wreck mysteriously turned up on eBay, where bidding for the medals quickly rose to $1,000 a piece.

The seller claimed that she had acquired them from a former boyfriend who had been engaged in construction work on the island and who had been legally permitted to dive and collect artifacts at the site of the wreck. Fortunately, the medallions were spotted by Don Mitchell, a lawyer associated with the Anguilla Archeological and Historical Society; the F.B.I. was thus notified and the artifacts secured. In March 2009 they were returned to Anguilla; the cache currently constitutes one of the largest collections of eighteenth-century religious medallions in the world. The circumstances under which the artifacts were acquired raised a number of troubling questions, however, and concerns about the securing and preservation of the island's patrimony remain.

Turning to my left, Scrub Island and its companion, Little Scrub, glinted in the sharp blaze of noonday sunshine. These small satellites (the former is only about three square miles) mark the northeastern extremity of the Caribbean archipelago; to the east there is only the Atlantic and eventually the African coast. Sometimes, Africa does not feel especially far away, however. In the summer months, when the skies in the Eastern Caribbean frequently become a bit hazy, the cause is often tiny grains of dust and earth (the so-called Sahara Sands) carried high into the atmosphere and across the Atlantic from the place where the Trade Winds (and hurricanes) are born. Crocus Hill may be higher than the peak at Windward Point but the view from the latter spot is possibly the most spectacular on Anguilla; the island both diminishing and broadening into the distance beneath you, the round bow of Savannah Bay blinking to the southwest, barely visible beyond its sentinels of Royal Palm. The savage, broken Windward coast and the stunning ultramarine gorge that is Captain's Bay lie below, as relentless salt-fragrant winds buoy aloft the frigate birds in all their effortless grace and the submerged ghost of the wrecked and ransacked vessel dissolves into warm, fish-fretted waters. I stood for a long time atop Windward Point, watching as the surf detonated into white clouds along the perimeter of sand and cactus and gray stone hot to the touch; looking down upon the sort of hard, desiccant landscape that your imagination might easily people with biblical patriarchs, strange visionaries and anchorites silent as the grave.

The descent from Windward Point proved easier than the climb and instead of traveling again through the valley of cactus and coral I turned toward the coast, seeking to follow the shoreline back in the direction of the path upon which I had begun my trek. I thought of taking a quick plunge into the ocean to cool off but there was no place where this could be done safely, for the surf roared upon the sharp, wet rocks and rendered any attempt to enter the sea impossible. The violence of the ocean nevertheless created myriads of tiny pools that I stopped to examine, struck as I was by the contrast between the pounding waves and those delicate, miniature ecosystems that flourished along the perimeter of this coral-blasted beach: fragile networks of trickling watercourses and small, shallow basins teeming with life. Eel grass grew here and there, sometimes concealing miniscule sea urchins and tiny crabs. There were limpets and mussels and gray-green chitons with their serried armor plates, each of the pools a kind of time machine providing a glimpse of the gradual and ungainly first movements of living things from the sea to the land. After mounting a large projection of exposed rock I came across something that took me by surprise, something I had not noticed from atop Windward Point and which offered respite from the searing heat of the early afternoon. Between two low, sandy hills a large, shallow tidal pool appeared. The water was very calm—a pale, sandy green in color—and graced at various points with small, craggy islets peeking above the still surface. A barely visible ridge of limestone separated the pool from the roiling, deep blue tumult of the Atlantic, yet the ominous white-crested rollers were suddenly reduced to diminutive, playful ripples as they washed over this limestone barrier. Little appeared to move in the pool save the broken, crystalline squares of dancing sunlight upon the sandy bottom. There was no way to *plunge* into the water, for—despite its width (perhaps a hundred yards) and breadth—the basin was a shallow one, never deeper than four feet. As I sat comfortably in the water, or paddled from one small submerged reef to another, I saw that the pool was teeming with living things that had formerly escaped my attention. Spiny black sea urchins huddled in the rocks and tiny fish—mostly translucent and hard to identify, but a few juvenile sergeant majors—scurried around and hid themselves amidst the thin shadows that were available. I imagined that life here involved something of a trade-off for these creatures: free from the jaws of larger marine predators, the fish that inhabited the pool would probably find themselves short of food and easy prey for visiting gulls and terns, who would not have to look hard (or dive deeply) to find them. After lounging in the water for a while, I walked out to the edge of the limestone ridge where the once-prodigious waves were diminished to trickles of seawater that barely brushed over my toes. A mere fifteen feet from where I stood was the Atlantic—the mad adversary, abode of Leviathan—yet just behind me all was quiet and still. The tidal pool here is the accidental and collaborative work of men and nature: before such activity was banned, sand was removed from the beach here for mixing into concrete. It is inevitably a temporary phenomenon too, for when the coralline barrier collapses, many centuries from today, the basin will be inundated and eroded away. I had discovered this place at a moment of fortuitous equilibrium. Where there is only ocean and sky we sometimes grow quiet, observing things strangely, with gratitude. Alone in the bright sunlight—alongside the primordial, sand-swept and ocean-bruised coastline—I felt that I was present at a remote epoch of pre-history. The only sound belonged to the surf, bridled for a small moment and tentatively held in check.

*

Island Harbour has been called the "gateway" to Anguilla's rugged East End; certainly it is the last sizable settlement to be seen on the journey out to Windward Point. The Valley—with its banks and shops and government offices, its citified busyness and its agreeable entrepreneurial clutter—constitutes the political and financial center of Anguilla. But Island Harbour is altogether different, its situation more isolated, its voice softer, its character more deeply and obviously tied to the sea. The community is gathered around a startling and often windswept bay of indigo and apple-green water; low-lying Scilly Cay hovers at the center of the bay, surrounded by a jouncing cavalcade of colorful, stalwart vessels. Some are yellow with green trim, others blue with red trim (or the reverse), some sport salt-paled canopies above the steering consoles, some have tattered seats, some none. These are the ships that bring to port most of the fish eaten here, and the dock that juts out into the bay is often lined with coolers of red snapper or grouper on ice, the little beach nearby piled high with lobster traps. Such a scene may seem typical of the little Leeward Islands but a bit of reading and a conversation or two soon reveal that Island Harbour has a few surprises up its sleeve. As local surnames like Webster and Harrigan might suggest, many residents here have long claimed Celtic ancestry in addition to African roots, asserting that their Irish forbears first came ashore when a vessel carrying indentured servants foundered and sank off the northwestern coast sometime in the eighteenth century. While particular facts remain in dispute there is a general understanding on Anguilla that the name Island Harbour is itself a corruption of *Ireland* Harbor and it is still not uncommon to catch something of an Irish lilt in the speech of the community's older residents (or at least to think that you have). 'God bless you, darlin', God bless you,' said one very old black woman I had stopped to transport to a friend's house on an especially hot afternoon. She was wearing a woolen skirt, long sleeves and a kerchief wrapped around her head, sounding for that moment like any little old lady you might meet between Cork and the Giant's Causeway. Island Harbour is fringed by several turquoise and coral-colored homes situated within brakes of elegant palms; it was here that, until recently, the return of the fishing fleet was announced by the blowing of conch shells, and it is still not unusual to find the national dish of salt fish and Johnny Cakes served here on sea grape leaves. As Island Harbour native Denise Crawford recounts, it was the old Hilltop Baptist Church here that screened some of the first movies ever shown on Anguilla, with a generator used to power the film projector and a white sheet hung from the pulpit as a screen.

Behind the harbor and beyond the beach, across a narrow road that runs into the settlement, there is a former gas station and a second establishment—a kind of bar and eatery *cum* curiosity shop—both formerly owned and operated by Euton ("Smitty") Smith: beloved restaurateur, former member of the legislative assembly, benign godfather and tireless promoter of Island Harbour. A tall, thin man with a high forehead topped by dark wiry hair, Smitty's charm is irresistible, his age indeterminate, his manner warm and playful. He is also a strong-willed and successful businessman. When his celebrated beach restaurant was destroyed by Hurricane Luis in 1995, Smitty purchased the shell of an old nightclub across the street and within a few months had it up and running, offering plates of fish, shrimp, chicken and sea lice (the local name for a creature more commonly called Spanish lobster). He knows everyone in the Eastern Caribbean: most of these count themselves as friends, all probably owe him a few favors. Smitty smiles easily and after a few words with you his dark eyes will narrow, his weathered, chestnut brown face will wrinkle and ruffle into a roguish grin. Yet there is also a kind of melancholy behind the real charisma and good-natured blarney: in quiet moments, as he sits in a chair beside his restaurant and glances out toward the cay, an impossibly sad and faraway look will sometimes cross his face, his silence on such occasions just a little unsettling, as is invariably the case when a genial and voluble man grows wistful and quiet.

It was Smitty who arranged for a trip to Scrub Island. Having viewed the place from the top of Windward Point I was determined to pay a visit. I soon discovered that this is not so easily done, however. Scrub is uninhabited, the surrounding seas unsettled and difficult to navigate; thus, with the exception of those local fishermen who sometimes make the crossing, this island sees very few visitors. Fortunately, I came across Smitty one morning as I passed through Island Harbour and not surprisingly he said that he could "make something happen." A flurry of cell-phone inquiries followed, authoritative requests joined with coy imprecations and puckish admixtures of flattery and mockery. On this particular expedition I was accompanied once more by Erin, no doubt an advantage, as Smitty seemed genuinely pleased at the opportunity to chivalrously fulfill the requests of a pretty lady and her beau. The phone pressed to his ear, there was a reckoning of what was owed to whom, a general squaring of accounts, followed by earnest (if playful) entreaties. 'I got two people here wanna go over Scrub. What you can do?' At last, success. 'Kenneth? Uncle Smitty, here!' Following a brief conversation, Kenneth agreed to take us across and we promised that we would meet him at Smitty's gas station in the morning, "promptly at eight." When we arrived we found Kenneth—a powerfully built man in a taciturn and business-like mood—gassing up his boat and preparing to put her in the water. Smitty was a playful interlocutor, presenting our credentials to the man amidst much glad-handing and hugs all around. 'You bring water?' asked Kenneth. 'It's hot out there; no shade. You pass out.' He nodded approvingly when I pointed out the cooler we had brought. Smitty told us that there was absolutely no question of payment before our departure; we could settle accounts with him after our return.

Once underway we motored out past the colorful boats of the fishing fleet, beyond the cay with its ring of white sand and out along the leeward shore, headed north. Once past Island Harbour the coast turned rocky and purple-gray, pocked with tiny inlets of clear water and trimmed with small trees. As we approached Windward Point I was surprised to see that below the tall cliff upon which I had once stood was an enormous cavern where the limestone undercarriage of the escarpment had been eaten away by centuries of wild winds and turbid waters. The point which had once seemed so adamant and solid now appeared utterly tenuous and fragile, with only a few feet of rock separating the audacious climber from the yawning hole beneath him, from the little clouds of whirling bats and a great tumble into the roiling sea. The water of the channel was choppy but the passage today was an uncharacteristically easy one, particularly for Kenneth, who is known as an expert sailor. As we moved into the channel there was one more surprise: a military helicopter appeared on the horizon and headed directly toward us. Junior slowed his boat, and looked up. Erin and I were unsure what was happening.

The helicopter banked to the left and circled us; on its side was the distinctive white, red and blue bull's eye insignia identifying the craft as belonging to the United Kingdom. The pilot waved to us through the helicopter's open door and Kenneth waved back. 'He recognize me,' said Kenneth. After another pass and a jaunty salute the chopper flew off again and Junior fired the outboard. 'There's a ship out there,' he said to us, pointing toward the northwest. 'He come around now and then.' This encounter represented the residue of a proud and storied past. The Royal Navy, which once maintained a sizable West Indies squadron, continues to station one of its nineteen frigates and destroyers in West Indian waters at all times. This guard ship, as it is called, is part of the Atlantic Patrol Task (North), and is most often engaged in counter-narcotics operations. In fact, in the summer of 2013, the *Wave Knight* intercepted some $14 million worth of marijuana, when she overtook and boarded a small craft called the *Miss Tiffany*. Perhaps the helicopter that the three of us had seen returned to the *Wave Knight* or perhaps to the *Lancaster* or the *Argyll,* for each of these vessels has recently served as the West Indies guard ship, patrolling those waters formerly secured by storied admirals like Rodney, and Nelson.

Kenneth pulled his boat up close to shore and Erin and I hopped out, wading just a short distance onto the beach. Kenneth pledged to return and pick us up in four hours (these arrangements seemed so informal and *ad hoc* it was impossible not to feel that we were having a little adventure). The beach here was utterly pristine and its drop was dramatic. Four or five steps from the shoreline into the water and you find yourself unable to touch bottom; a mere twenty feet from shore, and you are in very deep water, indeed. The fish here seem larger and less skittish than those you find on Anguilla itself, although exploring below the surface of the water can be a little unnerving. As the sandy bottom quickly becomes more remote the expansive blue of the bay begins to feel somehow limitless, the lone swimmer solitary and utterly exposed, wildly vulnerable to whatever might lurk behind the round wall of teal (and with only a desolate beach behind him). With the exception of two local fisherwomen who waved to us from their seats far out along a natural jetty that bounded the bay to one side, Erin and I had the island to ourselves.

As no boat was visible we assumed that the two women had been ferried to Scrub and left here, just as we had been. After a swim we decided to head into the interior, crossing to Scrub's windward side in order to catch a glimpse of the evocatively named Dead Man's Cay. Once off the beach the island becomes remarkably hot and dry. Scattershot klatches of baked and mummified prickly scrub, along with scorched and thorn-bedecked clumps of dead trees, are all blown into weird and impossible configurations by the inescapable wind. And there are bones in the uplands—jawbones, femurs, skulls—bones everywhere, and all picked clean. Many years ago someone brought a herd of goats to the island, constructing for them a large stone corral which still stands (though long abandoned) deep within the interior. There are still goats on Scrub, heard infrequently, and less often seen. The island is just large enough that at its center the sea is lost to view; passing through the tall grass and the stony ruins here the heat seemed to grow even more intense. With the ocean having vanished it was easy to forget that we were on an island in the West Indies and I began to feel a strange sort of disorientation: we might just as easily have been trekking across the Serengeti. Presumably, there were no lions in the vicinity. We looked around, hoping to find a tree tall enough to provide some relief from the scorching sunlight; there was none. Erin and I paused for a moment to catch our breath, with a field of bones and the wailing wind for ambiance. We came upon the windward shore about fifteen minutes later (the journey from coast to coast took just over half an hour), and gazed out across a strand of barren stone toward the restless, hammering surf, the ghostly funnels of spray. Scattered about the rocky shore were several enormous boulders, one about the size of an automobile, each facing the sea with the sort of austere indifference and rugged vitality that brought to mind the ancient monoliths of the British Isles or the *Moai* of Easter Island. It seemed so unlikely that these massive rocks were arranged utterly at random that their presence here began to feel just the slightest bit sinister, as if a strange, autochthonous people forgotten by history had placed them here long ago in the organization of some unspeakable rite. Pocked and pitted by driving wind and rain—peculiarly shaped, with their unsettling profiles and weird warrens of holes—the stones seemed oriented toward Dead Man's Cay, where a range of roiling blue waves rolled and rolled again into the desolate estuary. As we approached the cay, tendrils of sea grapes straggled and grasped their way toward the ocean like the expiration of some alien thing amidst the sage-gray landscape, the stunted loblolly pine. From where we stood we could just make out the remains of a small airplane that had crashed on the other side of the bay some years earlier.

It was a reminder that during the early 1980s Scrub Island served as an important link in the transshipment of narcotics from Colombia to the United States. The usual procedure was for a small American aircraft to rendezvous at this spot with a plane from South America (after a local contact had snuck ashore and lit a few fires to mark a landing place). In 1983, after American drug enforcement authorities received word of an imminent transfer of cocaine on Scrub, the governor quickly dispatched the Royal Anguilla Constabulary, whose officers quietly took their positions in the dark and ambushed the smugglers, securing a quarter of a ton of cocaine, worth about $1 billion (at the time, the most valuable drug interdiction in the history of the Caribbean).

Erin and I hiked back to the leeward bay and enjoyed a swim in the deep, cool water. We were in no hurry to leave the island but we began to become a little concerned as the time for our departure came and went with no sign of Kenneth and no way of contacting him. We noted that the two fisherwomen were still seated out on the jetty, so we were not unduly alarmed (though we couldn't be certain that whichever boat came to retrieve them would also have room for us). After about a half-hour of scanning the horizon, we watched as a small fishing boat suddenly swept into the bay: a frothy white streak of foam unfolding behind, a tall, thin man in dungarees and a baseball cap at the console. It was not Kenneth. 'He must've come for them,' said Erin, nodding toward the women, but neither of the ladies moved from their perch. Several moments passed. Slowly the boat began to idle and spin listlessly as the man at the console called out to us. 'Kenneth send me. He say he can't make it. Swim out to the boat.' He gestured wildly with his right arm, as if leading a squad of marines in an amphibious attack. 'What?' I asked, uncertain if I had heard correctly. 'Swim out. Swim!' He was doing an enthusiastic facsimile of the breast stroke. 'Kenneth can't make it. He ask me come. Swim out. Pull you self up into the boat.' Erin looked toward the cooler we had brought with us. The pilot's proposal seemed impractical; even without the cooler, it was hard to see how we might swim out into some thirty feet of water and then pull ourselves up into a fishing boat that lacked a Jacob's Ladder (or anything else that we might use for leverage). 'I don't think we can do that,' said Erin. The boat continued to make slow circles in the bay, the pilot eyeing us with quizzical amusement. 'Hopeless nincompoops,' I imagined him saying to himself, or perhaps something more colorful in the parlance of the fishing fleet. 'Hey, hey,' we heard someone shout. The two women had left their seats and walked down the jetty toward the bay. They may have been grandmother and granddaughter. The old woman walked with a careful, wobbly swagger, her arms raised just slightly for balance, the young girl, plump and agile, bounded along at her side. 'Hey, hey,' shouted the old woman a second time, gesturing toward the fisherman in the bay, 'you bring that boat up here to the rocks now. How they gonna get in they?' Pointing to us and gesturing toward herself she called out, 'Come on now… here.' We obeyed. As we approached her I saw that the woman was very dark and even older than I had thought. She wore an oddly formal, faded pick blouse; her narrow, wizened face topped by a traditional West Indian straw hat, several wisps of frayed straw pointing upward and outward at peculiar angles. I guessed that the fisherman piloting the boat was not especially enthusiastic about driving the bow of his craft up onto the rocks, but the old woman had about her an air of absolute authority. As she shouted commands and gestured out the best approach to the jetty, the pilot of the vessel simply did as he was told. Erin and I stood anxiously to one side as the pilot brought his vessel thudding onto the rocks, a maneuver he carried out with a combination of delicacy, propulsive obedience, and clenched teeth. The bow of the boat thrust forward and dragged along the surface of the piled stones. Quickly the old woman bent over and pushed our cooler toward the side of the vessel. 'Step up,' she said. It was a decidedly inelegant method of boarding, but the only feasible one that any of us had thought of. As the round young woman sang out a religious hymn in her lovely voice, the elderly lady helped out with an additional and forceful shove administered to my rear end. I sprawled like a beached porpoise across the nose of the boat and was joined a moment later by Erin, who had been the beneficiary of a similar tactic in coming aboard. The young woman handed the cooler up to us, never once losing her melody; I took out two bottles of water that we hadn't drunk and quickly passed them down to her. The pilot reversed his outboard as the two women pushed the bow from atop the rocks; we all waved and laughed and thanked one another while the pilot brought the vessel into the bay and steered her in the direction of Windward Point just across the channel. Behind us the two women grew smaller and smaller as they trudged slowly back to their fishing poles, their nets and buckets. By the time we reached the middle of the channel they had melted into the stones, into the indigo and silver of a late West Indian afternoon. There were no seats on board the boat but the pilot gestured to a large cooler placed near the stern and invited us to make ourselves comfortable. Only the last button of his shirt was fastened, so that it billowed and snapped around his very thin yet muscular frame. He shouted to us over the driving wind, apologizing for the confusion and responding to my queries with an assertion that it was no problem at all for him to ferry us back to Island Harbour, he was headed there in any case. With a grin that was somehow both self-satisfied and self-deprecating, he pointed down to his cooler. 'Look in there,' he said. The entire container was crammed with yellow-tailed snapper. 'Good day today,' he shouted, nodding his head. 'I take them around to the restaurants.' As we rolled into the harbor Kenneth called the man, whose name was Carleton, and asked to speak with us; Carleton handed me his cell-phone, which was sealed inside a clear plastic bag. 'Sorry I get tied up,' he said, 'but Carleton take good care of you?' I said that he had, omitting any details concerning the unwieldiness of our departure from Scrub. 'He catch some fish today, yeah?' 'I think so,' I said. 'Good,' said Kenneth. 'Good, good.' We soon came to the dock.

*

It is a small and unpretentious building located near the reclaimed ruins of the old East End school; mud flats are spread out on the other side of a two-lane road. As you pass by this one-story building, even if you miss the sign reading "Heritage Museum," your attention will be captured by the colorful artifacts ranged around the grassy yard or on display in the veranda: small eighteenth-century cannon, old copper vats used in the boiling of cane juice, an industrial cotton gin from the 1920s. Five rooms crammed with additional objects are to be found within. If the place feels less like an institution and more like someone's private residence, there is a good reason. This was the family home of the museum's proprietor, Mr. Colville Petty, whose passion for the island's history and whose determination to secure her people's patrimony led him to amass perhaps the finest collection of artifacts to be found anywhere in the Leeward Islands. Gradually the house became a museum yet it also remains very much a home. Despite the careful, rigorous curatorial organization that is evident, the mood remains comfortable and domestic. When Mr. Petty meets you at the door—earnest, soft-spoken and gracious, with his bald head and his imposing white beard—you feel as though you are being welcomed into a gentleman's parlor and granted the quiet privilege of peering into a wonder cabinet full of precious objects. Religious totems called *zemi*—crafted by the island's earliest Amerindian inhabitants—sit beside a cornucopia of ocean treasures: tortoise shells, sea sponges, fossilized crustaceans and smooth fragments of luminous sea glass. There are desiccated whorls of driftwood wrought into fantastical calligraphic patterns, fretworks of majuscules and arabesques. Here there are a handful of religious medallions from the *Consejo*, there an inventory of slaves belonging to a former cotton plantation (sugar was never a great success on Anguilla, but cotton enjoyed some boom years, particularly in the wake of the American Civil War, a conflict which saw the destruction of Britain's traditional source of the crop). There are the remains of a 1927 Whippet, the first automobile driven on the island, and a photograph of Peter Alexander Carter, a decorated soldier who saw action on the Western Front while serving with the British West Indies Regiment in 1917. Then there are those artifacts that for me speak most eloquently to Mr. Petty's sensitivity as curator and scholar: traditional three-legged earthenware pots, a piece of coral once used as an egg beater, a sea fan sifter and the skin of an old wife fish (these deployed as scouring pads by many local people until only a decade ago).Where a less attentive person might have seen mere household instruments—quotidian and uninteresting— Mr. Petty was conscious of the apparatus becoming an artifact,

202

placing these objects here as points of entry into a past that is at once both remote and thoroughly familiar, a lived, worked and human past that is utterly accessible. A photo gallery of the island's centenarians lines the wall that leads to Mr. Petty's office; as you wander near the door you will sometimes hear him conversing with scholars from the West Indies and beyond, the smooth, melodic voice of the patriarch refocusing a question, correcting a misremembered date or a misapprehended observation with a combination of tact and complete assurance. Museum curator, journalist, author and scholar, his is the authoritative voice concerning all aspects of the island's past, a fact acknowledged by Queen Elizabeth herself when Mr. Petty was awarded the prestigious Order of the British Empire.

There is an entire room given over to the story of the Revolution. Here are rifles and handguns carried by the island militia, a series of newspaper articles detailing the events of 1967–69 (culled from West Indian, North American and British publications), a green, yellow and blue banner representing the ill-fated state of St. Kitts Nevis Anguilla (flown only once— surreptitiously—at Government House), and a passport issued by the short-lived Republic of Anguilla. The Revolution was a consequence of Britain's determination to liquidate her Caribbean holdings in the wake of her earlier failed attempt to create a West Indies Federation, an enterprise that foundered upon the rocks of mutual Jamaican and Trinidadian mistrust in the early 1960s. With the collapse of the Federation the individual islands would have to go it alone. Responding to increased calls for autonomy on the part of the people of St. Kitts, Britain began the process of transferring power to the government of that island, based in Basseterre, a government that would also assume administrative responsibility for the islands of Anguilla and Nevis. There was only one problem: Anguilla wanted no part of confederation with the larger island, an arrangement which was preferred not only by Britain but also by Premier Robert Bradshaw of St. Kitts. Anguilla had been compelled to accept union with St. Kitts as early as 1825, an administrative convenience for Whitehall but an arrangement which yielded little in the way of benefits for Anguilla itself. As late as 1967 the island remained astonishingly underdeveloped; there were no paved roads, no telephones and no proper port facilities. There was no electricity and no pipe-borne water. The suspicion was that St. Kitts always secured for itself all the development assistance it could get, with little left over for her smaller sister islands. Now that the (minimal) oversight exercised by London was soon to be a thing of the past, fears rose that the cost of union with St. Kitts would grow even more burdensome, and quickly. The politically gifted and generally astute Bradshaw (subject of Mighty Slinger Bryan's satirical calypso "No Finny Hand Man") did not help matters with the sort of inflammatory rhetoric that played well to his constituents on St. Kitts but only served to frighten and enrage many of the people of Anguilla. His infamous threats to turn "into a desert" an island already so desperately impoverished only seemed to add insult to injury.

Following a series of disturbances that erupted in connection with the celebration of what proponents of confederation called Statehood Day, the contingent of policemen dispatched to the island by the government of St. Kitts found itself on high alert. In one of the Revolution's most celebrated events, a hostile crowd of Anguillians surrounded police headquarters on May 30th 1967. They disarmed the police, marched the officers to Wallblake Airport and flew them off to St. Kitts (when the pilots who flew the aircraft were themselves taken into custody at Basseterre they were subsequently rescued in a daring aerial operation carried out by the indefatigable Captain Pipe). The Anguillians promptly formed a peacekeeping committee and worked to administer the island themselves. Determining that the best defense was a good offense, several members of the committee authorized a clandestine landing at Half Way Tree on St. Kitts with the intention of attacking police headquarters and the Defense Force headquarters at Basseterre, while kidnapping Bradshaw himself. The attack fizzled but may very well have served to keep Bradshaw from deploying his Defense Force against the "insurrectionists" on Anguilla. While there was unanimity amongst the leaders of the Revolution when it came to rejecting the union with St. Kitts, there remained some disagreement as to what governmental or administrative model should take its place. Certain men, like the charismatic and courageous Ronald Webster (regarded as the Father of Anguilla), initially supported full independence for the island and the creation of a republic. Others—like Aitlin Harrigan and Emile Gumbs—called instead for direct ties with Great Britain and a form of self-government organized under the auspices of the Crown. As the two camps bristled (and while a belligerent Bradshaw cried foul on St. Kitts), Britain appointed an administrator named Tony Lee to work with the Anguilla Council in the implementation of its objectives and to act as a kind of liaison with Basseterre. With the expiration of his mandate at the end of 1968—and with St. Kitts and Anguilla no closer to a way out of the impasse—Lee withdrew. At this point the so-called radicals—led by Webster—began to move forward with their own plans for establishing an independent republic. When the heads of the Commonwealth of Caribbean Countries called on Britain to secure the territorial integrity of St. Kitts Nevis Anguilla (and following the expulsion of Minister William Whitlock, who had attempted a last-minute intervention in order to defuse the crisis) Britain launched what amounted to an invasion of her own territory. About 400 British troops stormed onto the island in the early hours of March 19th, 1969, including a detachment of crack Red Devil paratroopers. The frigates *Minerva* and *Rothesay* put in at Road Bay. While there was much hysterical speculation at home— the *Daily Mail* wondered whether Castro's communists might have been supporting the Anguillians, along with "American gangsters and Black Panthers"—there were ultimately no fatalities on either side during the operation. In fact, with a firm British presence finally established on the island, the leaders of the Revolution felt that they had at last secured the attention of the home government. After several stops and starts the Anguilla Act was passed in 1971, which laid the groundwork for the establishment of a ministerial system of government on the island, with a governor, an Executive Council and a House of Assembly. Anguilla finally became a separate Crown colony with its own constitution in December 1982 (399 years after Britain took her first non-European colony of Newfoundland); a few months later the state of St. Kitts Nevis celebrated her independence from Great Britain. Though the people of Nevis had themselves sought a similar separation from St. Kitts, London firmly declined to take upon itself the administration of another overseas territory. One volatile and fraught divorce amidst the twilight of empire was enough.

*

The afternoon before I was to leave the island, at about the moment when the sun enters that quarter of the sky from which it no longer drives you to shelter yourself in the shade or the ocean—when the strange inland silence of a West Indian afternoon dissolves again into the sad calls of doves, the rustling of unseen ground lizards in the dry grass—I found a seat upon a dilapidated old bench just off an unfrequented tributary of macadam that loops into the island's main thoroughfare, and gazed out upon Road Bay and its shallow salt pond many feet below. The village of Sandy Ground is carefully situated upon a narrow strip of land that runs between North Hill and the tall limestone precipice upon which I sat. To the west a quiet and mollified ocean lolls ashore, composing a crescent of deep blue and shattering white as it ambles along the sand. Behind the town lies the pond, shifting from cinnamon brown to amber and finally to a white-flecked pink as the sun falls toward the sea and the late-afternoon breeze begins to rise. The day drew on; a few more sailboats and catamarans took their positions amidst the handful of local vessels that had already returned from the fishing grounds out beyond Scrub Island or out past Dog and Seal. Sandy Ground is an important commercial port and a bustling fishing village; it is also the site of several of the island's most popular restaurants, these very different milieus mingling here with more ease and grace than might be found in other parts of the Caribbean. Behind me, I could hear the slap and shuffle of dominoes upon a resin table-top; it was Friday and a group of old men had gathered for what would no doubt be a tournament of several hours' duration, laughing and shuffling the bones back and forth in anticipation of the evening's contests. A few lights began to blink on beneath the palm trees of the village below. I could just make out the pitch of the shingled roof atop the elegant two-story bungalow of nonagenarian and revolutionary hero Sir Emile Gumbs, its graceful veranda and fine fretwork slumbering amidst the penumbra of green leaves and approaching dusk. The turquoise façade of the police marine base turned to a deep navy as the sun vanished behind the diminutive profile of Sandy Island into the western sea. Then it was night.

MONTSERRAT

The small plane hung in the sky like something forgotten by gravity. A few moments earlier the aircraft had idled and rattled atop the tarmac at Antigua's Vere Cornwall Bird International Airport, our pilot waiting for clearance to throttle forward and climb aloft. The airport, today one of the major hubs in the eastern Caribbean, began its life as the United States' Coolidge Army Air Force Base in 1942, part of a network of airfields that served to provide warplane convoys as a counter to very effective German U-boat operations in the Caribbean Theatre during World War II (despite these air stations—and despite increasingly successful naval escorts in the region—German submarines would sink some 400 Allied merchant vessels in Caribbean waters by wars' end). In 1949 Coolidge Army Air Force Base was handed over to Antigua for use as a civil airfield; it would play a vital role in opening the island to North American and British tourists, beginning in the early 1960s. Unfortunately the airport's later history has been somewhat troubled. Goats have repeatedly penetrated the airport fence, sometimes preventing planes from landing or taking off, while navigational equipment employed at the air traffic control tower has been described as antiquated. Most troubling was the crash of a Fly Montserrat airplane in October of 2012, an accident which resulted in three fatalities. According to several newspapers, subsequent investigations revealed a number of worrisome facts: there was allegedly a three-foot drop at the end of an unfinished runway (a runway that was nevertheless in use), while a windsock had been absent from the end of this runway for some time. Supposedly there were dark threats that the airport might very well lose its U.S. Federal Aviation Administration ranking, a serious blow to Antigua's tourism sector. Needless to say, a major campaign has since been launched to improve safety and infrastructure (apparently with some success) though the airport still looks a little tired and worn around the edges, cluttered with mazes of open cement stairways and small stores nestled into dark corners. I found a deserted and down-at-heel sort of shop which sold a variety of unrelated items: neglected black dolls dressed in the national colors of the various islands, salt and pepper shakers adorned with the image of Horatio Nelson, dog-eared copies of Jean Rhys' *Wide Sargasso Sea*, alongside an assortment of religious titles like *Where Will You Spend Eternity?* and *He's Watching,* the latter successfully combining the earnestly spiritual with the decidedly Orwellian. There were a few CDs featuring Montserrat's own Mighty Arrow which looked as if they had been packaged (if not duplicated) at someone's home. For those traveling to tiny Montserrat from North America, Antigua (and its rough and tumble air facility) constitute the necessary gateway, a gateway that seemed to me to be characterized by a kind of vague disquiet as well as an undeniably colorful past.

At 108 square miles Antigua was the largest of Britain's Leeward holdings, while English Harbour, with its excellent anchorage, served for two centuries as the Royal Navy's home port in the West Indies. It was from Antiguan waters that His Majesty's warships sailed into battle against their French foes throughout the bellicose eighteenth and early nineteenth centuries; it was from English Harbour that British naval escorts sailed during the troublesome days of the American War for Independence, seeking to protect homebound merchant vessels and their cargoes of sugar from molestation by Franco-American privateers. After the war Nelson took command of the fleet at English Harbour—a station he seems to have despised—carrying out his unpopular campaign against North American and British Caribbean smugglers. There was always something a bit dangerous and unruly about the island, however, despite its administrative and military importance: when the deeply unpopular Governor Daniel Parke ran afoul of his local wards in 1710 he was brutally murdered (the assassins themselves were never punished, indeed, they were never even identified). Many years later it was Sir Reginald St.-Johnston who first saw the potential of Antigua as a destination for tourists; as sugar prices plummeted during the early 1930s, St.-Johnston sought alternative sources of revenue for the increasingly abject and desperate Leeward Islands. He thus spearheaded work to develop Antigua's first tourist hotel and began the rehabilitation of English Harbour (derelict following its abandonment by the Admiralty in 1889), transforming it into one of the region's first cultural sites: the elegant and visitor-friendly Nelson's Dockyard. With tourism coming as early as it did to Antigua concerns about overdevelopment as well as overdependency upon offshore dollars and investors have long been raised here; like many of her sister islands, Antigua has struggled to balance the demands of the tourist industry and its opportunities for employment with quality of life and environmental concerns, work best achieved within a healthy, transparent political environment. As Jamaica Kinkaid has reminded us, however, throughout much of the latter half of the twentieth century Antiguan politics could hardly have been so characterized. During these years the Bird family kept its hands clasped with alarming firmness to the levers of power. The founder of this dynasty, Vere Cornwall Bird, took control of the Antigua Labor Party in the 1950s. Building upon trade union support he rose to become Chief Minister in 1961 and the island's first Prime Minister following full independence twenty years later; having played a pivotal role in moving the nation toward full sovereignty, Bird is still revered by many on the island as the Father of Antigua (the airport was renamed in his honor in 1985). Nevertheless, the subsequent career of this national icon is a bit more checkered, as Bird and his sons would come to control not only the government and all of its important ministries, but nearly all of Antigua's arable land, its two most influential radio stations and its only cable television station. Political opponents were sometimes imprisoned, elections—if not precisely rigged—were subtly managed and massaged to the benefit of the Birds. Things became more complicated for the first family when V.C. Bird's favored successor—his son, Vere Jr.—was dismissed from office following accusations of weapon smuggling in support of Colombia's Medellín drug cartel. V.C. Bird's younger son, Lester, led the Antigua Labor Party to victory in 1994 but charges of fraud, corruption and intimidation continued to dog the Birds. Many observers agree that following the ascendancy of Baldwin Spenser in 2004 this island of 80,000 people finally began to enjoy a more normatively democratic political life (in testament to which, it would seem, the island's highest point—Boggy Peak—was rechristened Mount Obama in 2009).

*

I was just passing, through, however, on my way toward what had long seemed to me one of the most exotic, most remote and most woebegone of the little Leeward Islands. The southernmost of Britain's Caribbean holdings (its sharp profile and lush interior evocative of the lofty peaks and dense jungles of the more southerly Windward Isles), Montserrat lay evocatively just below the watery horizon that I gazed out upon from the tinted windows of Antigua's airport terminal; its three lingering syllables winding from the hushed and open *Mont* into a sharp, serrated landscape (the *a* is most often a short *a* when the island is named by its residents) that closes with a hard, decisive click upon the upper palate. There is something ancient and liturgical in the appellation, summoning for me an image of the craggy mountains of Catalonia in faraway Spain, where one will find the Benedictine monastery which has bequeathed its name to this cloistered, wistful Caribbean island. It was at this same religious retreat that St. Ignatius Loyola, founder of the Jesuits and avowed enemy of Protestantism, dedicated himself to the Virgin Mary. It is said that, following the established conventions of knight errantry, he held an all-night vigil before her shrine at Montserrat in

213

1522. Merely travelers and no knights-errant, Erin and I were anxious to arrive upon the island for reasons more secular than sacred, although the name of the place served once again to remind us of those long-abiding associations between travel and pilgrimage: Church fathers offering to generations of the faithful a sense of the individual human being as *Homo Viator* or "Man on the Way," "Man the Journeyer." Travel reminds us that we are all transients of one kind or another, that we are all passers-by. Montserrat beckoned and inclined us to reflection. At the Fly Montserrat counter a glamorous and efficient airport attendant named Cheynne stepped up to take the role of acolyte or hierophant. Her eyes heavy-lidded and shadowed an azure blue—her red lips pursed into a glossy pout—she took decisive action: stamping this certificate, discarding that, tearing at the perforated lines of documents that had been distributed to us a few hours earlier at 30,000 feet, dispensing customs forms, stapling various pages and papers together, unbinding others, and hurling our bags onto a momentarily immobile conveyor belt. Her performance had about it the discipline and liquid gestures of deliberate choreography, and amidst the damp tropical heat she never for a moment lost either her professional demeanor nor her magazine-cover allure. A few moments later we found ourselves with six other passengers aboard a nine-seat Britten-Norman Islander, propellers abuzz in anxious anticipation as an enormous British Airways 747 concluded its transatlantic reverie and thundered down onto the tarmac just in front of us, kicking up a cloud of acrid smoke. After a moment, the Britten-Norman turned left onto the runway, streaks of burned rubber from previous landings converging toward the end of the tarmac, pointing us in the direction of

Montserrat. Suddenly the plane seemed to be hanging in the sky, hanging like something forgotten by gravity, as we headed south, plumes of white towering and scattering across the sky like rollers on a celestial ocean.

A few indolent raindrops pecked at the fuselage as Montserrat gradually emerged from the clouds and early summer haze, an equivocal island conjured by an uncertain magician, an aqueous shadow that expanded and glowered within a gray-green ocean that had been flattened and stilled by low-hanging clouds. Slowly the jagged profile of the Silver Hills grew sharper, while behind, the half-obscured harbor at Little Bay peeked surreptitiously through the brume that had gathered about the low cliffs and scrubland marking the northern terminus of the island. Montserrat lowered from out of the gloom as if someone was lifting a series of charcoal curtains, exposing range after range of rolling hills and serried peaks. The Silver Hills gave way to a broad plateau of small towns, crossroads amidst flinty pasturage and meandering flocks of spectral, diminutive goats. Sugar estates once dotted this plain but most of these had collapsed by the end of the nineteenth century, ruined by a combination of low rainfall and the Trade Winds that howl across the uplands with little here to impede their force, heaving the clayed soil across the island, into the air and out to sea. Beyond this plateau looms the higher, green-forested spine of the island: The Centre Hills. Half a million years younger than the Silver Hills, their labyrinths of primeval forest are marked here and there by ghostly plumes of sulfur and traversed by a network of gullies and streamlets, channels for tumultuous (if short-lived) cascades of water when the hard rains come. The monsters are more southerly still; only a pall of heavy, low clouds intimated the dark presence of the Soufrière Hills with its cluster of ominous lava domes, Chances Peak, Gages and Galway's. When the Soufrière Hills volcano rumbled to life in 1995 following some 20,000 years of dormancy, Montserrat entered a period of terrible and persistent crisis that nearly spelled the demise of the island and from which it has yet to fully recover. Even some twenty years later the mountain—though apparently going back to sleep—is still considered to be in a state of eruption, all geothermal activity carefully monitored by the Montserrat Volcano Observatory at Flemings (the island's current Hazard Level is set at 1 by the M.V.O.). The airplane crossed the island, banking sharply so that the white, blue and red roofs of Gerald's rolled from beneath us and filled the cockpit window to the right. In the course of our brief flight we discovered that the president of Fly Montserrat was one of the eight passengers aboard and that the pilot was thus determined to offer us something more than a merely competent approach and landing. He would be an impromptu tour guide as well. 'Davy Hill,' said the pilot as he nodded over his shoulder, then, pointing in the opposite direction as the plane completed another circle, he called out 'That's Cudjoehead.' He grinned broadly as the president nodded and leaned forward, shouting something to the pilot that I didn't hear amidst the whine of the propellers. Turning toward me the president winked and gave a thumbs-up sign of approval, driving his hand gently toward the earth as if to suggest that in a moment we would be on the ground.

The airport terminal was small, breezy, even elegant, despite its determinedly functional design. Arriving at six in the evening, ours was the last flight of the day. The little snack bar was thus in the process of being shuttered (the gift counter had already been closed) while the soft-spoken and unofficious customs officer turned off the light at her station and quietly closed the half-door after her, stepping out from behind the counter where a moment earlier she had pressed small green shamrocks into our passports. This stamp served officially to record our entry into "The Emerald Isle of the Caribbean," as the sign just beyond the louvred terminal doors proclaimed the place. Montserrat has long made much of its Celtic heritage; most of the island's first European settlers seem to have been Irish men and women from St. Kitts who arrived in the early 1630s. The precise date of their arrival remains uncertain, though it must have been sometime between the summer of 1631 and January of 1634. In July of the former year Sir Henry Colt reported that Montserrat was uninhabited by Europeans, while by the end of 1633 a traveling Jesuit priest wrote that a small community of Irish Catholics was to be found on the island (the settlement of Montserrat thus postdates the planting of Britain's other Leeward colonies, with the exception of Anguilla). It was the twentieth-century anthropologist John Messenger who first sought to demonstrate just how thoroughly the Irish influence permeated Montserrat; while not everyone agrees with his findings (he believed the influence to be deep and extensive), no one would deny that a Celtic flavor has long imbued the life of the island, often manifesting itself in surprising ways. In the middle of the nineteenth century, for example, an Irish sea captain named Donavan stopped off on Montserrat and was astounded to find so many black men and women speaking Gaelic to one another. Today the island remains the only nation outside of Ireland where St. Patrick's

217

Day is celebrated as a national holiday. This is not to say that these celebrations retain the same sort of Celtic flavor as those performed in Ireland itself or in North America. Beginning in the mid-1980s, what had been a one-day, largely religious-themed commemoration of Montserrat's Hibernian past was gradually transformed into a week-long celebration of the island's African patrimony, commemorating especially one particular instance of black resistance: a slave revolt that was set to coincide with the Irish planters' celebration of St. Patrick's Day in 1768 and which was detected by the slave owners and aborted. The plotters themselves (if such they were, for the truth is hard to come by) were transported or executed. These days the construction of a "Slave Village" with local foods for sale at various stalls is a beloved component of the holiday. Beside the shops traditional storytellers perform and children are taught to play old-time games with hand-made spinning tops. Later in the week masked street dancers move to the brisk and festive sound of fifes and drums, tall, elaborate headdresses with their eerily rendered red masks purling in odd-angled pirouettes above wheeling, parti-colored tassels of flying fabric. In a faintly disturbing touch, these masqueraders also carry whips which they twirl and snap along the parade route; the slave-owner transformed into a ludicrous, strutting (but never quite harmless) figure of ridicule and contempt, or perhaps, as others have suggested, the crack of the whip is African in origin and an attempt to ward off evil spirits. Despite the *bonhomie* associated with such occasions, the relationship between the island's African and Irish patrimony is complex and fraught; performances associated with the latter often decried as manifestations of a retrograde self-image. Many who live on the island have come to feel that assertions of Montserrat's Celtic character function as subtle repudiations of its African roots, undertaken in order to circulate a tourist-friendly picture of the place for white North Americans who find the Irish diaspora more romantic and more familiar than the African. Slaves and Irish indentured servants probably identified with one another just as often as they sought to set themselves apart from each other, both maneuvers necessarily delicate and undertaken for particular, tactical reasons. The bristling ambivalences of seventeenth-century race relations would thus seem to be replicated in those tensions that characterize cultural performance in twenty-first century Montserrat. Even the stamp in our passports was politically charged and the enactment of Montserrat may thus be said to begin at the customs station.

*

As the airport was prepared for its night-time repose Erin and I climbed the wide concrete steps to the "waving gallery" atop the terminal. A fleet of two small planes lay idly upon the tarmac—tailfins emblazoned with sleepy palm trees—beneath a low-set air traffic control tower, its windows darkened and somnolent. The Centre Hills turned deep purple amidst an abrupt, bedimmed Caribbean sunset. The blue-white lights of Gerald's were just beginning to appear when a battered Ford pickup pulled into the empty airport parking lot below, a disembodied woman's arm waving up to us through the passenger-side window while a young man hunkered down in the back of the truck. 'Welcome to the Emerald Isle,' called out a female voice, laughing in the gloaming. 'Come on down, we'll get you something to eat!'

The truck rumbled through the narrow, empty streets of Davy Hill as David (no relation to the Hill) deftly kneaded the wheel, by turns accelerating and bringing the vehicle to a series of quiet, circumspect pauses as we inched around corners and through shadowy, tree-canopied defiles. He was a thin man with an open, sanguine face and a white beard, his blue eyes blinking in the dark with a combination of gentle sarcasm and good humor. 'I've been through a bunch of these islands,' he said, his voice pitched high but also touched with gravel-throated gravitas, 'and landing on Montserrat is always an adventure, seat of your pants. When they relocated the airport they put it right on the edge of a cliff.' Perhaps flying into Saba had steeled me somewhat, I suggested. 'Oh, Saba, sure. At least if you miss the runway there you end up in the drink. But here...' David waved his hand in the air and allowed the unpleasant possibilities to speak for themselves before dissolving into the dim island twilight. A moment later he honked the horn and waved to a few men seated around a table by the side of the road. The men waved back and one of them saluted the truck with a bottle of beer. 'Dominoes,' said Clover with a grin. 'It's the World Series around here every Friday.' Her hair flashed wildly like an electrical cloud of blond and pink and gunmetal gray in the rising dark. She looked back at us over her left shoulder and said, 'We're going to drop by Karishma's to do a little shopping. You can gather some food there if you want. Their samosas are really wonderful. Do you like Indian food?' We nodded, a bit surprised at the question. In the wake of massive emigration following the volcanic eruptions of the

220

late 1990s, many Guyanese of Indian extraction have moved to the island, several enjoying some success as grocery store operators and purveyors of formerly unknown comestibles: chicken pakora, lamb vindaloo, saag paneer. 'Right. And I have to pick up that tire,' added David. Clover glanced at us and rolled her eyes. 'We'll get you to Gingerbread Hill, I promise.'

Our hosts, we would quickly come to discover, were among the leading citizens of Montserrat, local celebrities, one might say, if that classification did not seem so at odds with their lack of self-importance and unaffected amiability. David and Clover first traveled to the region as Christian missionaries from the United States, residing on Montserrat since 1980. 'This seemed like a good place to raise a family,' Clover told us. But it was clear that running a guesthouse in the West Indies was no picnic. She and David have spent a lifetime here, scrambling, building and rebuilding, renovating, improvising, contributing mightily to the welfare of their adopted home and working hard to help preserve the island's cultural memory. David has become the leading chronicler of Montserrat's volcanic traumas, producing an eight-part video documentary called *The Price of Paradise*, as well as an educational series with Dr. Steve Sparks of Bristol University, former director of the M.V.O. 'Most of the images of the eruptions that appeared in *National Geographic*, *Discovery* or on *Dateline*, they were David's images,' said Clover. Proprietary images, they helped to save the entire enterprise at Gingerbread Hill during those long years when Montserrat was effectively closed to travelers. Clover paused for a moment. 'David also hoped that all the documentaries and television shows would help to inform the people overseas, the ones who had to leave the island, of what was happening here. We call it the Diaspora.' 'It was hard to find out at first,' confirmed David. There was a simple decency about the pair, an earnest, open-handed, almost hippie sensibility. You might even be tempted to misread their sincerity as naïveté were it not for David's clear-eyed capability and toughness, Clover's down-to-earth and steely resolve. Theirs is also a talented family to be sure, even beyond David's work with the camera. Clover herself is a vocalist and a poet; I quickly identified some of my favorite verses in the copy of her *Everyday Lady* that I found on a bookshelf at Gingerbread Hill. One of their children, Sunny, is also a local musician. The roads were dark now, and the communities we passed seemed less like towns than scattered settlements that had become sidetracked amidst the low hills and plateaus, a landscape peppered here and there with vagabond thickets of dusky trees that snaked amongst the solitary neighborhoods like curious night-time visitors. Small roadside snack huts (called "takeaways" here) festooned the dark with candles and fairy lights, laughter and catcalls, tiny wooden structures painted yellow and green or blue and red, fretwork dangling with flowers and windows ajar, kitchens gallantly expending themselves in plates filled with king fish and grouper, barbecued chicken and Goat Water, pungent aromas rising at every crossroads and haunting the liquid tropical night with spectral, savory dinners. Clover nodded to the back of the truck, where a young face glanced at us through the rear window of the cabin, shy but affable, with a curious smile and deep, attentive eyes. 'Noah is anxious for you to meet Pepper. Oh, she's a bark-a-holic, that dog. Let me tell you.'

The gingerbread at Gingerbread Hill refers to the guesthouse's architectural grace notes: the handsome fretwork and grille-work that frame and punctuate the comfortable simplicity of the place. There are several residential options at Gingerbread Hill, ranging from the Heavenly Suite, perched at the very top of the guesthouse, to the Mango Cottage on the ground floor and the Backpacker's Special, a one-room cottage situated in a banana grove at some distance from the main house. Erin and I were staying at the Villa: really a modest, if handsome, apartment lying just below the Heavenly Suite and a few steps above the Mango Cottage. Even to recall the ambiance of these rooms is to begin to succumb again to the gentle, dreamlike and vaguely mournful quality of the island. A mahogany fan lazes indolently above the great room with its curious corner bookshelf and its tiny windows framed by colorful plaid curtains; the grille-work that adorns the wrap-around porch is alive with small yellow bells that dance and tremble in the warm, tropical breezes. A pearly-eyed thrasher has built a nest in a corner of the balustrade that borders the Villa's elegant, tiled veranda (there is a single, turquoise egg in the nest, while the thrasher remains uncharacteristically quiet when he comes to the table to eye our breakfasts). Hummingbirds are regular guests, silent, quick-winged, emerald-and-sapphire habitués of Gingerbread Hill; so are the festive yellow warblers and bananaquits that flit about the balustrade and the porch swing in the drowsy afternoon heat. We saw no orioles; despite being the national bird, hardly anyone has seen them. After dark, bats haunt the eves and the shadowy tops of nearby trees—tall palms that murmur like the airy shades of night-time gossips—while in the nearby woods the little frogs chirp and gargle a playful, scolding accompaniment. Once we might have heard the distinctive lower-pitched yawping of the mountain chicken, a famously aggressive species of frog (and the largest in the Caribbean) living only on Montserrat and Dominica. Much of its habitat was lost as a result of volcanic activity, however, and these days its once-ubiquitous call is rarely heard on Montserrat. With daylight the enchanted profile of the island once again glimmers awake: a tumbling ocean of foliage alongside the smooth turquoise sea, hills ranging from olive to lime to peacock green soaring skyward then falling abruptly toward the rocky shore. White, coral and blood-red bouquets of frangipani, bougainvillea and poinciana dot the landscape, quavering in the soft, leeward winds; in the distance the square, graying bell-tower of St. Peter's rises oddly amidst the wild, flowering growth. Ringed with blanched headstones, the downcast and rock-wrought church gathers itself in grim anticipation of the island's merciless high-noon heat, otherworldly here in its aspiration to the medieval, its austere and runic grace. St. Peter's Church was one of the makeshift shelters that housed some 1,500 desperate refugees from the south of the island as the Soufrière Hills volcano continued to spew forth super-heated rock and gas and debris. This Parish of St. Peter's constituted then the front line in a battle with nature that had reached an unhappy and indecisive stalemate; her several shelters often *ad hoc* and under-resourced, dark, overcrowded and stiflingly close. There is little in this corner of Montserrat to recall those days but something—the chill and stillness of the early hours before sunrise, the weird greenish light that will sometimes bathe the leeward coast and its uplands toward evening, the handful of abandoned or unfinished buildings that you stumble upon in the bush—something preserves here a sense of sorrow and disquiet, a sense of many things having been lost or put away.

There is only a single white sand beach on Montserrat, located at Rendezvous Bay near the northern tip of the island. This is one of the only places on Montserrat that looks like anyplace else. More characteristic are the beaches at Bunkum and Woodland's Bay. Erin and I decided to walk to the latter, a hike of several miles along a desolate road that led through a series of small villages and along the edge of thick woods that rose gently toward the summit of Katy Hill. We passed from sharp sunlight into broken caverns of lilac-gray; the forest canopy high overhead was a vast vaulted ceiling pierced by watery shafts of lambent blue that glittered with small white butterflies. There were orchids, orange hibiscus and mammy apple trees, the occasional thud too as an overripe mango dropped to the ground. There were many of these littering the roadways and footpaths, sweetening the air with an almost sickly scent when the wind fell away and giving the impression of a plenteous, even prodigal, island, a place surfeited with flowering plants and fruit trees, with ravishing colors and fragrant, winding ways. Once we spotted an agouti beside the road, his eyes alert as he concealed himself beneath a tree and appeared to nibble at one of the fallen fruit; he resembled a squirrel or rabbit (perhaps a cross between the two), although the absence of a tail gave the small creature a unique, truncated appearance. These rodents may be found throughout the West Indies, descendants of larger deer- or bear-sized ancestors (the famed *Amblyrhiza* that once inhabited Anguilla apparently being one of these); they are called *hutias* in the Spanish-speaking Caribbean. On this island, however, the agouti is the recipient of special affection: he appears cheerfully on a $2.75 stamp issued by the Government of Montserrat and gave his name to a once-famous nightclub as well as to the musical group that played there, the Agouti Brothers Band. Woodland's Bay can be reached by a series of dirt paths that run through the forest and emerge onto a beach that is sheltered on one side by a series of crumbling, rust-colored cliffs. Black-sand beaches are quite common on volcanic islands and Montserrat is no exception; at Woodland's, the salt and pepper sand (unusually hot underfoot) blends into a startling mixture of obsidian and silver as the sun, passing its zenith, declines in the west. The peculiar color of the sand here alters the tint of the ocean as well and the sea at Woodland's Bay is an enchanted color: aquamarine touched with navy, or turquoise blended with sage and chartreuse. Perhaps there should simply be a color called Woodland's Green; it is unlike any other hue I know. Just offshore there is a marine reclamation project underway and a network of new reefs have been created: reefs with charming names like Spadefish, Seahorse Gardens, Crumbles and Cake. You can swim out to see the colorful reef-dwellers that have already begun to move in. The beach dwindles as you walk northward; here Erin and I passed into a stand of trees sheltering a fishing boat named *No Rush*, which apparently calls Woodland's Bay its homeport. The trees here begin to move closer and closer to the water's edge until they are perched directly beside the ocean, waves washing beneath the twisted branches that strain seaward as if to catch a glimpse of their reflection in the gentle swells that roll from the west. By the time Clover arrived at Woodland's in the Ford pickup, the few other bathers we met had gone home and bats were beginning to circle in the sunset canopy of the tall trees.

*

'I seventy-two years old, but you never guess that. Yes?' Indeed, the trim, affable man who had just returned to Gourmet Gardens to pick us up—and who had just slipped into a chair so that he might join us at our table while we waited for dessert—looked at least ten years younger than his age. Thomas Lee wore a pink cotton shirt that matched the color of the restaurant's clapboard exterior while the light cast by the hurricane lamp atop our table imparted a faint, playful glow to his bald pate. His eyes grew wide and his mouth hung open in feigned astonishment as if he had just surprised himself with the sudden recollection of his true age. Lee paused and appeared to grow more serious. 'No salt, no sugar, no greasy foods,' and his creased black hands fumbled with a napkin that he had taken from an empty table (they were all empty, save for ours), folding and refolding the bit of cloth. 'No secret,' he said, counting on his fingers as he reiterated, 'no salt, no sugar, no greasy foods.' He dabbed at his forehead with the napkin. 'Hot,' he said. 'Air very still.' Lee—who is better known on the island as "Fumbo"—told us that nights on Montserrat used to be much cooler, evening mists and heavy fogs more common, before the eruptions began. 'Now all those rainforests gone down there, Great Alps Waterfall, everything.' He changed the subject, telling us instead about his twelve children, about driving on Montserrat ('Just like playing the accordion,' hands frantically squeezing at empty air), and about famous

227

island Get Togethers from many years ago. After each jocund anecdote, however, he would relate a sadder story concerning the adversity that the island has endured, a report of its almost-uncanny hard-luck. 'All the trouble begin with Hugo,' said Lee. Hurricane Hugo slammed into Montserrat in September 1989, a Category Four storm with 150 mile-per-hour winds; more than twenty people were killed and three-quarters of the homes on the island were either completely destroyed or severely damaged. Twenty percent of the population was homeless. Sir George Martin's Air Studios—where musicians such as Paul McCartney, Jimmy Buffet, Phil Collins and the Rolling Stones once recorded—had been flooded, smashed by the high winds. The devastation was so great that the island was closed to nonessential visitors for many months while some neighborhoods spent an entire year without electricity. In response the British government launched a £17 million capital aid program to get Montserrat back on its feet. 'New schools, new library, new hospital,' said Fumbo, once more counting on his fingers for emphasis, 'new government buildings, too. Used to be some people talk about independence before Hugo. Not after.' Relief aid poured in and the island experienced an economic boom during the early nineties. 'The tourists come back. Construction happening everywhere; them jobs good. Some people want to sell they land, but they hold on, 'cause the price on they land keep going up-up.' The new hospital had not yet admitted a single patient and the new library was receiving its final coat of paint when—on July 18th 1995—steam venting began in the Soufrière Hills. The volcano crisis that would nearly destroy the island was underway. 'People here talk say "Old Montserrat, New Montserrat"; before the

228

volcano, after the volcano. Hugo was like you have a party on a Saturday night and the next day you do the dishes. But the volcano; everything different.' For the first time Fumbo Lee looked his age. When the passion fruit cheesecake arrived Erin and I asked if he would like a fork. 'No, no,' said Fumbo, gently patting his belly, 'I just had a big slice of coconut pie.'

*

The Caribbean is quite active geologically, containing something like eighteen live volcanoes (about half of this number found on Dominica alone). The archipelago constitutes a partially submerged mountain range extending from South America to the Florida Strait; the islands exist at all because of the tectonic forces that are at work deep below the earth's surface. In the eastern Caribbean two tectonic plates—vast blocks of the earth's crust that slide along a bed of molten rock—come together and generate friction on a massive scale, the Atlantic plate rolling beneath the Caribbean plate as the latter (over the course of many millions of years) moves eastward. The friction caused by this process generates a great deal of super-heated matter (molten rock, magma and gas) which rises to the surface and is discharged in the form of a series of volcanic blasts. The first regional eruption recorded by Europeans occurred on the island of St. Kitts in 1692; since then there have been around twenty volcanic "events" in the Caribbean. No doubt the most terrible of these occurred in 1902 on the island of Martinique where the town of St. Pierre was obliterated in a matter of minutes, resulting in some 28,000 fatalities. It was Frank Perret, the father of volcanology, who first noted that

Montserrat's Soufrière Hills were apparently waking up after many centuries of dormancy. Visiting the island several times throughout the 1930s he noted that Gages Peak had apparently been reactivated by a strong earthquake that rocked Montserrat on November 11th 1935, discussing his findings with the curious (if faintly distressed) Governor-General St.-Johnston. He also observed that the household silver he kept at Gages had a strange habit of turning black, the result of exposure to sulfur gas. Though in his public statements Perret claimed that a surface eruption was unlikely he issued a confidential report to the government which pointed out that the volcanic activity he had measured in the Soufrière Hills was ominously close to the surface. He wondered if such disturbances might not continue, perhaps in thirty-year cycles. The earthquakes that occurred in 1966 appeared to validate such speculation; the venting which began in the summer of 1995 was confirmation.

*

It was mid-morning and we were rumbling along the windward coast in Sunny's truck. A fine salt mist hung in the air and coated the seaside cactus there; Jack Boy Hill rose to our right as we headed south toward the boundary that marked the end of habitable Montserrat. Since the latest venting began the island has been divided roughly in half, with the southern portion designated an exclusion zone; only accredited scientists who are studying or monitoring the volcano may travel into this region. Offshore, while vessels are permitted to transit through coastal waters, stopping or otherwise delaying one's passage is not allowed. The problem was that in Old Montserrat nearly everyone lived in the south. When the evacuations started, people thought, "Maybe a week or two." No one was looking at—what is it?—sixteen years.' Sunny thought for a moment and changed down. 'Forever, I guess. No one's ever moving back down there.' I heard that Montserrat had grown in size since the eruptions began and asked Sunny about this. 'Right,' he said, 'now it's about forty square miles, up from thirty-six. The government is even working on long-term plans to assess who can claim what land, when the day comes. Not in my lifetime.' He grinned somberly. Sunny laughed easily, speaking with quiet assurance about the island's past. He was tall, with a head of dirty-blond hair and penetrating, almost uncanny, gray-blue eyes. His muddy work boots and thick blue jeans contrasted appealingly with the sensitivity of his bearing and his overall appearance: an open unguarded face, long feminine eyelashes, the delicate and dexterous hands of the musician. 'The day the volcano went up, I was headed to summer camp off-island. The governor was coming back from Barbados or somewhere; they closed the airport just a few minutes after he landed. Not the one where you came in, the *old* airport. That's where we're headed.'

There are no real towns along the desolate windward coast and even in the days when the entire island was still open to settlement hardly anyone lived in the southeast, the area beyond the South Soufrière Hills that quickly became known as Behind God's Back. Part of the problem in the old days— here as elsewhere—was the difficulty of bringing to shore a large sailing vessel amidst the full force of the Atlantic winds. With very few adequate harbors, the windward coasts of the West Indian islands remained (and continue to remain) generally under-populated. For the early European colonists on Montserrat there was an additional concern when it came to eastern settlement; the Kalinago Indians. The French on nearby Guadeloupe (who were usually on better terms with the Amerindians than were their English rivals) enthusiastically allowed the Kalinago to use that island as a home base for raids upon Montserrat. Throughout the first decades of British settlement such attacks occurred with some frequency, beginning with a terrifying raid in 1651. Because the Kalinago used oars rather than wind power to propel their war canoes, they might strike anywhere, particularly along the windward coast where settlers had at first felt themselves relatively safe from seaborne assault. Add to this unsettling reality the generally (though perhaps incorrectly) held belief that the Kalinago were cannibals who cooked and ate their defeated foes, and one might begin to grasp the fear of the first European settlers (as well as their general unwillingness to live Behind God's Back or anywhere on the island's eastern coast). In fact, during the 1660s and '70s Governor William Stapleton (an able Irish politician and a notorious Indian hunter) began the construction of a series of coastal watchtowers that would ring the island and provide a first line of defense against Kalinago attack.

The Great North Road began to deteriorate into a ragged and pot-holed track little wider than a footpath as the thick, inhospitable growth closed in on us. 'This is empty country,' said Sunny, 'always has been. You won't see anybody out here.' Nearly true, but as the truck rounded the very next ragged curve, Fumbo himself stepped out of the bush, his eyes wide, his mouth open in surprise before drawing itself into a broad grin as he held aloft bunches of root vegetables. 'I'm just checking on me yams!' he shouted triumphantly by way of explanation. 'You with my pupil,' he added, stepping up close to the window and gesturing toward Sunny, 'I teach him everything he know.' Then he laughed, turned his back and was swallowed up once more by the jungle. Sunny explained that Fumbo was the exception that proved the rule. 'He's kind of an institution here,' said Sunny, 'he's everywhere and he's got a million stories.' Erin asked if Fumbo had in fact taught Sunny everything he knows. 'Sure,' Sunny confirmed, then grinned. 'Let's say a whole lot anyway.' Clusters of startled cactus continued to glide past as Sunny drove forward, salt spray off the roiling windward ocean spattering the windshield and the road narrowing before us in serpentine and increasingly fractured curves.

Everything stopped, however, as we approached a lookout point at the edge of the exclusion zone: the truck, the road, the jungle, everything alive and recognizable and rendered to familiar scale. To our right one of the last of the forested hills exhaled plumes of sulfur from its wounded side. Sunny called our attention to this mountain rising some eighty or ninety feet above us. 'It's active,' he said. 'That wasn't even here before 1995, it's grown up all in the last fifteen years. I watched it. Sometimes day to day you could see it expand, the jungle sort of move up the flanks.' The view directly before us was even more dramatic and disconcerting. Bramble Airport was gone, buried under several layers of rock and debris extending eastward into the Atlantic, a barren promontory of pale yellow and gray ringed by white surf and blue ocean. The airport, closed in 1995, fell victim to a powerful lateral blast that took place in February 2010; this explosion generated a mudflow consisting of volcanic material—called a lahar—that finally buried the facility and built up the nearby bulwark of land. The terrain was lifeless and lunar in appearance, making it difficult to get a sense of precisely what we were seeing. A small tower of brick poked above the dry, rocky landscape; a chimney, as it turned out, all that could be seen of what was once the boiling works belonging to an old sugar plantation. Sunny pointed to what seemed to be a small stone dropped between the chimney and the snowy, silent shoreline. 'That thing's probably about the size of a school bus,' he said. Just out of sight were the ruins of Spanish Point and the remains of the devastated village at Farms, one of the three communities that bore the brunt of the fatal eruption on June 25th 1997. 'Dad was volunteering at the M.V.O. that day,' said Sunny. 'He told us that the seismographs suddenly started going crazy, "like the mountain was having babies", he said.' That afternoon, between 12.57 and 1.08 the volcano expelled three separate bursts of super-heated debris, each one of these forming a fast-moving and rapidly expanding wall of fiery rock and blistering dust rising into billows over one hundred feet high. Eerily, these pyroclastic flows (and the accompanying ash cloud surges) moved in utter silence, engulfing roads and hills, buildings and people, without warning and without mercy. The first of these reached the village of Bramble, stopping at the Paradise River, about three miles from the volcanic dome. The second flow was fast, covering just over four miles in seven minutes and laying waste the towns of Trant's and Farms. The third flow was the quickest yet: traveling at fifty miles per hour it burst beyond the little valley formed by the Paradise River and spread out over the nearby plain toward Bethel, stopping just shy of the airport runway. Nine people died at Farms, while an elderly man named Beryl Grant was killed at Harris. Three people perished on the road beyond Farrell's as they sought to outrun the pyroclastic flow. Six more fatalities would eventually be confirmed, bringing the grim total to nineteen. Most of the dead had been roasted by temperatures that soared in a matter of seconds to some 932°F. Those who survived were said to be living "a second life." An evacuation of Harris—where twenty people had been trapped by one of the flows—was quickly undertaken. An emergency operations command post was established by Governor Frank Savage in the town of Olveston. Several of the most seriously wounded persons were flown to trauma centers in Guadeloupe and Martinique while the British guard ship HMS *Liverpool* would soon be dispatched in order to support relief operations on Montserrat. Something still confused me, however. If the southern half of the island had already been evacuated what were all those people doing in places like Farms, Trant's, and Harris, towns situated well inside the exclusion zone? 'No, they weren't supposed to be there, but, you know, these folks had been living with relatives in the north or crowded into some shelter; nothing serious had happened at the mountain for a while. Sometimes they would go home for a night or for a weekend, just for some privacy or peace and quiet. Other people needed to keep up their farms; the banks still wanted their money every month, so folks needed to work the land, grow crops, raise livestock.' 'What about the police?' asked Erin. 'Sure, they should have stopped people from crossing in, but, you know, the constable is your nephew or your brother-in-law. Is he really going to keep you out?' The wind wailed plaintively as we all fell silent, swells rolling many feet below against the edge of that strange new land the volcano had made.

*

The Leas operate a community center and café at Fogarty's Hill which has become a kind of unofficial museum dedicated to the memory of Old Montserrat. We were on our way across the island—from windward to leeward, one end of the exclusion zone to the other—and in the midst of our transit Sunny decided to stop off at the Hilltop Café, which gave Erin and me a chance to view the collection of artifacts there. Scattered throughout an otherwise cheerful and brightly painted veranda were the ghostly remains of another age: a charred sign for Radio Antilles (R DIO NTILLES, it reads today), a warning posted at the Montserrat Golf Club that "Animals are not permitted to graze on the golf course," and a sign for the Montserrat Springs Hotel. The first two sites are simply gone, the last is abandoned and rusticating within the exclusion zone at Richmond Hill. There was also a colorful, be-flowered and hand-drawn advertisement for Niggy's Guesthouse—fifteen U.S. dollars for a single room, twenty-five dollars for a double—that called particular attention to the hotel bar with its "old time jazz" and "congenial atmosphere." I was told that the moniker was the stage name of a celebrated chanteuse of Old Montserrat. But this is not a museum proper and there is thus no curatorial commentary. These objects are simply given the space to speak for themselves, each of them retaining a kind of guileless, unself-conscious character. They simply go about their business of warning, admonishing, directing or selling, as blithely unaware of the former cataclysm as they once were of the cataclysm to come. It is an eclectic assortment; about the only thing the various signs and placards have in common is that they all belong to a world that has vanished. The attitudes, life and busyness of former times still seem present within them, tangible as well in the room given over to their presentation, framed in gingerbread, adorned with baskets of hanging pink flowers and dangling feeders for the hummingbirds that come and go. Sometimes older visitors—local people—will come up to the café just to walk through the veranda and quietly remember Old Montserrat. 'Maybe places where they lived and worked,' said David, who stepped in from the kitchen, 'people who they knew. Lots of memories, maybe good and maybe not so good.'

As we returned to the lunch counter for a light snack Erin and I had a near-encounter with a local celebrity. 'You missed him,' said Sunny, nodding in the direction of a black man in a white cotton shirt and khaki trousers who had just stepped through the door and was headed back down the outer stairway. 'Who was that?' I asked. 'One of the guys who played on the national soccer team in 2002. They called it "the Other Final." Somebody even made a documentary.' It is not hard to understand why. In that year Montserrat shared with Bhutan the ignominious distinction of fielding the lowest-ranked soccer team in the world, according to F.I.F.A. Amidst what was then a full-blown crisis on Montserrat—with displaced persons huddled into shelters and the beginning of a massive exodus that would cut the island's overall population by more than fifty percent—the national team known as "the Emerald Boys" quickly became a much-beloved source of pride. It had long been a hard-luck club; founded in 1973, the Emerald Boys lost every match until 2012 (with the exception of a narrow win and a tie, both at the expense of Anguilla). Local fans nevertheless sported the green and white with panache, particularly as they prepared to depart for South Asia. Bhutan had endured its own national tragedy less than two years before the match when a series of devastating floods and landslides caused by weeks of heavy rain killed hundreds of people and shook the small Himalayan kingdom to its core. Hoping to provide some diversion for the desperate citizens of these troubled lands, it was decided that Montserrat and Bhutan would face off on the same day as the World Cup final between Germany and Brazil in a good-natured attempt to determine which club was *not* the worst. The match was played at Bhutan's Changlimithang Stadium on June 30th 2002, where Montserrat was crushed, 4-0. Nevertheless the players returned home to an enthusiastic reception, their campaign having secured international attention and esteem for the beleaguered people of Montserrat. Some of the former players still claim that the thin Himalayan air did them in, demanding (perhaps only *half* in jest) a rematch on their own low-lying home soil. 'It's a cool story,' said Sunny, 'most of those guys had never even left the islands. Then there they were flying to Asia.' Several of the players had been local policemen serving in the constabulary, he told us. So who was policing the island while the team was in Bhutan? 'Good question.' Sunny grinned. Then he shrugged. 'There's hardly any crime here, anyway.' Brazil defeated Germany 2-0 in the 2002 World Cup final, but nobody cares or remembers on Montserrat. 2002 was the year of the Emerald Boys.

*

After lunch we continued south along the leeward coast, passing through church-bedecked Salem and skirting the elegant, garden-fringed homes of Old Towne, nestled quietly between Happy Hill and Old Road Bluff, the latter drifting gently southward toward the frond-skirted curve of Isles Bay and Foxes Bay (the ocean a-glimmer and bisected here by the invisible edge of the exclusion zone). Then we were rolling once more through thick green scrubland interspersed with isolated bands of lofty trees. There was something peculiar about this region of the island, however; the road looked out of place—too broad and full of aspiration for such a wilderness—while the land round about seemed a mixture of failed cultivation and riotous virgin forest. Just as the mood of this place was making itself felt, the truck passed out from beneath a bedraggled canopy of trees into the bright sunshine, dropping suddenly onto a broad, narrow plain of dirt and rock that snaked between low green hills and vanished in the direction of a concealed and secretive Caribbean Sea. 'Believe it or not, this used to be the old golf course,' said Sunny as he carefully and deliberately steered his truck across the winding, desolate terrain, 'and the main road to Plymouth came right through here.' The soil—beige and sorrel, irradiated by a hostile white sun—had the consistency of beach sand mixed with flaky bread crust; convocations of gray stones threaded the landscape like wandering pilgrims drawn toward the emerald peaks that glimmered to our left in the trembling tropical heat. Sunny continued to thread the truck along an invisible trail that hedged across the treacherous, broken earth. Isolated courses of packed soil lay atop shallow beds of solid rock that supported the passage of heavy vehicles above; any deviation from this network of concealed bedrock, however, would almost certainly sink the truck in a morass of gravel and sand. This was what remained of the Belham Valley, once a pleasant green swale of countryside and pretty homes, watered by a gentle stream that trickled down from Molyneaux and Windy Hill. Today the valley is buried beneath a dry river of volcanic boulders and debris that is often remobilized during heavy rains, becoming then a ferocious running trench of mud and rock that cuts through the land, lurches into the nearby Belham River then heaves itself toward the sea. There the slurry of muck fans out into the ocean and falls beneath the waves, an undulating, undersea delta of shifting, sodden earth and rubble. When the volcano began erupting, successive waves of ash and dust rolled into the valley and covered it. Rains only bring more of the mountainside down into the area, as the treeless flanks of the high surrounding hills are now incapable of holding on to the soil there. The houses to the south of the valley atop Garibaldi Hill are cut off from the rest of the island when this river of debris becomes remobilized. 'Sometimes folks have no power up there for weeks,' Sunny informed us. 'Lots of them have had their houses on the market for years, but no takers.' One of these homes was planted along the lowest edge of the hill, mere yards from where the broad trail of flattened, lifeless earth snaked past. The house was lovely, its whitewashed walls and West Indian shutters capped by a green roof and embowered by cheerful-looking fruit trees. A stone's throw from its elegant lawn, however—just within the perimeter of the dry riverbed—scowled the broken remains of the Crowe House. Here the yellow walls are topped by eaves whose red shingles have dropped away, exposing the wooden frame of the roof (its underside still adorned here and there with bits of gingerbread, dangling teeth suspended from a fractured upper jaw). Framed by sagging green shutters, the shattered and empty windows stare out upon the land like vacant and darkened eyes. Only the formerly handsome third story of the Crowe House remains visible; its two lower floors lie buried in the dead earth below. As we passed out of the serpentine plain and into the low, lush margins of Garibaldi Hill we learned about the final evacuation of Plymouth in the spring of 1996, and the destruction of the former capital which began four months later, with eruptions that rained some 600,000 tons of ash upon the southwest corner of the island. We were heading for the lookout point at the top of Garibaldi Hill; from there the story would tell itself.

Sunny stopped the truck at the end of a narrow dirt track that ended abruptly in a splash of gray-green scrub and meager, sickly looking trees. Under a dense ceiling of low clouds that had just begun to press down upon the island, the wind seemed to be keening as it tumbled seaward into the desolate valley below. In the near distance were the remains of Richmond Hill, once a high-end suburb just beyond the capital. This neighborhood was spared the full fury of the ash falls and pyroclastic flows that devastated the majority of southwest Montserrat, but it was evacuated along with the capital and today remains closed to resettlement. Trees, scrub and exotic wildflowers—insurgent and irresistible—had taken possession of the streets and structures here: breaking into homes, devouring floors and walls, inundating furniture in endless webs of green. A strange colonization was underway, anarchic, inexorable and silent. It was as if the rich growth that had been so savagely laid waste just beyond Richmond Hill here enjoyed a vicarious satisfaction at the expense of what the neighborhood's former inhabitants had left behind. Trees grew through broken roofs and had begun to overtop the stone foundations of old windmills. I thought of how stalks of cane were once pressed here by the same breezes that now mourned in the branches of the vigorous woodlands of Richmond Hill. In the far distance stood the half-interred remains of Plymouth. Formerly one of the finest and most-storied old towns of the eastern Caribbean, she is today a melancholy collection of ghostly roofs. Everything else lies buried beneath a vast mound of earth that has swept down from the Soufrière Hills, expanding toward the sea with a terrible, silent sublimity. The leeward shore was lifeless beneath a frowning sky, its still and leaden ocean the bruised color of ebony and violet. The rough mud-packed landscape behind Plymouth was broken by an enormous fissure, really a kind of canyon, that has begun to yaw and widen across what was once the city's eastern suburbs, circling seaward in a strange echo of the bay's own bow-like bend. Successive lahars have been burying the city for more than twenty years and in some places the former capital is entombed in deposits of earth some twenty-five feet deep. With each subsequent ash cloud or rainfall, the internment continues. Third floors have become ground floors while church steeples peek above the soil like vast tomb markers in an abandoned cemetery. Once richly hued in a profusion of colors, the roofs of the various structures have all faded to a cadaverous ash-white while the buildings themselves (or what may be seen of them) appear frozen in attitudes of morbid amazement, still startled to find themselves abandoned beneath a crumbling, dry ocean of rock and debris. A dust devil whirled itself many feet into the air, spinning glumly in the low light like some weird desert apparition. Invisible beneath its trackless path were the remains of George Street and Parliament Street, the pretty wharf and the once-proud war memorial; things and places that linger here like the empty space left by a wound. Nothing else moved—or breathed— within this strange, grim and sepulchral landscape. Plymouth has been called the Pompeii of the Caribbean. Unlike its Italian namesake, however, this site is closed to visitors; the view from Garibaldi Hill is about as close as you may come to the ruined city, for the earth remains unsettled there and likely to swallow up careless wanderers. There were ghosts of other towns still further south; St. Patrick's and Galway's were utterly consumed and lost. Atop this lookout point Erin and I began to feel oddly like interlopers or trespassers, gawking and snapping pictures seemed a desecration while claiming and mourning a past that was not ours seemed intrusive and glib. We chose reverence, reflection and a quiet departure.

*

Following the loss of Plymouth, Montserrat has become a state without a capital. Government offices and public buildings may be found throughout the northern part of the island, at Brades, at Little Bay and at Carr's Bay. There is a long-term project underway to transform Little Bay into the new capital of Montserrat; some 223 acres have been set aside there and construction is already underway, spearheaded by the Montserrat Development Corporation. There are plans for a luxury hotel and condominiums, retail space and an expansive marina capable of accommodating sixty large vessels. Renowned architect Lane Pettigrew has designed the waterfront and marina. Some concerns and conflicts have already arisen, however. Nearby Piper's Pond is the island's only remaining mangrove swamp and several local activists have strongly protested its demise. Still others have spoken of the need to preserve Little Bay as a cultural site; it was the major point of disembarkation for thousands who were forced to abandon Montserrat during those years when the volcano crisis was at its worst. To some local people luxury high-rises and chic eateries seem a poor way of commemorating those hard years and lost countrymen. Others argue that this sort of development is precisely what is needed to bring those expatriates back home to Montserrat, but there is also a good deal of suspicion on the island that the project will ultimately fail to materialize. Lying amidst a set of low hills that hem the scrub and pasturage just behind Little Bay, the island's Cultural Center has already been completed. An elegant whitewashed structure with proud colonnades and a brilliant coral-colored roof, the building was paid for by Sir George Martin (long a resident of Montserrat). Further out is the Marine Village, a collection of newly completed but still mostly vacant rooms for shops and restaurants. A fish market has recently opened for business there. On the opposite side of the valley lies the new National Museum with its salmon-colored exterior, its quiet and cordial garden walk. The lowlands here are typical of northern Montserrat: dry and silver-gray, filled with tall grass and scraggly trees, with brushwood and thickets of thorny shrubs that run down to the shoreline, pressing there against the narrow perimeter of sand that lies between boscage and ocean. Flowering plants are few to be seen and the occasional goat is lean and hungry, yet there is a hard and scanty sort of loveliness about the place, a spare, inimical allure. It is hard to imagine a marina with boutique shops and a skyline topped by sleek penthouse apartments. It is hard to imagine and it is hard to want to imagine.

The museum was still being fitted out with its assortment of artifacts and its expansive rooms felt half-empty when Erin and I stopped by late one afternoon. The various displays positioned throughout the large exhibition gallery looked as if they had just arrived and had not yet made themselves at home there, while strange shadows congregated throughout the gallery, falling upon the still, contorted figures of the displays and imparting to them a disconcerting aura of animation and vitality. A gleeful devil and a grinning Moko Jumbie seemed to turn their heads slightly toward us as we walked beneath them and across the tiled floor. Each figure was composed of tattered fabric matched with what looked like *papier-mâche*, the devil with a bright red face topped by a pair of goat-like horns, the Moko Jumbie planted high upon a pair of stilts, with a wide, drooping mouth and weird, bulging eyes. Particularly important players in Montserrat folklore, jumbies may also be found (in various guises) throughout the English-speaking West Indies, a diffuse and complex cultural phenomenon. Usually they represent the spirits of the deceased; the *wicked* deceased, most-commonly, called to serve after death the same malevolent forces they honored in their lives. In the French Caribbean they are called zombies (the two terms are etymologically related). Here they are most often depicted as mere unfortunates brought back from beyond the grave to work on the old sugar plantations, although on Haiti some suspected Papa Doc's dreaded *Tonton*

Macoutes of being zombies (a zombie's eyes are believed to turn wholly white and the bloodthirsty *Macoutes* concealed their eyes behind dark sunglasses). These manifestations of the undead seem to reflect West African origins while their various permutations in Caribbean and North American popular culture suggest something of their profound adaptability. In American movies the zombie has wandered far from its roots, becoming both a lumbering ghoul reawakened by nuclear radiation and a fleet-footed virus-infected, flesh-eating signifier of dystopia. Jumbies are not quite so well-traveled, but are often manifested in distinctive and characteristic ways upon the several islands of the eastern Caribbean. On Dominica there is a legend that the jumbie of Père Labat haunts particular byways throughout the island while on Anguilla there is a traditional belief that sweeping your floor after dark invites a visit from the jumbies. In the British Virgin Islands I have often heard jumbies identified with the restless spirits of drowned sailors. Yet jumbies are not always malevolent. On Montserrat there is a traditional dance that calls them up as benign mediators that are capable of bridging the chasm that separates the living from the dead; in such cases the jumbies may even become conflated with the deceased loved ones themselves (this is also true on Anguilla, where the jumbie associated with a particular individual may go walking about or climbing trees even *before* the ailing man or woman in question is quite dead, often with mischief in mind). There were also other, less numinous figures displayed at the museum: figures like "the guppy" (not to be confused with the Jamaican "duppy," a ghost). This female carnival character is usually represented by a male performer who dresses in a duster or a fine house coat and wears elaborate make-up; carried away by the bacchantic spirit of carnival, this proud, imperious "lady" is made ridiculous when she hikes up her skirts and flashes various revelers assembled along the parade route, revealing "her" undergarments and nether regions.

Music plays an enormous role in the cultural life of the island and not only at carnival time. Montserrat is, after all, the birthplace of the legendary musician known as the Mighty Arrow. Born into a solidly middle-class family (his birth date given variously as 1949 and 1951), Alphonsus Cassell began his career competing in local calypso contests, following in the footsteps of his brother, Justin. In 1970 Cassell released his first album, *Arrow on Target*, after which he headed for Trinidad where he came under the influence of the superstar calypsonian known as Sparrow. As a result Arrow began developing his own celebrated fusion of Trinidadian *soca* (itself a mixture of calypso and funk) with Latin salsa, merengue and *zouk* (the last originating in the French islands) to produce a playfully sexual, utterly exuberant, and hard-driving dance music: gleefully irreverent, but also amiable and benign. Because he subsequently turned away from calypso's more acerbic tone and its politically minded ethos, several Caribbean intellectuals distanced themselves from the performer and his later work, but Arrow was never especially troubled by this. His critics may not have been wrong that he had an eye on album sales (given that his biggest record—*Hot, Hot, Hot*—sold some 75,000 copies in 1982 and became the biggest *soca* hit of all time, he probably needed two eyes) but Arrow also claimed that his greatest satisfaction as an artist was in simply bringing people joy. When I think about this rather one-sided spat between

Arrow and his critics, it sometimes reminds me of the squabble that sprang-up when Bob Dylan "went electric" and forswore working on Maggie's Farm. In any case, Arrow's later work can hardly be dismissed. From the brash celebration of youthful vigor, "That's How We Are," to the humane encouragement of "Have a Little Faith"—his 1990 post-hurricane entreaty to the people of Montserrat—from the surprisingly poignant "I Just Can't Run Away" to "Don't You Touch My Tempo," the artist's insistent musical claim to his own autonomy, Arrow has amassed an impressive body of work over a period of four decades, becoming the island's best-known and most-celebrated personality. In 2000, he even became a Member of the British Empire. Sadly, Arrow would later be diagnosed with cerebral cancer, dying quietly at his home on Montserrat in 2010, at age sixty.

Arrow was not simply synthesizing various sounds, however, he was also building upon a tradition of indigenous music grounded in the gamesome, "industrial" sound of the local Iron Bands. These bands are usually composed of a blend of standard musical instruments (saxophone, cow bell and a "big drum") with decidedly less conventional "found" instruments like graters and the worn discs from broken-down automobiles. Artifacts associated with some of the more celebrated Iron Bands were featured at the National Museum, along with instruments belonging to the darker, more shamanic Goat Skin Bands. These troupes were most often associated with old-time Christmas and wedding entertainments. Performances began with tunes played upon a fife, accompanied by a *bobja* (a small drum) and a mouth organ. As the evening drew on a concertina often took the place of the fife and a large goat-skin drum called a French Weed appeared; the latter was apparently brushed with *rassum*, a local wax, so that the drum produced a strange moaning sound when it was played. As midnight approached, what had been simply a series of musical diversions seems to have evolved imperceptibly into something more numinous. The French weed was believed to work upon an "interpreter" who danced himself into a trance in order to commune with certain spirits who would help him to determine if anyone in the assembly was bewitched and needed to consult a "black doctor." For some reason Erin and I were unable to play the recordings of the Goat Skin Band that were included as part of the exhibition, though the weird cry of the wind purling beneath the building's high eaves provided an effective, unsettling substitute.

*

Along the water's edge at Little Bay you will also find one of the most delightful restaurants in all of the Leeward Islands. There is almost nothing pretentious or grandiloquent about Montserrat; its ways are generally quiet and unaffected. In the heyday of high-end tourism the island touted itself as "the way the Caribbean used to be." In the wake of the volcano crisis this slogan is once again quite apt, although in a very different sense. Whereas formerly it was intended to evoke the sort of old-world luxury and pampered seclusion that the other islands were no longer able to provide, the catchphrase points now to a place that lacks a conventional tourist infrastructure, a place of simplicity and of unaffected charm. The high-end resorts and restaurants that are found virtually everywhere on Nevis or Anguilla are absent here; Montserrat is thus not the sort of place where a visitor feels "catered to" so much as "looked after" in a friendly and unfussy fashion, an island that does not pretend to exist for the satisfaction of tourists and where every undertaking is a kind of improvisatory adventure. Pont's Beach View Restaurant is a fine example of the simple, forthright—though decidedly gracious— ambience of Montserrat. There was an impromptu flavor to our evening there. While meandering around Little Bay, Erin and I spotted a sign for the restaurant sprouting amidst an abundance of trees and tropical vegetation. The hours posted on the sign were twelve to three in the afternoon; we were thus right on time for the lunch barbecue that we had heard so much about but the place appeared to be closed (dinner was apparently not an option during the off-season). Back at Gingerbread Hill I decided to call the number for Pont's and inquire as to whether there was any possibility of an evening meal. A decorous and quiet voice sounded on the other end of the line. I explained that this was to be our last night on Montserrat and that we would be sorry to miss visiting a restaurant that we had heard such a great deal about. Was there any chance that the Beach View bar might at least be open for drinks later in the evening? Someone had mentioned that this might be a possibility. 'Your last night? You come on in, I'll open up for you. I have ribs and King Fish tonight. Can you stop by around seven, then?' It felt less like making a reservation and more like we had been invited to stop by a friend's house for a meal. Gratefully we confirmed the time and began to prepare for dinner.

The restaurant is tucked into a quiet corner of Little Bay,

where a small footpath ducks into a patch of woodland that runs down from the low hills and up to the water's edge. A handful of young men were gathered around a car, drinking and laughing and singing along with the radio while someone inside the car snapped photos with an old thirty-five-millimeter camera. The group was illuminated by an electric light that hung from the edge of a pale cement building with empty windows. Someone kept shouting, 'There's nothing here, no, there's nothing here,' as if he was singing the lyrics to a song. The others laughed. One of the men saw us and waved formally. 'Good evening,' he said. The others waved too, raising their bottles in silent salute. Beyond them was the shadow of the dock where passengers embark for Antigua, the site of somber migration during the worst of the volcano crisis. As we walked along the path to the left we slowly drew near to a low, irregular structure nearly consumed (or so it seemed) by tall trees and exuberant tropical growth. Upon entering we were greeted by the proprietor and chef, John Ponteen, courtly, but unaffected. We were led out onto an octagonal back porch that extended just past some nearby cliffs and out over the murmuring of the waves that washed back and forth beneath us. Here we chose our meals—Erin the ribs, King Fish for me, while both of us ordered the pumpkin soup—and were left to enjoy our drinks while an electrical storm flashed and stabbed in the offing, faraway and silent across the dark water. The only sounds were the sibilant muttering of the surf, the click of the breeze-addled leaves and palm fronds, the light patter of pans from the kitchen. Once our meals had been prepared we were ushered back into the dining room, though this term belies the magic and whimsy of the place. It was only at this point that we realized there were no real walls here, nor a true ceiling, unless the thick, flower-bedecked foliage embracing and overtopping the restaurant might be thought of as a wall or a ceiling. There were a few wrought-iron gates and railings that framed the establishment but these mostly acted as supports for various growing things: lobster claws and salvia, hibiscus and bird of paradise: a burgeoning West Indian blazonry. It was difficult to know where the restaurant ended and the forest began, but what might be called the interior was further adorned with a profusion of little fairy lights—red, blue and yellow—that meandered through a garden of hanging nets and dangling buoys. Curious and unusual objects caught the eye at several points: bits of gnarled driftwood peeking from within suspended tin cups, a teapot sprouting a riot of colorful flowers, an artfully arranged assortment of wicker-wrapped demijohns and glowing sea glass. A particular point of pride for the proprietor was a little coconut suspended from the ceiling and sporting an eye patch, a goatee and a red bandana wrapped around the top of its head. The coconut spun slowly around and around as we enjoyed our meals, its one good eye trained now upon us, now upon the kitchen. The pumpkin soup was light and spicy, the King Fish cooked in butter and garlic; simple, but delicious. The ribs were prepared with the restaurant's signature barbeque sauce, piquant and smoky and not too sweet. The simplicity of the meal and the casual, easy-going ambience of the place may mislead you as to the expertise of the proprietor himself: John Ponteen was for several years the chairman of the Montserrat Tourist Board, with a degree in hospitality management from Westminster University. Such credentials do not, however, compromise the easy good humor, the unfussy geniality, of either the owner or his enchanted Beach View Restaurant. 'The captain himself,' grinned John Ponteen as he called our attention to the dangling pirate's-head coconut, 'the captain himself.'

*

Perhaps there is nothing stranger about Montserrat than its small, uninhabited satellite called Redonda. Erin and I could see its low, purple mass humped above the horizon as we sat on our porch swing at Gingerbread Hill, though it took us some time to identify the rocky, inhospitable islet. It was David who named the place for us, saying that it had long been claimed by both Antigua and Montserrat (a third claimant—the island of Nevis—had long ago abandoned its occasional assertions of suzerainty). In 1872 Antigua even went so far as to formally annex the island, for its phosphate deposits made this otherwise undesirable piece of real estate a profitable acquisition during the nineteenth century (the same is true of several of the Leeward Island's outlying cays, including Anguilla's Sombrero Island). By the time of the First World War, however, mining operations ceased on Redonda and its few inhabitants left for their various homes. What these men never realized, however, is that while they had lived and worked on the island they were apparently the subjects of a science-fiction writer named M.P. Shiel; not the subjects of his several tales, but individuals who were subject to the political authority of Shiel himself. Born on Montserrat in 1865, Shiel later emigrated to Britain, where he became one of the more volatile and wildly experimental of the *fin de siècle* Decadents, making his name with collections of short stories like *Prince Zaleski* (1895) and *Shapes in Fire* (1896), compendia featuring weird, futuristic tales that some scholars argue exercised an influence upon more-celebrated authors like H.G. Wells. One of his greatest successes was a novel entitled *The Purple Cloud*, published in 1901: a post-apocalyptic adventure concerning a redoubtable explorer named Adam Jeffson who returns from an expedition to the North Pole only to find that all humanity has been mysteriously wiped out. There is something of a dark side to the author himself, as he was charged with inappropriate sexual activity involving a thirteen-year-old girl and prosecuted under the provisions of the Criminal Law Amendment Act of 1885, the same act (with its infamous Labouchere Amendment) that was used in the prosecution of Oscar Wilde for "gross indecency." Found guilty, Shiel spent sixteen months in prison. Later he befriended the poet John Gawsworth, to whom he bragged that he had been installed as King Felipe I of Redonda back in 1880, when he was fifteen years old. Installed by whom and for what purpose were unclear but following Shiel's death in 1947 this title was bequeathed to (or claimed by, or something) Gawsworth himself over a few pints in an English pub, the poet taking the name of King Juan I. Gawsworth—or King Juan—is believed to have maintained a strong attachment to Shiel—or King Felipe—even after the latter's death, apparently keeping his ashes in a biscuit tin over the fireplace. Following the demise of Gawsworth, Jon Wynne Tyson—celebrated author, philosopher and founder of Centaur Press—was installed as King Juan II; as of this writing, he remains the island's sovereign. King, perhaps, but not the uncontested authority, for in 1978—one suspects in part to counter such peculiar goings-on—the government of Antigua installed a post office and a single caretaker on Redonda. This has not stopped King Juan II from consolidating his control, however, as he has subsequently created an honorary aristocracy composed of an order of knights to attend (at least metaphorically) upon him. Perhaps the most celebrated member of this estimable body is the Italian novelist and philosopher Umberto Eco, author of *Foucault's Pendulum*, *The Name of the Rose*, and *The Island of the Day Before* along with a mountain of other work. Even the official nautical map for Redonda and its surrounding waters is full of unexplained peculiarities: a "Centaur's Cave" is clearly delineated near the windward coast while a stretch of the leeward shore is identified as the spot where someone observed a "Paranoic-Critical Apparition of [the] Guardian's Face on [a] Cliff." Whatever that might mean, the little island seems the sort of place that generates apparitions, poetical fantasies and half-mystical, half-nonsensical reveries, an island rich and strange, full of wonderful weirdness and delightful nautical balderdash.

*

At least in passing, however, it seems necessary to note the truly astonishing cultural sophistication of tiny Montserrat, an island with a claim to artistic and scholarly achievement that is belied by its small size and disproportionately hard times. Beginning in 1952 the island was home to Radio Montserrat, the first national radio station in the Leeward Islands (maintained for the better part of a decade by a wholly unpaid, deeply dedicated broadcasting committee). Until its evacuation and destruction,

Plymouth—with a total of three radio stations, including the influential Radio Antilles)—was very much a powerful media center in the region. Local scholar and historian Howard Fergus has long been a one-man guarantor of the island's past and its memory. Author of some fifteen books, sometime Speaker of the Legislative Council and director of the Montserrat Theatre Group for the better part of a decade, Fergus is nothing less than a giant, his scholarship unimpeachable, his politics reasonable and progressive, his voice humane and generous. Most decidedly not to be overlooked is the island's impressive and celebrated author, Edward Archibald Markham. While he first pursued a career as a dramatist, Markham (who moved to the United Kingdom in 1956) became particularly renowned for his poetry and short stories (*Lambchops*, *Human Rites*, *Living in Disguise*), while his characteristically prickly, deeply intellectual voice was leavened by an earthy, buoyant wit. Markham was especially fascinated with the shifting nature of identity, developing a fictional persona named Sally Goodman. The writer—himself black, goateed and utterly authoritative— once famously described her as "Welsh... young... white... blue-eyed [and] blonde... very much in a way like me." He died of a heart attack in 2008 in Paris. Perhaps it is in part the influence of the island's traditional "tea meetings" and "penny concerts," the former were salons held in respectable, middle-class homes of the nineteenth century, the latter robust street entertainments associated with musical performances and populist rhetorical debates. Perhaps it is the abiding influence of Ireland and her enduring poetry-madness or memories of a lost West African intelligentsia long since decimated by slavers and rum, bibles and disease. Or maybe there's something in the water of the ghauts; your guess is as good as mine. What is undeniable, however, is the small island's impressive cultural life and integrity, very much alive amidst all the loss. It still leaves a lump in my throat.

*

On the morning of our departure Erin and I traveled one final time down the leeward coast of Montserrat, past Woodlands and the ruins of the Duberry Estate to a place called Runaway Ghaut, where a streamlet trickles from the hillside and shuffles toward the sea. The site of a bloody engagement between invading French forces and the island militia in 1712 (when the latter fought a holding action that allowed fleeing civilians to escape up into the nearby hills), local lore tells that anyone who drinks of the waters here will return to Montserrat. A large green and white sign boldly proclaims the legend these days. It made me think of another tall story. There was once a beautiful mermaid who lived in a deep blue lake atop Chance's Peak. Every day she sat beside her cache of gold and combed out her golden hair with a magical golden comb, all the while singing a ravishing but melancholy air. She had as her companion a diamond snake who guarded both the mermaid's comb and her pot of gold, the latter secreted away long ago in some unknown corner of the island. It was said that if someone could steal the comb and reach the sea before being caught by the diamond serpent, the mermaid's gold would belong to them. This was a tale of Old Montserrat. The mermaid's lake is gone now, along with most of Chance's Peak, obliterated by volcanic blasts. Many things have disappeared here or, like the last of the island's mangrove swamps, are in the process of going away. I hope that Montserrat—and all of the little Leeward Islands—will not be left simply with stories about things that have been lost. Time will tell. One hopes that Montserrat will work with care as it opens itself once more to the tourist market and that those who come to see the place will remember that the island is not a resort but a home, one characterized by an abiding Afro-Celtic melancholy and a quiet endurance, by laughter and tall tales, by heartbreak and humor and a national bird that hardly anyone has seen. They used to say that you couldn't outrun the guardian snake, that the secret was to travel slowly and attentively and with great care. Should you do so, they used to say, rare and precious things might appear for you to wonder at and carry with you. I think they were right. Erin and I drank the water. Then it was time to go.

ADDITIONAL READING

Below is a list of works that may be of interest for further reading. It is hardly a complete list, and must be considered highly idiosyncratic, but it does include a wide range of Caribbean literature: novels, and works of history, memoirs, collections of plays, and poetry, along with a delightful catalogue of the work of Heleen Cornet, the celebrated painter of Saban churches and cottages. Some titles are focused upon a single island of the several I have visited, while others consider the West Indies more broadly. Some are quite simply classics of Caribbean literature that should not be missed by those interested in the region. The works of the West Indies' two Nobel laureates would undoubtedly fall into this category, with Naipaul's wry, meticulous prose a counterpoint to Walcott's archetypal, yet intimate verse. There are a handful of scholarly works: Braithwaite's anthropological study of Jamaica and Dunn's *Sugar and Slaves* represent pivotal contributions to the field of Caribbean studies, so too does *Capitalism and Slavery*, written by Trinidadian historian and politician Eric Williams. No serious consideration of the many challenges posed by tourism in the contemporary Caribbean would be possible without the work of Polly Patullo, especially her groundbreaking study called *Last Resorts*. A few are travel books, and while their inclusion here runs the risk of placing my own work indubitably in the shade, I cannot in good conscience omit a laudatory and heartfelt acknowledgment of these particular books, nor take the chance that I might contribute to anyone who loves the Caribbean possibly missing out on them. *The Traveller's Tree*, in particular, is an unalloyed delight: profound, exhilarating, prodigal in its gifts to the reader. Most of the works below served as comrades and colleagues during my travels through the little Leeward Islands; if you are looking for a travel companion, you could do worse than any of these titles. Some books deal only in part with the West Indies, but represent especially insightful, authoritative, and exuberant considerations of the Caribbean, its history and culture. Barbara Tuchman's *The First Salute*, for example, contains a vivid and deeply learned exploration of the role of the island of St. Eustatius during the American War of Independence. Hugh Thomas—whose focus in *Rivers of Gold* is the Spanish Empire during its first decades in the New World—provides an excellent account of early European exploration and settlement of the West Indies. Likewise, Simon Winchester explores all the remnants of Britain's former empire in his book *Outposts* (including Hong Kong, which still belonged to Britain at the time of the book's publication), treating each of Her Majesty's West Indian holdings in delightful detail. To paraphrase the poet: Read only for pleasure. Follow your own nose.

Akenson, Donald Harman. *If the Irish Ran the World: Montserrat, 1630–1730.* Liverpool: Liverpool University Press, 1997.

Aspinall, Algernon. *West Indian Tales of Old.* New York: Negro Universities Press, 1969.

Braithwaite, Edward Kamau. *The Development of Creole Society in Jamaica, 1770–1820.* Oxford: Clarendon Press, 1971.

Burns, Sir Alan. *History of the British West Indies.* London: George Allen and Unwin Ltd., 1954.

Cestero, Jacqueline A. *From Bananaquits to Boobies. A Photographic Gallery of the Wild Birds of Anguilla.* Anguilla: published by the author, 2009.

Cornet, Heleen. *Saban Cottages.* Saba: published by the author, 1991.

Crawford, Denise. *Island Harbour Village.* Anguilla: published by the author, 2014.

Dunn, Richard S. *Sugar and Slaves. The Rise of the Planter Class in the English West Indies, 1624–1713.* Chapel Hill: University of North Carolina Press, 1972.

Dyde, Brian. *Out of the Crowded Vagueness. A History of St. Kitts, Nevis, & Anguilla.* London: Macmillan Caribbean, 2005.

Fergus, Howard A. *History of Alliouagana. A Short History of Montserrat.* Plymouth, Montserrat: University Center, 1975.

Fergus, Howard A. *Montserrat, Emerald Isle of the Caribbean.* London: Macmillan Caribbean, 1983.

Fermor, Patrick Leigh. *The Traveller's Tree.* London: John Murray, 1950.

Fermor, Patrick Leigh. *The Violins of Saint-Jacques.* London: John Murray, 1953.

Froude, James Anthony. *The English in the West Indies, or the Bow of Ulysses.* London: Longman's, Green and Co., 1888.

Glissant, Édouard. *Poetics of Relation.* Trans. Betsy Wing. Ann Arbor: University of Michigan Press, 2010.

Goodfield, June. *Rivers of Time.* Leicester: Matador, 2008.

Harrigan, Colonel. *Little Ole Anguilla. A Collection of Plays and Skits. Vol. 1.* Anguilla: published by the author, 2009.

Harrigan, Colonel. *De Ole Rock. A Collection of Plays and Skits. Vol. 2.* Anguilla: published by the author, 2010.

Harrigan, Colonel. *Tell Me 'Bout it. A Collection of Plays and Skits. Vol. 3.* Anguilla: published by the author, 2011.

Hartog, Dr. J. *History of Saba.* Saba: Saba Artisan Foundation, 1975.

Jones, S.B. *Annals of Anguilla.* Belfast: Christian Journals, Ltd., 1976.

Kinkaid, Jamaica. *At the Bottom of the River.* New York: Farrar, Straus and Giroux, 1978.

Kobbé, Montague. *The Night of the Rambler.* New York: Akashic Books, 2013.

Labat, Jean-Baptiste. *Memoirs of Père Labat.* Translated by John Eaden. London: Frank Cass & Co. Ltd., 1931.

Latimer, Jon. *Buccaneers of the Caribbean. How Piracy Forged an Empire.* Cambridge, Massachusetts: Harvard University Press, 2009.

Mais, Roger. *Brother Man.* Jonathan Cape: London, 1954.

Naipaul, V.S. *The Middle Passage. The Caribbean Revisited.* New York: Vintage Books, 1962.

Naipaul, V.S. *The Mystic Masseur.* New York: Vintage Books, 1957.

Oostindie, Gert. *Paradise Overseas. The Dutch Caribbean: Colonialism and its Transatlantic Legacies*. Oxford: Macmillan, 2005.

O'Shaughnessy, Andrew Jackson. *An Empire Divided: The American Revolution and the British Caribbean*, Philadelphia: University of Pennsylvania Press, 2000.

Patullo, Polly. *Fire From the Mountain. The Tragedy of Montserrat and the Betrayal of Its People*. London: Constable, 2000.

Patullo, Polly. *Last Resorts. The Cost of Tourism in the Caribbean*. London: Cassell, 1996.

Paton, William Agnew. *Down the Islands. A Voyage to the Caribbees*. New York: Charles Scribner's Sons, 1896.

Petty, Colville L. *Bless our Forbears*. Anguilla: published by the author, 2008.

Petty, Colville L. *A Handbook History of Anguilla, 2nd edition*. Anguilla: published by the author, 2015.

Petty, Colville L. & Nat Hodge. *Anguilla's Battle for Freedom, 1967–1969*. Anguilla: published by the authors, 2010.

Phillips, Caryl. *The Final Passage*. New York: Penguin Books, 1985.

Phillips, Caryl. *A State of Independence*. New York: Vintage International, 1986.

Richardson, Bonham C. *Igniting the Caribbean's Past: Fire in British West Indian History*. Chapel Hill: University of North Carolina Press, 2004.

Rhys, Jean. *Wide Sargasso Sea*. New York: W.W. Norton, 1966.

Shaw, Jenny. *Everyday Life in the Early English Caribbean: Irish, Africans, and the Construction of Difference*. Athens: University of Georgia Press, 2013.

Sorton, Raphael. *An Inside Look*. Saba: published by the author, 2012.

St.-Johnston, Sir Reginald. *From a Colonial Governor's Note-Book*. London: Negro University Press, 1936.

Thomas, Hugh. *Rivers of Gold. The Rise of the Spanish Empire from Columbus to Magellan*. New York: Random House, 2003.

Tuchman, Barbara W. *The First Salute. A View of the American Revolution*. New York: Alfred A. Knopf, 1988.

Walcott, Derek. *Omeros*. New York: Farrar, Straus, Giroux, 1990.

Walcott, Derek. *Dream on Monkey Mountain and Other Plays*. New York: Farrar, Straus and Giroux, 1976.

Waugh, Alec. *A Family of Islands*. Garden City, New York: Doubleday & Company, 1964.

Waugh, Alec. *The Sugar Islands. A Collection of Pieces Written About the West Indies Between 1928 and 1953*. London: Cassell, 1958.

Westlake, Donald E. *Under an English Heaven*. London: Hodder and Stoughton, 1972.

Williams, Eric. *Capitalism and Slavery*. Chapel Hill: University of North Carolina Press, 1994.

Winchester, Simon. *Outposts. Journeys to the Surviving Relics of the British Empire*. New York: HarperCollins, 1985.

Zacek, Natalie A. *Settler Society in the English Leeward Islands: 1670–1776*. Cambridge: Cambridge University Press, 2010.